Physics
for the IB Diploma

Workbook

Mark Farrington

CAMBRIDGE
UNIVERSITY PRESS

CAMBRIDGE
UNIVERSITY PRESS

University Printing House, Cambridge CB2 8BS, United Kingdom

One Liberty Plaza, 20th Floor, New York, NY 10006, USA

477 Williamstown Road, Port Melbourne, VIC 3207, Australia

4843/24, 2nd Floor, Ansari Road, Daryaganj, Delhi – 110002, India

79 Anson Road, #06 -04/06, Singapore 079906

Cambridge University Press is part of the University of Cambridge.

It furthers the University's mission by disseminating knowledge in the pursuit of education, learning and research at the highest international levels of excellence.

www.cambridge.org
Information on this title: www.cambridge.org/9781316634929 (Paperback)

First published 2017

20 19 18 17 16 15 14 13 12 11 10 9 8 7 6 5 4 3 2 1

Printed in Spain by GraphyCems

A catalogue record for this publication is available from the British Library

ISBN 978-1-316-63492-9 Paperback

Contents

How to use this book

Chapter outline

Each chapter begins with a Chapter outline to briefly set out the learning aims and help with navigation through the topic.

> **Chapter outline**
>
> In this chapter, you will:
> - Sketch and interpret graphs of *displacement*, *speed*, *velocity* and *acceleration* against *time*; and use them to solve problems involving instantaneous and average values of velocity, speed and acceleration.
> - Use the SUVAT equations of motion for uniform acceleration to solve problems involving projectiles and the Earth's gravitational field strength near the surface of the Earth.
> - Sketch and interpret free-body force diagrams, understand and be able to use coefficients of friction and be able to describe qualitatively the effect of fluid resistance of falling objects, including the concept of terminal speed.
> - Sketch and interpret graphs of force against distance, their gradients and their areas, solve problems involving the concept of power as the rate of doing work and incorporate the concept of efficiency into calculations involving the transformation of energy.
> - Use Newton's second law in terms of a rate of change of momentum, interpret graphs involving force and time, including the meaning of impulse, use the conservation of linear momentum in a range of practical situations and distinguish between elastic, inelastic and super-elastic collisions.

Key terms and Key formulae

A list of Key terms and Key formulae at the start of each chapter provide clear, straightforward definitions for the Key vocabulary. Key formulae can be referred to throughout the chapter, to help with Exercises and Exam-style questions.

> **KEY TERMS**
>
> **Internal energy:** The sum of the kinetic energies and the potential energies of all the particles in a sample of a substance.
>
> **Specific heat capacity:** The amount of energy required to raise the temperature of 1 kg of a substance by one kelvin.
>
> **Specific latent heat of fusion/vaporisation:** The amount of energy required to change the state of 1 kg of a substance from solid/liquid to liquid/gas without a change in temperature.
>
> **Boyle's law:** For a fixed amount of gas at a constant temperature, the pressure of the gas is inversely proportional to its volume; $P \propto \dfrac{1}{V}$.
>
> **Charles's law:** For a fixed amount of gas at a constant pressure, the volume of the gas is proportional to its absolute temperature; $V \propto T$.
>
> **The pressure law:** For a fixed amount of gas at a constant volume, the pressure of the gas is proportional to its absolute temperature; $P \propto T$.
>
> **Ideal gas:** A gas that can be considered to have no potential energy in its atoms. In practice this is not possible, but it can be approximated by a gas at a low pressure and temperature.
>
> **Mole:** One of the SI base units, defined as the amount of a substance that has the same number of particles as there are atoms in 12 gram me of $^{12}_{6}\mathrm{C}$.
>
> **Ideal gas equation:** There are several ways of expressing this important equation: $PV = \dfrac{1}{3} N \, \overline{mc^2}$, $PV = n \, R \, T$, and $P = \dfrac{1}{3} \rho \, \overline{c^2}$.
>
> **Kinetic energy and temperature:** $\dfrac{3}{2} kT = \dfrac{1}{2} m \overline{c^2}$, where the Boltzmann constant, $k = 1.38 \times 10^{-23}\,\mathrm{J\,K^{-1}}$.

Exercises

Each chapter contains a number of Exercises that relate to each chapter topic. Exercises can help to practise and consolidate learning.

Exercise 4.1 – Oscillations

1 Explain what is meant by:
   a time period of an oscillator
   b frequency
   c amplitude
   d equilibrium position
   e displacement.

2 Figure 4.1 shows the displacement of an oscillating body about its equilibrium position.

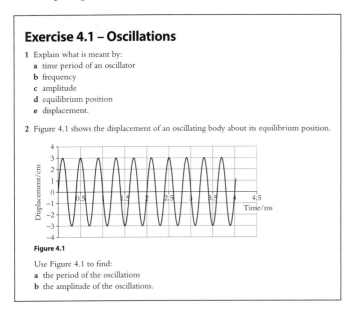

Figure 4.1

Use Figure 4.1 to find:
   a the period of the oscillations
   b the amplitude of the oscillations.

Exam-style questions

Each chapter concludes with a list of Exam-style questions. These Exam-style questions provide an opportunity to practise what has been covered in each topic, and prepare for the types of question that will appear in the IB Physics Diploma exams.

? Exam-style questions

1 Which of the following statements about simple harmonic motion is *false*?
   A The period of the oscillation is constant.
   B The amplitude of the oscillations decreases with time.
   C The period of the oscillations is independent of the amplitude.
   D The total energy of the oscillator is constant.

2 What is the best estimate for the time period of a simple pendulum of length 1 m?
   A 0.1 s
   B 1 s
   C 10 s
   D 100 s

3 A mass of 10 kg, attached to a vertical spring of spring constant, k, oscillates in a vertical direction. If the time period of the oscillations is 4 s, what is the best estimate for the spring constant of the spring?
   A 1 N m^{-1}
   B 8 N m^{-1}
   C 16 N m^{-1}
   D 25 N m^{-1}

Introduction

This workbook supports students studying the physics content of the International Baccalaureate® (IB) Diploma Programme (DP). It provides standard and higher level questions for all topics including the four options. The questions develop understanding, test knowledge and provide exam-style question practice.

The workbook orders topics as in the Physics guide (First assessment 2016). Each topic includes a chapter outline and a selection of key terms.

Students following the IB Physics course do so either at Standard Level (SL) or at Higher Level (HL). The Core material is covered by both SL and HL students. The Additional Higher Level material is covered by the HL students only. Core material consists of Chapters 1–8 inclusive whereas Chapters 9–12 are additional HL material. The Option Topics A–D contain both SL and HL material, with the HL material indicated by a symbol next to each exercise.

Students do not have to complete the course in this exact order. However, it seems sensible for higher level (HL) students to cover core topics before the additional higher level (AHL) ones. Some HL students and teachers may find that tackling some topics in pairs enables a more accessible 'flow' through the course: chapters 4 and 9, 5 and 10, and 7 and 12 complement each other.

Each topic develops knowledge and understanding by including a range of question types: some require simple recall, others develop an idea from base principles, and some require detailed explanations or application of ideas and concepts.

The skills grid maps questions against examination command terms. Students should become familiar with these. The grid also links each question with its assessment objective.

The nature of science (NOS) is now formally assessed as part of the written examination. To address this, some questions consider aspects of physics not previously covered. Similarly, some questions require consideration of how a physicist would 'know' something – this theory of knowledge (TOK) forms an important part of the IBDP. These questions add philosophical credibility and richness to the variety of this workbook.

Answers are provided with their workings. It is important to look closely at these workings; it helps develop a formal method for solving problems in physics, as well as an appreciation of the detail required in examinations.

AO	Command Term	1. Measurement and Uncertainties				2. Mechanics					3. Thermal Physics			4. Waves					
1	State/List	1.1.1 1.1.2 1.1.3 1.1.7 1.1.9 1.1.10 1.1.11 1.1.12 1.1.13 1.1.14 1.1.16 1.1.24			9	2.1.6 2.1.9	2.2.2 2.2.6	2.3.2 2.3.3 2.3.8	2.4.1	12 13	3.1.19	3.2.4 3.2.7 3.2.8 3.2.12 3.2.15 3.2.22	4 5	4.1.10 4.1.14	4.2.4 4.2.7 4.2.8	4.3.8 4.3.12	4.4.4 4.4.6 4.4.10 4.4.11	4.5.3	1 3 5 10 12
1	Draw/Sketch			1.3.3 1.3.4 1.3.5 1.3.6 1.3.12	5 8	2.1.9 2.1.11	2.2.5 2.2.6 2.2.7		2.4.6					4.1.13 4.1.15	4.2.3	4.3.3 4.3.5 4.3.7 4.3.9 4.3.13	4.4.1 4.4.2 4.4.6 4.4.8	4.5.3 4.5.4	8 12
1	Label/Annotate		1.2.23							8 10									8
1	Define		1.2.16	1.3.2		2.1.7		2.3.3			3.1.14	3.2.17					4.4.3		7
2	Outline										3.1.25	3.2.1 3.2.3 3.2.5 3.2.9 3.2.13 3.2.14	6 10	4.1.3 4.1.11 4.1.12	4.2.5		4.4.7 4.4.16		
2	Calculate/Show	1.1.4 1.1.5 1.1.6 1.1.7 1.1.8 1.1.17 1.1.18 1.1.19 1.1.20 1.1.21 1.1.22 1.1.23 1.1.25 1.1.27 1.1.28 1.1.29 1.1.30	1.2.7 1.2.8 1.2.9 1.2.14 1.2.15 1.2.19 1.2.20 1.2.21 1.2.22 1.2.24	1.3.4 1.3.5 1.3.11 1.3.14	5 8 9 11 12 13	2.1.2 2.1.3 2.1.4 2.1.6 2.1.9 2.1.10 2.1.11 2.1.12 2.1.13	2.2.3 2.2.4 2.2.5 2.2.11	2.3.1 2.3.2 2.3.4 2.3.5 2.3.8 2.3.10 2.3.11 2.3.12 2.3.14 2.3.15	2.4.2 2.4.3 2.4.4 2.4.6 2.4.8 2.4.9	5 6 7 9 12 13	3.1.7 3.1.8 3.1.15 3.1.16 3.1.18 3.1.19 3.1.20 3.1.21 3.1.22 3.1.23	3.2.6 3.2.11 3.2.16 3.2.17 3.2.18 3.2.20 3.2.21 3.2.22 3.2.23 3.2.25	6 7 8 9 10	4.1.4 4.1.5 4.1.7 4.1.8 4.1.12	4.2.4 4.2.6 4.2.8	4.3.12	4.4.4 4.4.18		4 9 11

AO	Command Term	1. Measurement and Uncertainties				2. Mechanics					3. Thermal Physics			4. Waves					
2	Describe		1.2.17		8	2.1.4 2.1.14	2.2.8 2.2.10				3.1.1 3.1.2 3.1.3 3.1.4 3.1.5 3.1.6 3.1.12	3.2.2	2		4.2.1 4.2.2 4.2.9	4.3.2 4.3.6 4.3.11		4.5.2	
2	Estimate	1.1.26			1 2 3 4														2
3	Suggest	1.1.15	1.2.5 1.2.24 1.2.25		6 7 9 12				2.4.5	13	3.1.13 3.1.25		9			4.3.14	4.4.8		10 11 12
3	Determine/ Analyse		1.2.1 1.2.2 1.2.3 1.2.4 1.2.9 1.2.10 1.2.11 1.2.12 1.2.13 1.2.19 1.2.20 1.2.21 1.2.22	1.3.6 1.3.7 1.3.8 1.3.9 1.3.10 1.3.12 1.3.13 1.3.15	5 6 8 9 11	2.1.5 2.1.8 2.1.15	2.2.8 2.2.9 2.2.10 2.2.12	2.3.6 2.3.7 2.3.9 2.3.13	2.4.5 2.4.6	1 2 3 4 8 11 12 14	3.1.17 3.1.24	3.2.21 3.2.24	1 3 6 7 9	4.1.2 4.1.9		4.3.4 4.3.5	4.4.5 4.4.6 4.4.12 4.4.14	4.5.3 4.5.4	6 8 9
3	Explain		1.2.6	1.3.1	12	2.1.1	2.2.1 2.2.5 2.2.7 2.2.10	2.3.2 2.3.3 2.3.4	2.4.1 2.4.4 2.4.7	8 10 13	3.1.9 3.1.10 3.1.11 3.1.13	3.2.7 3.2.10 3.2.13 3.2.19 3.2.22 3.2.24	7 8 10	4.1.1 4.1.6 4.1.13		4.3.1 4.3.4 4.3.10	4.4.9 4.4.11 4.4.13 4.4.16 4.4.17	4.5.1 4.5.5	10 11
3	Discuss		1.2.18		10 11				2.4.9			3.2.5							

AO	Command Term	5. Electricity and Magnetism					6. Circular Motion and Gravitation			7. Atomic, Nuclear and Particle Physics				8. Energy Production		
1	State/List	5.1.1 5.1.2 5.1.3 5.1.8 5.1.9 5.1.10 5.1.11 5.1.13 5.1.16 5.1.17 5.1.19 5.1.25 5.1.28 5.1.31	5.2.1 5.2.2 5.2.10 5.2.11 5.2.18 5.2.19 5.2.20	5.3.1 5.3.6 5.3.9	5.4.3 5.4.4 5.4.7 5.4.10 5.4.11 5.4.14 5.4.15	8	6.1.2 6.1.15 6.1.18 6.1.20 6.1.22 6.1.24 6.1.25 6.1.27	6.2.4 6.2.5 6.2.7 6.2.12	5	7.1.3 7.1.4 7.1.5 7.1.11 7.1.12 7.1.15 7.1.16 7.1.17 7.1.23 7.1.24 7.1.28 7.1.29 7.1.35 7.1.36 7.1.41 7.1.42 7.1.43		7.3.2 7.3.3 7.3.4 7.3.5 7.3.6 7.3.7 7.3.10 7.3.12 7.3.13 7.3.14	5 7 9 10 11	8.1.3 8.1.13 8.1.14 8.1.19	8.2.7 8.2.8 8.2.10 8.2.15 8.2.19 8.2.20	1 8 13
1	Draw/Sketch	5.1.9 5.1.18 5.1.23 5.1.25	5.2.1 5.2.10	5.3.6	5.4.1 5.4.2 5.4.3 5.4.11	6 7 9	6.1.16 6.1.17 6.1.25 6.1.26	6.2.2 6.2.11 6.2.13	7	7.1.7 7.1.18 7.1.36	7.2.12	7.3.15 7.3.17 7.3.18		8.1.9		9
1	Label/Annotate	5.1.30			5.4.4		6.1.14 6.1.27			7.1.18 7.1.33	7.2.12	7.3.5 7.3.6 7.3.12		8.1.6	8.2.14	
1	Define	5.1.8 5.1.16 5.1.19 5.1.34	5.2.2 5.2.5		5.4.8		6.1.1 6.1.7	6.2.2			7.2.1 7.2.7			8.1.4	8.2.18	
2	Outline			5.3.1 5.3.2 5.3.3 5.3.7	5.4.6		6.1.19	6.2.1		7.1.39 7.1.41	7.2.13 7.2.15	7.3.1	5 6	8.1.12 8.1.17 8.1.18 8.1.20 8.1.21 8.1.24 8.1.27	8.2.3 8.2.24	
2	Calculate/Show	5.1.3 5.1.10 5.1.14 5.1.15 5.1.16 5.1.20 5.1.21 5.1.26 5.1.27 5.1.28 5.1.29 5.1.31 5.1.32 5.1.33 5.1.35 5.1.36 5.1.37 5.1.38 5.1.39 5.1.40	5.2.3 5.2.5 5.2.6 5.2.7 5.2.8 5.2.9 5.2.12 5.2.13 5.2.14 5.2.16 5.2.20 5.2.21 5.2.22 5.2.23	5.3.4 5.3.5 5.3.8	5.4.5 5.4.9 5.4.12 5.4.13 5.4.14	6 7 10 11 12 14	6.1.3 6.1.4 6.1.5 6.1.6 6.1.7 6.1.8 6.1.9 6.1.10 6.1.12 6.1.21 6.1.23 6.1.25 6.1.27	6.2.3 6.2.5 6.2.9 6.2.10 6.2.11 6.2.12 6.2.13 6.2.14 6.2.15	8	7.1.6 7.1.8 7.1.9 7.1.10 7.1.14 7.1.15 7.1.18 7.1.30 7.1.33 7.1.36 7.1.40	7.2.3 7.2.4 7.2.5 7.2.9 7.2.10 7.2.11 7.2.14		5 6 7 8 9 10 11	8.1.4 8.1.9 8.1.15 8.1.16 8.1.23 8.1.25	8.2.11 8.2.12 8.2.13 8.2.15 8.2.17 8.2.21 8.2.23	7 9 10 11 12

AO	Command Term	5. Electricity and Magnetism					6. Circular Motion and Gravitation			7. Atomic, Nuclear and Particle Physics				8. Energy Production		
2	Describe	5.1.6			5.4.3					7.1.1 7.1.3 7.1.13 7.1.25 7.1.31 7.1.39	7.2.12	7.3.14			8.2.1 8.2.21	
2	Estimate					4			1 7	7.1.27						4 5 6 10
3	Suggest		5.2.10 5.2.21 5.2.23	5.3.2	5.4.2 5.4.4	6 7 11 12				7.1.3 7.1.7 7.1.8 7.1.14 7.1.26 7.1.38 7.1.40	7.2.3	7.3.13 7.3.18	4 7	8.1.15 8.1.23 8.1.26 8.1.29	8.2.18 8.2.19 8.2.20 8.2.21 8.2.23 8.2.24	8 11
3	Determine/ Analyse	5.1.23 5.1.24 5.1.34 5.1.36	5.2.4 5.2.15 5.2.17 5.2.18 5.2.19	5.3.9	5.4.13	1 2 3 5 8 13	6.1.11 6.1.20 6.1.22 6.1.26 6.1.27	6.2.6 6.2.8 6.2.11 6.2.12 6.2.14	2 3 4 6	7.1.7 7.1.8 7.1.18 7.1.20 7.1.22 7.1.33 7.1.35 7.1.36 7.1.37 7.1.41	7.2.2 7.2.6 7.2.8	7.3.8 7.3.9 7.3.11 7.3.16 7.3.17	1 2 3 6	8.1.8 8.1.10 8.1.11 8.1.22 8.1.23 8.1.25 8.1.28	8.2.3 8.2.16	2 3
3	Explain	5.1.1 5.1.2 5.1.4 5.1.5 5.1.6 5.1.7 5.1.8 5.1.12 5.1.22 5.1.38	5.2.1 5.2.10 5.2.21 5.2.22	5.3.1 5.3.5	5.4.2 5.4.10	8 9	6.1.13 6.1.22 6.1.23 6.1.25 6.1.26 6.1.27	6.2.4 6.2.5 6.2.10		7.1.1 7.1.2 7.1.4 7.1.5 7.1.19 7.1.21 7.1.26 7.1.31 7.1.32 7.1.34 7.1.38 7.1.44	7.2.8	7.3.3 7.3.7 7.3.10	5 9	8.1.1 8.1.2 8.1.5 8.1.7 8.1.15	8.2.2 8.2.4 8.2.5 8.2.6 8.2.7 8.2.9 8.2.14 8.2.15 8.2.19 8.2.24	13
3	Discuss						6.1.27				7.2.4 7.2.9					13

AO	Command Term	9. Wave Phenomena						10. Fields			11. Electromagnetic Induction				12. Quantum and Nuclear Physics		
1	State/List	9.1.1 9.1.2 9.1.5 9.1.10 9.1.14	9.2.2 9.2.3 9.2.7	9.3.2 9.3.6 9.3.7 9.3.9 9.3.14 9.3.15 9.3.16 9.3.18	9.4.1 9.4.2 9.4.6	9.5.2	1 5	10.1.1 10.1.9 10.1.10 10.1.13 10.1.18 10.1.19	10.2.6 10.2.7 10.2.10 10.2.12 10.2.15 10.2.16	2 4 7 8	11.1.3 11.1.7 11.1.8 11.1.13	11.2.1 11.2.3 11.2.4 11.2.7 11.2.9	11.3.1 11.3.6 11.3.14 11.3.15	8 9	12.1.9 12.1.11 12.1.18 12.1.23 12.1.24	12.2.3 12.2.4 12.2.11	
1	Draw/ Sketch	9.1.14	9.2.3	9.3.6 9.3.9				10.1.10 10.1.12 10.1.16 10.1.17 10.1.18 10.1.19				11.2.7 11.2.14 11.2.15 11.2.16 11.2.17	11.3.15		12.1.9 12.1.10 12.1.25		
1	Label/ Annotate	9.1.14						10.1.16 10.1.17 10.1.18 10.1.19	10.2.2	7		11.2.16 11.2.17		8			
1	Define	9.1.4 9.1.7 9.1.10						10.1.10						4 5			
2	Outline	9.1.12								10		11.2.7 11.2.13 11.2.14	11.3.4		12.1.3 12.1.12 12.1.13 12.1.22	12.2.4 12.2.6 12.2.15	
2	Calculate/ Show	9.1.3 9.1.5 9.1.6 9.1.7 9.1.10 9.1.11 9.1.13	9.2.4 9.2.6	9.3.4 9.3.5 9.3.11 9.3.12 9.3.13 9.3.20	9.4.1 9.4.4 9.4.5 9.4.6 9.4.7	9.5.2 9.5.4 9.5.5 9.5.6	7 9 10	10.1.4 10.1.5 10.1.6 10.1.7 10.1.8 10.1.9 10.1.11 10.1.13	10.2.1 10.2.3 10.2.5 10.2.8 10.2.9 10.2.10 10.2.11 10.2.12 10.2.13 10.2.14 10.2.15	7 8 9 10	11.1.4 11.1.5 11.1.9	11.2.4 11.2.5 11.2.6 11.2.9 11.2.10 11.2.11	11.3.3 11.3.9 11.3.13 11.3.14 11.3.16	12	12.1.1 12.1.2 12.1.6 12.1.8 12.1.11 12.1.14 12.1.15 12.1.16 12.1.17 12.1.18 12.1.19 12.1.20 12.1.23 12.1.24	12.2.2 12.2.3 12.2.5 12.2.6 12.2.7 12.2.11 12.2.12 12.2.13	6 7 8 9 10 11
2	Describe				9.4.1	9.5.1 9.5.5	7				11.1.1 11.1.2 11.1.14 11.1.16		11.3.1 11.3.7	7	12.1.5 12.1.17	12.2.9	
2	Estimate						2 3										1
3	Suggest			9.3.18 9.3.19					10.2.5	11	11.1.11 11.1.15 11.1.16	11.2.8 11.2.9	11.3.2 11.3.7		12.1.3 12.1.19 12.1.21 12.1.22 12.1.25	12.2.5 12.2.7	7 9

AO	Command Term	9. Wave Phenomena						10. Fields			11. Electromagnetic Induction				12. Quantum and Nuclear Physics		
3	**Determine/ Analyse**	9.1.5	9.2.1	9.3.7 9.3.10 9.3.14 9.3.18	9.4.1 9.4.3 9.4.5 9.4.7 9.4.8	9.5.1 9.5.2	4 6 8 9 10	10.1.13 10.1.15	10.2.1 10.2.4 10.2.8 10.2.12 10.2.17	1 3 5 11	11.1.3 11.1.6 11.1.10 11.1.12	11.2.1 11.2.2 11.2.11	11.3.2 11.3.5 11.3.7 11.3.8 11.3.10 11.3.11 11.3.12 11.3.14 11.3.15	1 2 3 6 8 10 11 12 13	12.1.6 12.1.7 12.1.8 12.1.10 12.1.14 12.1.15 12.1.16 12.1.19 12.1.20 12.1.22 12.1.24	12.2.1 12.2.3 12.2.7 12.2.8 12.2.9 12.2.12 12.2.14 12.2.16	2 3 4 5 6 7 8 10 11
3	**Explain**	9.1.4 9.1.8 9.1.9	9.2.5	9.3.1 9.3.3 9.3.9 9.3.17	9.4.2	9.5.3	6	10.1.2 10.1.3 10.1.10 10.1.12 10.1.14 10.1.16 10.1.17	10.2.2 10.2.4 10.2.10	9 11	11.1.3 11.1.10 11.1.11 11.1.12 11.1.14 11.1.16	11.2.7 11.2.8 11.2.12 11.2.14 11.2.15 11.2.16	11.3.2 11.3.13	7 11	12.1.3 12.1.4 12.1.5 12.1.9 12.1.14 12.1.17 12.1.21 12.1.22 12.1.24	12.2.5 12.2.6 12.2.8 12.2.10 12.2.11 12.2.14	6 8 10
3	**Discuss**			9.3.13		9.5.6										12.2.2	

AO	Command Term	A. Relativity						B. Engineering Physics					C. Imaging					D. Astrophysics					
1	State/List	A.1.1 A.1.2 A.1.4 A.1.5 A.1.7	A.2.1 A.2.2	A.3.2 A.3.6 A.3.12	A.4.7 A.4.9	A.5.3 A.5.5	4 5	B.1.7 B.1.10 B.1.16 B.1.17 B.1.19 B.1.22 B.1.23	B.2.1 B.2.2 B.2.3 B.2.12 B.2.13 B.2.16	B.3.3 B.3.4 B.3.5 B.3.6 B.3.7 B.3.8 B.3.14	B.4.4	4 5 7	C.1.1 C.1.2 C.1.3 C.1.9 C.1.10 C.1.11 C.1.14 C.1.17 C.1.18 C.1.19 C.1.20 C.1.22 C.1.28 C.1.29	C.2.1 C.2.3 C.2.7 C.2.9	C.3.1 C.3.2 C.3.8 C.3.9	C.4.3 C.4.4 C.4.6 C.4.10 C.4.11 C.4.13	1 2 5 6 7 8	D.1.2 D.1.11	D.2.3 D.2.9 D.2.12 D.2.13 D.2.20 D.2.22	D.3.1 D.3.4 D.3.10		D.5.8	2 3 4 6
1	Draw/Sketch		A.2.6	A.3.5 A.3.10 A.3.13	A.4.6	A.5.9	1	B.1.3	B.2.12 B.2.13		B.4.2 B.4.4		C.1.4 C.1.6 C.1.7 C.1.15 C.1.20 C.1.22	C.2.4 C.2.6 C.2.7	C.3.7		2 5	D.1.3	D.2.1 D.2.3 D.2.7 D.2.22			D.5.6 D.5.7	3
1	Label/Annotate			A.3.5 A.3.6 A.3.8 A.3.9 A.3.10 A.3.11			1	B.1.22			B.4.4	5	C.1.3 C.1.5 C.1.6 C.1.7 C.1.8 C.1.10 C.1.18 C.1.19 C.1.31	C.2.1	C.3.1	C.4.14	1 3 7		D.2.7				1
1	Define		A.2.10 A.2.11		A.4.1 A.4.7			B.1.2 B.1.7 B.1.10	B.2.17	B.3.7	B.4.1		C.1.29		C.3.9 C.3.11	C.4.11		D.1.11					
2	Outline		A.2.1	A.3.4 A.3.7 A.3.12		A.5.1 A.5.5 A.5.6 A.5.8 A.5.12 A.5.13	5			B.3.13	B.4.2	6	C.1.8 C.1.28 C.1.31	C.2.8 C.2.10	C.3.5 C.3.6	C.4.1 C.4.2 C.4.6 C.4.8 C.4.9 C.4.12	5 7		D.2.7 D.2.8 D.2.15 D.2.18	D.3.9	D.4.6 D.4.10 D.4.11	D.5.5	3 6 7
2	Calculate/Show	A.1.2 A.1.4 A.1.6	A.2.2 A.2.4 A.2.5 A.2.7 A.2.10 A.2.13 A.2.14 A.2.15 A.2.16 A.2.17	A.3.4 A.3.6 A.3.8 A.3.13	A.4.1 A.4.2 A.4.3 A.4.4 A.4.5 A.4.6 A.4.7 A.4.8 A.4.9 A.4.10 A.4.11	A.5.4 A.5.5 A.5.7 A.5.10 A.5.11 A.5.12	2 3 4 5 7	B.1.1 B.1.2 B.1.4 B.1.5 B.1.6 B.1.7 B.1.9 B.1.12 B.1.13 B.1.14 B.1.15 B.1.16 B.1.17 B.1.18 B.1.19 B.1.20 B.1.21 B.1.23	B.2.1 B.2.4 B.2.5 B.2.9 B.2.10 B.2.11 B.2.14 B.2.17 B.2.18	B.3.1 B.3.2 B.3.6 B.3.7 B.3.8 B.3.9 B.3.10 B.3.11 B.3.14	B.4.3	1 2 4 5 7	C.1.2 C.1.11 C.1.14 C.1.21 C.1.23 C.1.24 C.1.25 C.1.29 C.1.30	C.2.2 C.2.10	C.3.1 C.3.2 C.3.4 C.3.9 C.3.10 C.3.11	C.4.4 C.4.5	4 6 8 9	D.1.2 D.1.4 D.1.5 D.1.6 D.1.12 D.1.13 D.1.14 D.1.15 D.1.16 D.1.17 D.1.18 D.1.19	D.2.5 D.2.6 D.2.10	D.3.3 D.3.6 D.3.7 D.3.14		D.5.3	4 6

AO	Command Term	A. Relativity						B. Engineering Physics					C. Imaging					D. Astrophysics					
2	Describe			A.3.1 A.3.8 A.3.10	A.4.1	A.5.3 A.5.9	1	B.1.10	B.2.3 B.2.8 B.2.11 B.2.15 B.2.16 B.2.18				C.1.3 C.1.17 C.1.26 C.1.27 C.1.29 C.1.31	C.2.3 C.2.7 C.2.10		C.4.13		D.1.1	D.2.1 D.2.3 D.2.14 D.2.23	D.3.1 D.3.15	D.4.9	D.5.1 D.5.7	
2	Estimate											3							D.2.17				
3	Suggest	A.1.4 A.1.5 A.1.7	A.2.13			A.5.2 A.5.5 A.5.8 A.5.9 A.5.11 A.5.12	7	B.1.9 B.1.12 B.1.21	B.2.14 B.2.15 B.2.16	B.3.14	B.4.4	6 7	C.1.12 C.1.17	C.2.3 C.2.5 C.2.6 C.2.9 C.2.11	C.3.5 C.3.7	C.4.1 C.4.6 C.4.10 C.4.11	1 4		D.2.2 D.2.4 D.2.5 D.2.6	D.3.4 D.3.8		D.5.4 D.5.8	1 2 3 4
3	Determine/ Analyse	A.1.2 A.1.3 A.1.4 A.1.5 A.1.6 A.1.7	A.2.3 A.2.4 A.2.5 A.2.6 A.2.8 A.2.9 A.2.12 A.2.14	A.3.3 A.3.4 A.3.7 A.3.9 A.3.13		A.5.2 A.5.3 A.5.4 A.5.5	2 3 5 6	B.1.3 B.1.8 B.1.16 B.1.17 B.1.20	B.2.7 B.2.8 B.2.10 B.2.11 B.2.13	B.3.1 B.3.2 B.3.3 B.3.4 B.3.5 B.3.7 B.3.8 B.3.14 B.3.15	B.4.3 B.4.4	3 4 6 7	C.1.6 C.1.7 C.1.9 C.1.12 C.1.13 C.1.14 C.1.30	C.2.1 C.2.3 C.2.8 C.2.9	C.3.3 C.3.9	C.4.7	8	D.1.4 D.1.8 D.1.9	D.2.11	D.3.5 D.3.11	D.4.2 D.4.4	D.5.2 D.5.3	5 7
3	Explain	A.1.1 A.1.2 A.1.4 A.1.5 A.1.6 A.1.7	A.2.3 A.2.10 A.2.12 A.2.14 A.2.16 A.2.17	A.3.2 A.3.4 A.3.11 A.3.12 A.3.13	A.4.6	A.5.2 A.5.3 A.5.4 A.5.6 A.5.7 A.5.8 A.5.9 A.5.10 A.5.11 A.5.13	1 4	B.1.8	B.2.6 B.2.9 B.2.10 B.2.11 B.2.12 B.2.17	B.3.12 B.3.14	B.4.2	5 6	C.1.6 C.1.7 C.1.19 C.1.26 C.1.27	C.2.3 C.2.5 C.2.8 C.2.11	C.3.5 C.3.6	C.4.1 C.4.7 C.4.11 C.4.13	1 2 3 5 9	D.1.3 D.1.7 D.1.10	D.2.4 D.2.5 D.2.13 D.2.16 D.2.19 D.2.21	D.3.1 D.3.2 D.3.9 D.3.12 D.3.13 D.3.15	D.4.1 D.4.3 D.4.5 D.4.7 D.4.8 D.4.9	D.5.1	1 3 4 5 7
3	Discuss				A.4.11			B.1.11 B.1.21															

Measurement and uncertainties 1

Chapter outline

In this chapter, you will:
- Know and understand how to use the SI system of units.
- Perform simple arithmetic calculations without the use of a calculator, express and use numbers in standard form, and give answers to calculations using the correct number of significant figures.
- Understand the concepts of random and systematic uncertainty and be able to calculate and use absolute, fractional and percentage uncertainties.
- Develop the use of error bars in graphs and be able to find a gradient and its associated uncertainty on a linear graph.
- Understand the difference between vector and scalar quantities and be able to find components of vectors in mutually perpendicular directions, add components of vectors to find a resultant vector, and perform simple addition and subtraction of vectors both graphically and by using trigonometry.

KEY TERMS

Fundamental unit: one of seven units that form the basis of all other units used to measure quantities in physics, i.e. a fundamental unit is not *defined* in terms of any other units.

Standard form: expressing the magnitude of a quantity as a number between one and 10 along with a power of ten; for example, 1.5×10^4.

Random uncertainty: the statistical variation in a set of measurements of the same quantity.

Systematic uncertainty: a constant value of uncertainty, or offset, that is independent of the actual value measured.

Absolute uncertainty: the actual uncertainty associated with any measured value; this may be the smallest increment on a measuring instrument.

Fractional uncertainty: the proportion of the measured value that is its uncertainty; usually given as $\frac{\Delta x}{x}$.

Percentage uncertainty: the fractional uncertainty expressed as a percentage; i.e. $\frac{\Delta x}{x} \times 100\%$.

Components of a vector: two (or three in three dimensions) mutually perpendicular vectors that, when added together, form the vector itself – in practice, this usually involves the use of trigonometry: $v_x = v \cos\theta$, $v_y = v \sin\theta$, where θ is the angle between the vector and the x-axis.

Exercise 1.1 – Measurement in physics

1 State what is meant by the terms *fundamental unit* and *derived unit*.

2 The International Baccalaureate Diploma Programme (IBDP) physics courses use six SI fundamental units. (The seventh – the candela – is not a part of the specification.) These SI fundamental units are:

metre, kilogram, second, ampere, kelvin and mole

Which quantities are measured using the following units?

a metres

b kilograms

c seconds

d amperes

e kelvin

f moles

3 We usually measure speed in metres per second, $m\,s^{-1}$.

What are the units of the following quantities?

a acceleration

b force

c kinetic energy

d momentum

e charge

4 The SI unit of pressure is the pascal, Pa. Show that 1 Pa is the same as $1\ kg\ m^{-1}\ s^{-2}$.

5 The SI unit of energy is the joule, J.

a Newton's second law states that $F = ma$. Use this equation to find the SI base units of the Newton.

b Work done (as a measure of energy) = force × distance. Use this equation to show that the SI base units of energy are $kg\ m^2\ s^{-2}$.

c Kinetic energy, $KE = \frac{1}{2}mv^2$. Use this equation to find the SI base units of the joule.

6 The SI unit of power is the watt, W.

$$power = \frac{energy}{time}$$

Use this information to find the SI base units of the watt.

7 A volt, V, can be described as a joule per coulomb, $J\,C^{-1}$.

a Show that 1 C is the same as 1 A s.

b State the base units of energy.

c Show that 1 V is the same as $1\ kg\ m^2\ A^{-1}\ s^{-3}$.

8 A kilowatt-hour (kW h) is the amount of energy used by an electrical device rated at 1 kW (1 kW = $1000\ J\ s^{-1}$) when used for one hour. Use standard form to express 1 kW h in joules.

9 Units of quantities are often accompanied by a single letter prefix. It multiplies the unit by a power of ten. For example, we are familiar with the use of k (kilo) to mean that the unit is multiplied by 10^3, as in 1 km = 1000 m.

Look at the following prefixes. What are their proper names, and what power of ten do they multiply quantities by?

a m

b M

c μ

d n

e G

10 Physicists often use standard form to write numbers. For example, the number 130 is written in standard form as 1.3×10^2, and the number 0.053 is written as 5.3×10^{-2}. Express the following quantities in their appropriate base unit. Write your answers in standard form to two significant figures:

a 5.67 cm

b 13 μm

c 741 km

d 532 nm

e 53.7 g

f 43 minutes

g 998 g

h 45.6 ns

11 Complete the following statements by filling in the blank spaces with the appropriate power of ten:

a There are _____ mm in 1 km.

b There are _____ μJ in 1 GJ.

c There are _____ ms in 1 μs.

d There are _____ kg in 1 ng.

e There are _____ cm in 1 Mm.

12 Write the following quantities as numbers in standard form to the correct number of significant figures.

a 223 pF

b 4.5 kV

c 1.32 GW

d 503 MJ

13 There are 8457 pupils in a school in China. Give this number of pupils to:

a three significant figures

b two significant figures

c one significant figure.

14 A student measures the length of a road. It is 1359.457 m. Give the student's measurement to:

a one significant figure

b one decimal place

c two significant figures

d two decimal places.

15 Suggest a reason why one student might be able to give a measurement of length to three decimal places, whereas another student might only be able to give a measurement of length to two decimal places.

16 Write the following numbers in standard form.
   a 412
   b 320 000 000 000
   c 0.0087
   d 0.000 000 0001
   e fifty million

17 Without using a calculator, find the value of:
   a $10^{-2} \times 10^{-5}$
   b $10^6 \div 10^2$
   c $10^8 \div 10^{-3}$
   d $10^{-9} \times 10^9$
   e $10^6 \times 10^3 \times 10^{-5}$
   f $10^6 \times 10^3 \div 10^{-5}$
   g $(10^{-5} \div 10^{-3}) \times 10^4$
   h $10^{-5} \div (10^{-3} \times 10^4)$.

18 Complete the following calculations without using a calculator. It will help if you first write each number in standard form.
   a $40\,000 \times 0.02$
   b $0.000\,06 \times 0.003$
   c $50\,000 \times 41\,000$
   d 8 billion × fifty five

19 Use a calculator to complete the following calculations. Give your answers to an appropriate number of significant figures:
   a $53 + 6.047$
   b $2\pi \times 0.65$
   c 6.44^3
   d $360 \div 2\pi$
   e $3^2 \times 2.1$

20 Complete the following:
   a $(1.6 \times 10^{-27})^2$
   b $1 \div (6 \times 10^6)^2$
   c $(1.5 \times 10^{11}) \div (3 \times 10^8)$

21 Write the following numbers in standard form and to an appropriate number of significant figures.
   a 360
   b 0.004 400
   c 56 000
   d 0.000 0059
   e 32×66.87

22 Complete the following calculations without using a calculator.

  a $3 \times 10^8 \times 3.5 \times 10^7$

  b $2 \times 10^{-6} \times 8 \times 10^5$

  c $4.0 \times 1.7 \times 10^{-27}$

  d $5.0 \times 10^6 \times 1.6 \times 10^{-19}$

  e $(8.0 \times 10^{12}) \div (4 \times 10^4)$

  f $(1.2 \times 10^7) \div (3.0 \times 10^6)$

23 Use standard form to solve the following calculations without a calculator.

  a $\sqrt{1600}$

  b $(5 \times 10^{-3})^2$

  c $\sqrt{(400)^2 + (300)^2}$

  d $(3.0 \times 10^{-15})^3$

  e $\sqrt[3]{8 \times 10^{-12}}$

24 Physicists tend to quote the size of quantities to the nearest power of ten. This is called an *order of magnitude*. For example, the order of magnitude for the number 200 is 10^2, and the order of magnitude for the number 7×10^{-5} is 10^{-4}. What is the order of magnitude of the following numbers?

  a 2 000 000

  b 4300

  c 6.4×10^{-9}

25 The diameter of a nucleus is of the order 10^{-15} m. To what power of ten is the volume of the nucleus?

26 What is the order of magnitude of the following quantities?

  a The number of hours in a year.

  b The distance (in metres) from the Earth to the Sun.

  c The number of molecules of hydrogen gas, H_2, in 2 g of the gas.

  d The number of metres in a light-year.

27 One mole of hydrogen atoms has a mass of 1.0 g. There are about 6×10^{23} atoms in a mole. What is the mass of one hydrogen atom, to the nearest power of ten?

28 The unified atomic mass unit, u, is defined as the mass of $\dfrac{1}{12}$ of the mass of a $^{12}_{6}C$ atom. Calculate u in kg. Give your answer to an appropriate number of significant figures.

29 The density of copper is 8900 kg m^{-3}. The molar mass of copper is 63.5 g mol^{-1}. Calculate the number of:

  a moles of copper atoms in 1 kg of copper

  b copper atoms in 1 kg of copper

  c copper atoms in 1 m^3 of copper.

30 The speed of light is approximately 3.0×10^8 m s^{-1}. Calculate how far light travels in one year. Give your answer to an appropriate number of significant figures.

Exercise 1.2 – Uncertainties and errors

1   A student measures the length of a desk to be 126 cm. Determine the following quantities.
   a The likely uncertainty in the student's measurement.
   b The fractional uncertainty in the student's measurement.
   c The percentage uncertainty in the student's measurement.

2   A student used an ammeter to measure a current of 1.5 A. The smallest increment on her ammeter was 0.1 A. Determine the following:
   a The absolute uncertainty in the measurement.
   b The fractional uncertainty in the measurement.
   c The percentage uncertainty in the measurement.

3   A rectangle measures 12 cm ± 1 cm by 5 cm ± 1 cm. What is the perimeter of the rectangle and the uncertainty of the value?

4   In a calculation involving temperatures, a student notes that $y = x - c$. He measures x to be 61.5 °C ± 0.2 °C and c to be 30.2 °C ± 0.4 °C.
   What is the value of y and its associated uncertainty?

5   The uncertainty in a measurement can be classified as a *random* (or statistical) uncertainty or a *systematic* uncertainty. Suggest some ways in which:
   a random uncertainty can occur
   b systematic uncertainty can occur.

6   Explain what is meant by:
   a zero error
   b parallax error.

7   The percentage uncertainty in the radius of a circle is 5%. What will the percentage uncertainty be of the following?
   a The circumference of the circle.
   b The area enclosed by the circle.
   c A sphere of the same radius and associated uncertainty.

8   A quantity, y, is given as: $y = xz$. If the percentage uncertainty in x is 5% and the percentage uncertainty in z is 3 %, what will the percentage uncertainty in y be?

9   A student measures a component's current as 0.25 A ± 0.01 A and its voltage as 4.0 V ± 0.1 V.
   a What is the resistance of the component?
   b What are the percentage and absolute uncertainties in the value of the resistance?

10 A quantity, g, is given as: $g = \dfrac{F}{m}$. The percentage uncertainty in F is 6% and the percentage uncertainty in m is 3%. What is the percentage uncertainty in g?

11 The equation for kinetic energy is $KE = \dfrac{1}{2}mv^2$. The percentage uncertainty in m is 3% and the percentage uncertainty in v is 5%. What is the percentage uncertainty in KE?

12 In a physics experiment, quantity h is found to be proportional to one other quantity, $\sqrt{d}$:

$h = 4\sqrt{d}$

If the percentage uncertainty in d is 10%, what will be the percentage uncertainty in h?

13 $T = 2\pi\sqrt{\dfrac{m}{k}}$ If the percentage uncertainty in m is 4% and the percentage uncertainty in k is 2%, what is the percentage uncertainty in T?

14 A student measures the base length of a right-angled triangle to be 5.0 cm ± 0.1 cm and the height of the triangle to be 4.0 cm ± 0.1 cm. Calculate the:
   a percentage uncertainty in the measurement of the base
   b percentage uncertainty in the measurement of the height
   c percentage uncertainty in the area of the triangle
   d area of the triangle
   e absolute uncertainty in the area of the triangle.

15 A girl measures her weight to be 500 N ± 1 N. If the value of g, the gravitational field strength of the Earth, is given as g = 9.81 N kg^{-1} ± 0.01 N kg^{-1}, what is the:
   a percentage uncertainty in the girl's weight?
   b percentage uncertainty in the gravitational field strength of the Earth?
   c percentage uncertainty in the girl's mass?
   d girl's mass?
   e absolute uncertainty in the girl's mass?

16 What is meant by:
   a accurate?
   b precise?

17 Give an example of a set of measurements that is:
   a accurate but not precise
   b precise but not accurate
   c accurate and precise
   d neither accurate nor precise.

18 What is the main reason for scientists taking repeat measurements?

19 This list shows some repeated measurements of the length of a banana:
   12.2 cm; 12.5 cm; 11.8 cm; 12.0 cm; 11.9 cm; 12.2 cm; 12.0 cm; 12.3 cm
   a What is the mean average length of the banana?
   b What is the range of the measurements?
   c What is the random uncertainty in the mean length of the banana?
   d Write the length of the banana and its associated random uncertainty.

20 In an experiment, the following data were measured:

| Mass / kg ± 0.01 | 3.24 | 3.22 | 3.16 | 3.26 | 3.23 | 3.28 | 3.22 |

a What is the mean average of the values of mass?
b What is the range of values?
c What is the random uncertainty in the mean?
d Is this random uncertainty bigger than the absolute uncertainty in the measurements?
e Write the mean value and its associated uncertainty.

21 In an experiment, the following data were measured:

| Time / s ± 0.2 | 4.1 | 4.2 | 4.1 | 4.1 | 4.2 |

a Find the mean average of the measured values.
b Find the random uncertainty in the mean.
c Which is larger: the random uncertainty in the mean, or the absolute uncertainty in the measurement?
d Write the mean value and its associated uncertainty.

22 Six students measured their height using two metre rulers. Both rulers had a scale with a smallest increment of 1 cm. The measurements were:
1.72 m; 1.84 m; 1,66 m; 1.88 m; 1.70 m; 1.75 m
a Calculate the mean average height of these students.
b Calculate half the range of the heights for these students.
c Write the average height and its associated random uncertainty.
d Find the percentage random uncertainty in the height of the students.

23 Look at Figure 1.1; it has five points plotted on it.

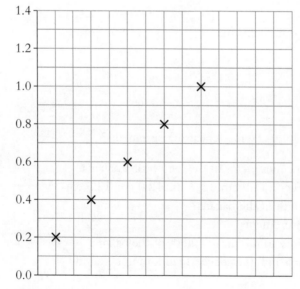

Figure 1.1

The uncertainty in the y-axis values is ± 0.2 for all points.

a Draw error bars on the graph to show these uncertainties.

b Draw the best-fit line that **passes through all of the error bars.**

c Draw a line that passes through all the error bars that has the **maximum** possible gradient.

d Draw a line that **passes through all the error bars** that has the **minimum** possible gradient.

24 A student carries out an experiment to find out how the time period of a simple pendulum varies with its length. She plots her results on a graph of *time period* against *length*, which shows a relationship of the form:

$$T = k\sqrt{l}$$

The student wants to draw another graph that has a relationship showing a straight line that passes through the origin.

a Suggest how she may process some of her data in order to draw this graph.

b If the percentage uncertainty in T was 5% and the percentage uncertainty in l was 4%, what would the percentage uncertainty in the values on her new graph be?

25 Figure 1.2 shows several different graphs.

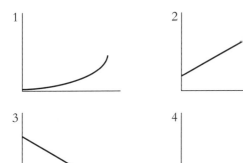
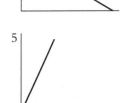
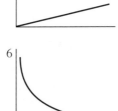

Figure 1.2

Which of the graphs shows a:

a linear relationship?

b proportional relationship?

c possible power law relationship?

d possible inverse relationship?

Exercise 1.3 – Vectors and scalars

1 Quantities in physics can be divided into **scalar quantities** and **vector quantities**.
   a Explain what is meant by a scalar quantity, and give one example.
   b Explain what is meant by a vector quantity, and give one example.

2 Here is a list of several quantities used in physics:
   mass; speed; time; velocity; force; weight; density; pressure; acceleration; temperature; kinetic energy; gravitational potential energy; momentum; volume; displacement; area; length; current; power
   Divide the list into **scalar quantities** and **vector quantities**.

3 Figure 1.3 shows two vectors, *a* and *b*.

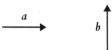

Figure 1.3

   Add together the two vectors graphically to find their sum, *a* + *b*.

4 Use the two vectors in question 3 to find, by drawing:
   a *a* − *b*
   b *b* − *a*

5 Use the two vectors in question 3 to find, by drawing:
   a 2*a* + 3*b*
   b 2*b* − 3*a*

6 A person's initial velocity vector is:

   and, after a short time, their final velocity vector is:

   What is the change in the person's velocity?

7 A ship that had been travelling north at 4 m s⁻¹ changes course so that it now travels west at 3 m s⁻¹. What was the change in velocity of the ship?

8 Vector *a* has magnitude 4 units and direction horizontally left-to-right, whilst vector *b* has magnitude 2 units in a direction vertically upwards. What are the magnitude and direction of the following?
   a *a* + *b*
   b *a* − *b*
   c *b* − *a*

9 The vector, p is:

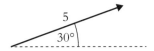

    a Find the horizontal component of p.
    b Find the vertical component of p.

10 A vector is described by its components as (6, 3), meaning that its horizontal component is 6 units and its vertical component is 3 units. Find the:
    a magnitude of the vector
    b direction of the vector.

11 Vector X has components: $X_{horizontal} = 5$ N and $X_{vertical} = 4$ N. Calculate:
    a the magnitude of X
    b the angle X makes with the horizontal.

12 The vector, P is:

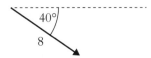

    Find the:
    a horizontal component of P
    b vertical component of P.

13 An object has three forces acting on it simultaneously:
An upwards vertical force of 6 N, a left-to-right force of 3 N, and another unspecified force.
If the object is in equilibrium, find the:
    a magnitude of the unspecified force
    b direction of the unspecified force.

14 A picture is hung on a wall by two strings. Each string makes an angle of 35° to the vertical. The tension in each string is 60 N. Calculate the weight of the picture.

15 A plane flies in a northwards direction at a speed of 300 m s^{-1}. If the plane experiences a westwards wind of 40 m s^{-1}, find:
    a the actual speed of the plane as observed by a spectator on the ground.
    b the actual direction that the plane is travelling in as observed by a spectator on the ground.
    c how much further west the plane will be after it has travelled for one hour.

1 Which of the following is the best estimate of the diameter of an atom?
   A 10^{-6} m
   B 10^{-8} m
   C 10^{-10} m
   D 10^{-12} m

2 Which of the following is the best estimate of the number of seconds in a year?
   A 10^4
   B 10^5
   C 10^6
   D 10^7

3 Which of the following is the best estimate of the speed at which Usain Bolt can run?
   A 10 m s^{-1}
   B 20 m s^{-1}
   C 30 m s^{-1}
   D 40 m s^{-1}

4 Which is the best estimate of the world's population in 2015?
   A 10^8
   B 10^9
   C 10^{10}
   D 10^{11}

5 a Use the data in Table 1.1 to draw a graph; plot time, t, on the x-axis. **[4]**

Time, t/s $\pm$ 0.2	0.0	2.0	4.0	6.0	8.0	10.0	12.0	14.0
Distance, x/m $\pm$ 1.5	0.0	4.1	8.6	12.0	16.2	19.9	24.2	28.3

Table 1.1

   b Add some error bars to your graph to show the uncertainty in the values of distance, x. (For this example, it is not necessary to plot the error bars for the values of time, t.) **[2]**
   c Draw the best-fit line and calculate the gradient of the graph. What physical quantity does this gradient represent? **[3]**
   d Draw the maximum gradient line that **passes through all of the error bars**. **[1]**
   e Calculate this maximum gradient. **[1]**
   f Draw the minimum gradient line that **passes through all of the error bars**. **[1]**
   g Calculate this minimum gradient. **[1]**
   h Find the value of half the range of the gradients. This will be your uncertainty in the best-fit gradient. **[1]**
   i Write an equation that links the distance, x, with the time, t, in the form:
      $x = (m \pm \Delta m)\ t$ **[1]**

6   Figure 1.4 shows the results from an experiment to find out how the distance of a dropped object varies with the time for which it has dropped. The error bars for these points have been omitted because they are too small to see. Using some computer software, the relationship for this graph is shown to be: $s = k\,t^2$

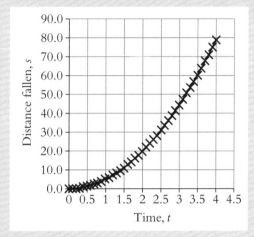

Figure 1.4

a   Suggest how these data could be processed, so that a new graph can be produced that shows a proportional relationship. **[2]**

b   In the second processed data graph, if the percentage uncertainty in s is 3% and the percentage uncertainty in t is 2%, what will the percentage uncertainties in the processed data be? **[2]**

7   A student measured how the time taken for a mass on a spring to oscillate varies with mass. He found a graphical relationship, as shown in Figure 1.5.

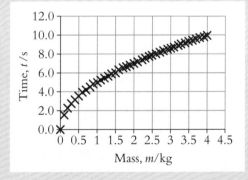

Figure 1.5

a   Suggest why the graph shows that the relationship between t and m is not proportional. **[2]**

b   Suggest how the student can process the data so a new graph showing a proportional relationship can be found. **[2]**

c   For the new graph, suggest how the student should propagate the uncertainties in the two axes. **[2]**

8   A student measures how much a length of copper wire stretches when she applies a tension force to it. Her results are shown in Table 1.2.

Force, F / N ± 2	10	20	30	40	50
Extension, x / mm ± 0.1	1.4	3.1	4.7	6.1	7.6

Table 1.2

a   Plot a graph of the student's results with force on the *y*-axis and extension on the *x*-axis, including error bars for all your points. [5]

b   What kind of relationship do the data suggest? [1]

c   Draw a best-fit line for the data on the graph, ensuring that your line passes **through all of the error bars**. [1]

d   The stiffness of the copper wire is given by the gradient of this graph. Calculate the stiffness of the student's piece of copper wire. [2]

e   Now, by drawing in the maximum and the minimum possible gradients (**remember that these two lines must pass through all of the error bars**), find the uncertainty in the stiffness of the student's piece of copper wire. [3]

9   A student investigates how the power supplied to a hair drier affects the speed of the air that the hair drier blows. Figure 1.6 shows the experimental arrangement.

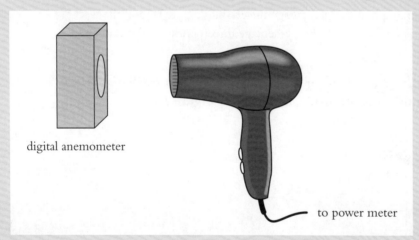

digital anemometer

to power meter

Figure 1.6

a   For this student's investigation:

   i   state the independent variable

   ii   state the dependent variable

   iii   suggest one control variable that the student will need to consider and what effect this variable will have on the dependent variable. [4]

The student notes that the uncertainty in the measurement of power, *P*, is ± 1 W and the uncertainty in the measurement of air speed, *v*, is ± 0.1 m s^{-1}.

The student plots a graph of the air speed, *v*, against the power supplied to the hair drier. Figure 1.7 shows the graph.

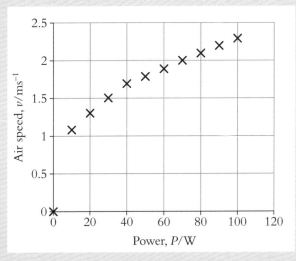

Figure 1.7

b For the points corresponding to a power of 10 W and a power of 80 W, add error bars to the air speed axis on the student's graph. **[2]**

c Calculate the percentage uncertainty in the air speed for the two points in **9b**. **[2]**

One hypothesis is that the data follow the relationship:

$$v - AP^{\frac{1}{3}}$$

d Suggest why plotting a graph of v^3 against P will be a suitable test for this hypothesis. **[1]**

e Using some graph paper, plot a graph of v^3 against P. You may need to process any relevant data. **[5]**

f Calculate the uncertainty in the value of v^3 for the power value of 10 W. **[2]**

g Use your graph to find the value for A. **[2]**

h State the units of A. **[1]**

10 **How can we know when we have made enough measurements?**

11 **This question is about uncertainties.**
In an investigation, a student plots a graph of y against x and notices that the graph is a curve. One of the points on the graph is given by the co-ordinates (12.0, 18.0).

a If the percentage uncertainty in x is 8.5 %, determine the absolute uncertainty in x. **[1]**

The student suggests that the relationship between x and y is of the form: $y = A x^2$, where A is a constant. The student suggests that a plot of y against x^2 will produce a straight line that passes through the origin.

b Comment on whether the student's suggestion is sensible. **[2]**

The student carries out the plot and finds that the previous point has now become (144, 18).

c Calculate the size of the uncertainty in the value of $x^2 = 144$. **[2]**

d Determine the value of A. **[1]**

12 A group of students measures the length and width of a piece of A1 sized paper. According to the ISO, a piece of A1 paper is supposed to be 841 mm ± 3 mm long and 594 mm ± 2 mm wide. Table 1.3 shows their measurements.

Student	David	Anna	Tim	Sophie	Joy	Charles
Length / mm ± 1	835	840	847	841	837	844
Width / mm ± 1	595	593	600	594	604	597

Table 1.3

a Calculate the mean value of the students' length measurements. [1]
b If the students want to quote the value of their average measurement of length along with its uncertainty, suggest, with a reason, the value of the uncertainty they should choose. [2]
c Sophie claims that Tim has a systematic uncertainty with his measurements. Suggest, with a reason, whether Sophie is correct in her thinking. [2]
d Calculate the percentage uncertainty in the mean width measured by the students. [2]

13 This question is about a swimmer who is trying to get across a river.
A swimmer swims directly towards the other side of a river at a steady speed of 2 m s^{-1} through the water. The river has a current that moves the water along at a steady speed of 3 m s^{-1}. If the river is 12 m wide:
a Calculate how much time it takes for the swimmer to reach the other side of the river. [1]
b Using your answer to **13a**, determine:
   i   the distance downstream from the point directly opposite where the swimmer began, to the point where the swimmer arrives on the other side of the river
   ii the actual distance that the swimmer has travelled on the journey across the river
   iii the actual velocity at which the swimmer moved during the journey. [5]

Mechanics 2

Chapter outline

In this chapter, you will:
- Sketch and interpret graphs of *displacement*, *speed*, *velocity* and *acceleration* against *time*; and use them to solve problems involving instantaneous and average values of velocity, speed and acceleration.
- Use the SUVAT equations of motion for uniform acceleration to solve problems involving projectiles and the Earth's gravitational field strength near the surface of the Earth.
- Sketch and interpret free-body force diagrams, understand and be able to use coefficients of friction and be able to describe qualitatively the effect of fluid resistance of falling objects, including the concept of terminal speed.
- Sketch and interpret graphs of force against distance, their gradients and their areas, solve problems involving the concept of power as the rate of doing work and incorporate the concept of efficiency into calculations involving the transformation of energy.
- Use Newton's second law in terms of a rate of change of momentum, interpret graphs involving force and time, including the meaning of impulse, use the conservation of linear momentum in a range of practical situations and distinguish between elastic, inelastic and super-elastic collisions.

KEY TERMS

Acceleration: A vector quantity defined as the rate of change of velocity; $a = \dfrac{\Delta v}{\Delta t}$

SUVAT equations:
$$v = u + at$$
$$s = ut + \tfrac{1}{2} a t^2$$
$$v^2 = u^2 + 2 a s$$

where, u = initial velocity, v = final velocity, s = displacement/distance moved, a = acceleration, t = time

Newton's laws of motion:

First: A body will continue to move with a constant velocity, or remain at rest, unless it is acted upon by an unbalanced force.

Second: Force equals rate of change of momentum; $F = \dfrac{\Delta p}{\Delta t}$.

Third: If body A exerts a force, F, on body B, then body B exerts the same size force, F, on body A, but in the opposite direction.

Coefficient of static friction, μ_s: The maximum value of the ratio, $\dfrac{F}{R}$, where F is the frictional force between a surface and a body and R is the normal reaction force, such that a body will not begin to slide; $\mu_s \leq \dfrac{F}{R}$.

Coefficient of dynamic friction, μ_d: The ratio of the frictional force, F, between a moving body and a surface and the normal reaction force, R; $\mu_d \leq \dfrac{F}{R}$.

Work done: The product of the force applied and the distance in the direction of the force through which a body moves – measured in joules, work done $= F s \cos \theta$, where θ is the angle between the direction of motion and the force applied.

Power: Defined as the rate of doing work. $P = \dfrac{\text{work done}}{\text{time taken}}$.

Efficiency: The ratio of the useful work done to the total energy supplied.
$\varepsilon = \dfrac{\text{useful work done}}{\text{total energy supplied}}$.

Principle of conservation of linear momentum: The total momentum in a system is always constant providing no external forces act on the system.

Impulse, I: The change of momentum, $I = F t$.

Exercise 2.1 – Motion

1 Explain the difference between *distance* and *displacement*.

2 Calculate the speed, in m s^{-1}, of a:
   a car that travels 200 km in 90 minutes
   b sound wave that reaches an observer's ears having travelled 1.5 km in 4.5 s
   c transatlantic liner that takes five days to travel 6000 km.

3 A high speed train travels between Beijing and Tianjin. If the train travels at a speed of 97 m s^{-1}, calculate the time it takes for the train to travel the 117 km journey.

4 Proxima Centauri is the closest star to our Sun. It is 3.78×10^{16} m from the Earth.
   a Calculate the time it takes for light to travel from Proxima Centauri to the Earth.
   b How else could the distance from Proxima Centauri to the Earth be stated?

5 Figure 2.1 shows a journey made by a pedestrian.

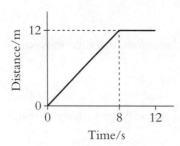

Figure 2.1

Use the graph to find the:
   a average speed of the pedestrian for the whole journey
   b speed of the pedestrian during the first eight seconds.

6 A molecule of nitrogen in the air travels 3 cm horizontally and 4 cm vertically in a time
   of 100 μs.
   a Calculate the overall displacement of the molecule.
   b Calculate the average speed of the molecule.
   c Calculate the direction in which it has travelled relative to the horizontal.
   d State its average velocity during the 100 μs period.

7 Figure 2.2 shows a velocity–time graph for a journey.

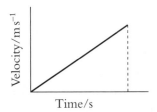

Figure 2.2

What aspect of the journey is shown by the:
a gradient of the graph?
b area under the graph?

8 Figure 2.3 shows a journey made by a cyclist.

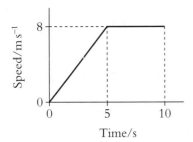

Figure 2.3

Use the graph to find the:
a distance travelled by the cyclist in the first five seconds
b value of the cyclist's acceleration during the first five seconds
c average speed of the cyclist for the whole journey.

9   Figure 2.4 shows a velocity–time graph for part of a journey made by an electric train.

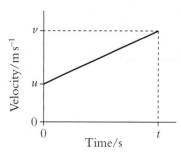

Figure 2.4

a   If the train had travelled at the same speed as its initial speed throughout the journey, state an algebraic expression for how far the train would have travelled.

b   Copy the graph and shade in the region of the graph that represents your answer to part **a**.
The remaining part of the graph shows the extra distance travelled by the train because it was accelerating.

c   Show that the acceleration, a, of the train can be given as $a = \dfrac{v - u}{t}$.

d   Show that the extra distance travelled by the train due to its acceleration can be expressed as $\frac{1}{2}at^2$.

e   Shade this region on your copy of the graph.

f   State the algebraic expression for the total distance travelled during the journey.

10 A passenger in a car starts a stopwatch when the car is travelling at 28.8 km h^{-1}. The car accelerates with a constant acceleration of 2 m s^{-2} for the next ten seconds. Calculate the:

a   speed of the car after 10 seconds of acceleration

b   distance that the car has travelled during the 10 second period.

11 A girl drops her mobile phone from a window that is 15 m above the ground. Taking the acceleration of the Earth's gravitational field to be 10 m s^{-2} and ignoring any effects of air friction:

a   Sketch a velocity–time graph for the phone from when it leaves the girl's hand to when it hits the ground.

b   Calculate the time it takes for the phone to hit the ground.

c   Calculate the phone's velocity just before it hits the ground.

12 A baseball pitcher practises by throwing a ball vertically into the air with an initial velocity of 30 m s^{-1} and catching it when it falls back. Ignoring any effects of air resistance, and assuming $g = 10$ m s^{-2}, calculate:

a   how much time it will take for the ball to reach its highest point

b   how far above the pitcher the ball reaches.

13 Two cricketers practise by throwing a cricket ball to each other, as shown in Figure 2.5.

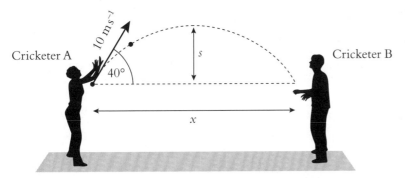

Figure 2.5

Ignoring any effects of air friction and assuming g = 9.81 m s^{-2}, calculate:
a   the vertical component of the ball's velocity as it leaves cricketer A's hands
b   the time it takes for the ball to reach its highest point
c   the height, s, that the ball reaches above the cricketer's hands
d   how far apart, x, the two cricketers are.

14 Describe an experiment you could carry out to determine the value of the Earth's gravitational acceleration, g, acting on a dropped object.
You need to include:
• the equipment you will require
• the measurements you will need to take
• how you will process your measurements to find g.

15 When a parachutist jumps from an aeroplane, he hits the ground with a landing speed of 6.0 m s^{-1}.
What is the minimum jump height required to simulate this landing speed?

Exercise 2.2 – Forces

1   Explain what is meant by the terms *inertial mass* and *gravitational mass*.

2   State:
a   Newton's first law of motion
b   the two conditions necessary for a body to be in equilibrium.

3   A mass of 5 kg is subject to an unbalanced force of 20 N. Calculate the resulting acceleration of the mass.

4   A bullet accelerates along the barrel of a rifle. Its speed changes from 0 m s^{-1} to 1500 m s^{-1} in a time of 0.1 s. The mass of the bullet is 0.05 kg. Calculate the average force acting on the bullet.

5 Figure 2.6 shows the free-body force diagram for a 12 gramme paper cone falling through the air.

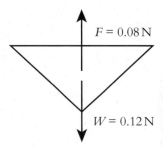

Figure 2.6

    a Calculate the acceleration of the paper cone.
    b Sketch a graph of *acceleration of the cone* against *time* for the next few seconds of its fall.
    c Explain the shape of your graph using Newton's laws of motion.

6 Consider an aeroplane flying horizontally at a constant velocity.
    a Sketch a free-body force diagram for the aeroplane.
    b What can you say about the relationships between the forces?

7 Consider a heavy box stationary on the surface of a table.
    a Sketch a free-body force diagram to show all the forces acting on the box.
    b Explain how your diagram reflects:
       i   Newton's first law
       ii Newton's second law
       iii Newton's third law.

8 Figure 2.7 shows the free-body force diagram for a box resting on the surface of a table. The two forces have been slightly displaced for ease of viewing.

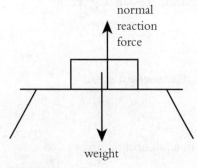

Figure 2.7

    a If a person pushes downwards on the box, what happens to the normal reaction force, N?
    b If a person pulls the box upwards with a force less than the box's weight, what happens to the normal reaction force, N?
    c What size force, and in which direction, must a person exert on the box if the normal reaction force is to be zero?

9   Just about every American SAT physics paper and university entrance exam seems to
    have a question about a person in an elevator. Consider, therefore, a person of mass
    60 kg standing on a set of weighing scales in an elevator.
    a   If the elevator is moving at a constant speed, determine the reading on the
        weighing scales.
    b   If the elevator is accelerating downwards with an acceleration of $0.25g$, determine
        the reading on the weighing scales. ($g = 9.81$ m s^{-2})
    c   If the elevator is accelerating upwards with an acceleration of $0.2g$, determine the
        reading on the weighing scales. ($g = 9.81$ m s^{-2})

10 Figure 2.8 shows a free-body force diagram for a book resting on an inclined slope.
    The book is not moving.

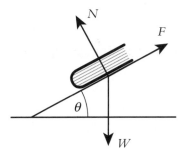

Figure 2.8

    a   By taking components of the forces along the slope and perpendicular to the
        slope, determine how F is related to N.
    b   How does your answer to part **a** relate to the coefficient of static friction, μ_s?
    c   Explain why the book will eventually slip down the slope if the angle of the slope
        to the horizontal is gradually increased.

11 Air freight is off-loaded from an aeroplane by allowing the containers to slide down
    an inclined ramp at an angle of 30° to the horizontal. The coefficient of static friction
    between the containers and the ramp is 0.45.
    Show that the containers are able to slide.

12 A box of mass 25 kg is being pulled across a horizontal surface at a constant speed by
    a rope at an angle of 40° to the horizontal. The tension in the rope is 150 N.
    Determine the coefficient of dynamic friction, μ_d, between the box and the
    horizontal surface.

Exercise 2.3 – Work, energy and power

1   The total energy of a body is the sum of its kinetic energy and its potential energy.
    Calculate the total energy of a:
    a   5 kg mass moving at 2 m s^{-1} along the ground
    b   4 kg mass sitting stationary on top of a cupboard of height 2 m
    c   3 kg mass moving horizontally through the air at a speed of 4 m s^{-1}, 5 m above
        the ground.

2 a A clumsy teacher drops her cup of coffee from a height of 1.5 m. The mass of the cup of coffee was 0.45 kg. Ignoring any effects of air friction, calculate the:

    i initial gravitational potential energy of the cup of coffee

    ii speed of the cup of coffee just before it hit the ground.

  b Would your answer to part **aii** be different if she had only dropped her spoon? Explain your answer.

3 a Define what a joule is.

  b State the principle of conservation of energy.

  c A pupil picks up a book from the floor and places the book on a table.

    i Has the book gained energy? Explain your answer.

    ii Has the pupil lost energy? Explain your answer.

    iii Why is it likely that the energy lost by the pupil is not the same magnitude as the energy gained by the book?

4 Figure 2.9 shows a large block of stone, of mass 3×10^3 kg, being pushed up a slope.

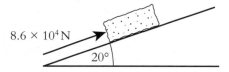

8.6×10^4 N

20°

Figure 2.9

The slope is 15 m long. The force used to push the block of stone is 8.6×10^4 N.

  a Calculate the work done in moving the block of stone.

  b Calculate the gravitational potential energy gained by the block of stone.

  c How do you account for the difference between your answers to parts **a** and **b**?

5 A driver applies the brakes of his 1400 kg car while travelling at 20 m s^{-1}. The car begins to slow down. If the average force of the brakes is 9 kN, calculate how far the car will travel until it comes to a stop.

6 Figure 2.10 shows how the force required to push a thumb tack into a poster board varies with distance (how far it is pushed into the board).

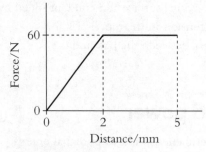

Figure 2.10

Use the graph to calculate the work done when pushing the thumb tack 5 mm into the board.

7   Consider a graph that shows how the force required to extend a spring varies with the extension of the spring.
    a   What physical quantity can be found from the gradient of the graph?
    b   What physical quantity can be found from the area under the graph?

8   a   State Hooke's law.
    b   For springs that obey Hooke's law, calculate the force required to extend a:
        i   spring of spring constant 25 N m^{-1} by 30 cm
        ii spring of spring constant 0.30 N m^{-1} by 2.5 mm.

9   a   The overall spring constant of three identical springs is series is 12 N m^{-1}. Determine the spring constant of one spring.
    b   The overall spring constant of two springs in parallel is 50 N m^{-1}. Determine the spring constant of one spring.

10 A children's toy comprises a plastic semi-sphere mounted on top of a spring of spring constant 5000 N m^{-1}. The total mass of the toy is 25 g. The toy is used by compressing the spring by 1 cm. When it is let go, it jumps into the air. Calculate how high the toy can jump into the air.

11 In a water well, a motor lifts a 40 kg bucket 30 m in 12 s. Calculate the:
    a   work done by the motor
    b   output power of the motor.

12 A small car, whose engine is rated at 15 kW, travels at a constant speed of 20 m s^{-1}. Calculate the effective driving force of the engine.

13 Three boys are arguing about who is the most powerful. They each time themselves to do some work. Their results are given in Table 2.1.

Boy's name	Work done / J	Time taken
Anton	3.25×10^3	15 minutes
Ravi	90	25 s
Joshua	11.5×10^3	1 hour

Table 2.1

Which boy is the most powerful?

14 When the driver of a car presses the accelerator pedal, more fuel is injected into the engine and the speed of the car increases. A car of mass 1.5×10^3 kg increases its speed from 20 m s^{-1} to 32 m s^{-1} in a time of 5.0 s.
    a   Calculate the increase in kinetic energy of the car.
    b   Calculate the output power of the car's engine
    c   If the car's engine is 55% efficient, how much energy did the fuel provide?

15 An athlete trains by running up a set of steps. The athlete, of mass 65 kg, runs up 5 m of steps in a time of 6 s.
    a   Calculate the power of the athlete.
    b   If the athlete's efficiency is 20%, how much energy has the athlete used?

Exercise 2.4 – Momentum and impulse

1 **a** State the principle of conservation of linear momentum.
  b Is the principle of conservation of momentum a universal law? Explain your answer.

2 Calculate the momentum of:
  a a girl of mass 50 kg running westwards at a speed of 6 m s^{-1}
  b an electron of mass 9.1×10^{-31} kg travelling at a speed of 2.0×10^7 m s^{-1} towards an anode
  c a hockey ball of mass 110 g travelling at 60 m s^{-1} towards a goal.

3 A body of mass 3 kg travelling horizontally at 4 m s^{-1} collides with, and sticks to, a stationary mass of 1 kg. Use the principle of conservation of momentum to calculate the speed of the combined masses after the collision.

4 A falling ball of mass 0.4 kg and speed 8 m s^{-1} hits the ground and bounces back upwards with a speed of 5 m s^{-1}.
  a Calculate the momentum of the ball *before* its collision with the ground.
  b Calculate the momentum of the ball *after* its collision with the ground.
  c How do you reconcile the principle of conservation of momentum?

5 In the alpha-decay of an americium–241 nucleus, a $^{237}_{93}$Np nucleus moves away at a speed, v, while the alpha particle moves away at a speed of 1.6×10^7 m s^{-1} in the opposite direction. The relative masses of the two particles are 237 and 4.
  a Determine the speed at which the $^{237}_{93}$Np nucleus moves after the emission of the alpha particle.
  b How does the kinetic energy of the alpha particle compare with the kinetic energy of the $^{237}_{93}$Np nucleus?

6 Figure 2.11 shows how the unbalanced force on an initially stationary object of mass 3 kg varies with time.

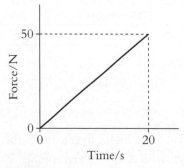

Figure 2.11

  a Use the graph to determine the impulse experienced by the object.
  b Sketch a graph of how the velocity of the object may be changing.
  c Calculate the final velocity of the object.

7 Explain how crumple zones on a modern car reduce the chance of injury to its passengers.

8 Newton's second law of motion states that force = rate of change of momentum. Show that, if a body's mass does not change during an interaction, Newton's second law can be written as $F = m\,a$.

9 In the famous 'Dirty Harry' movies, Harry Callahan (played by Clint Eastwood) uses a .44-Magnum gun because he claims it has more 'fire power' than ordinary police issue revolvers. The mass of a bullet from a .44 Magnum is about 250 g and it travels at 450 m s^{-1} from the barrel of the gun.

a Calculate the momentum of the bullet after it has been fired from the gun.

Now suppose that Harry shoots a bad guy, of mass 70 kg. The bullet hits the bad guy and lodges inside his body in a time of 0.1 seconds.

b Calculate the speed of the bad guy's body just after he has been shot.

c Now calculate the force that the bullet exerted on the bad guy.

d What do your answers to parts b and c tell you about the subsequent motion of the bad guy?

e Discuss whether the movies are an accurate portrayal of what you would expect to happen.

? Exam-style questions

1 **An object of mass 2.5 kg falls vertically through the air with a downwards acceleration of 4.81 m s^{-2}. Taking $g = 9.81$ m s^{-2}, the size of the air resistance force acting on the object is:**

A Zero

B 5.81 N

C 12.5 N

D 24.5 N

2 **Here are three statements about an object in motion:**

One: An object that is not accelerating must have a constant speed.

Two: An object that is travelling at a constant speed cannot be accelerating.

Three: An object that travels at constant speed for a period of time cannot have a zero displacement.

Which of the following combinations of these three statements is true?

A One only

B One and Three only

C Two and Three only

D One, Two and Three

3 **When two objects collide elastically, which of the following combinations of kinetic energy and momentum is correct?**

A Kinetic energy = conserved; Momentum = conserved

B Kinetic energy = not conserved; Momentum = conserved

C Kinetic energy = conserved; Momentum = not conserved

D Kinetic energy = not conserved; Momentum = not conserved

4   Here are three statements about an object:
    One: When all the forces acting on an object are balanced the object must be stationary.
    Two: When all the forces acting on an object are balanced the object cannot be accelerating.
    Three: When all the forces acting on an object are balanced the object can be changing direction as long as its speed is not changing.
    Which of the following combinations of the statements is correct?
    A One only
    B Two only
    C One and Two only
    D Two and Three only

5   An object starts from rest and accelerates uniformly at a rate of 5 m s^{-2} for six seconds. The distance travelled by the object after six seconds is:
    A 15 m
    B 30 m
    C 90 m
    D 180 m

6   An object of mass 25 kg collides with, and exerts a force of 900 N on, an object of mass 100 kg. Which of the following gives the magnitude of the force that the 100 kg mass exerts on the 25 kg mass?
    A Zero
    B 225 N
    C 900 N
    D 3600 N

7   A spring is stretched by a distance, x, and it stores E amount of elastic potential energy. Which one of the following gives the amount of elastic potential energy stored if the same spring is stretched by a distance $\frac{1}{2}x$?
    A $\frac{1}{4}E$

    B $\frac{1}{2}E$

    C $2E$
    D $4E$

8   Figure 2.12 shows the velocity–time graph for a ball thrown vertically into the air and then caught by the thrower.

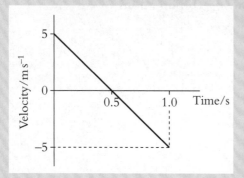

Figure 2.12

a Copy the graph and show on it where the ball has reached its highest point. **[1]**

b Use the graph to determine how high the ball reaches. **[2]**

c Explain how the graph shows that the overall displacement of the ball is zero. **[2]**

9 A projectile is launched horizontally at a speed of 40 m s^{-1} from the top of a hill, 50 m above the ground. Ignoring the effects of air friction, and taking $g = 9.81$ m s^{-2}, calculate the:

a time it takes for the projectile to hit the ground **[2]**

b horizontal distance from the hill that the projectile travels **[1]**

c **total** velocity vector of the projectile **just before** it hits the ground. **[3]**

10 Figure 2.13 shows the velocity–time graph for part of the journey of a skydiver after she has jumped out of an aeroplane. Air friction is not negligible.

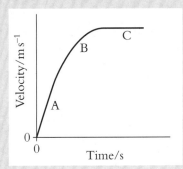

Figure 2.13

a Explain the shape of the graph at points A, B and C. **[3]**

b Copy the graph. Add what you would expect to happen when the skydiver opens her parachute. **[2]**

c Explain the shape of your graph. **[2]**

11 Figure 2.14 shows the force required to extend a spring plotted against the spring's extension.

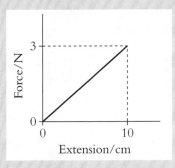

Figure 2.14

Use the graph to calculate the:

a spring constant of the spring **[2]**

b amount of elastic potential energy stored in the spring when it has been extended by 10 cm. **[2]**

12 **A body of mass 6 kg moving horizontally at a speed of 6 m s⁻¹ collides with, and sticks to, a stationary mass of 3 kg. The collision between the two masses lasted for a time of 0.2 s.**
   a Calculate the speed of the combined masses after the collision. **[2]**
   b Show that the force experienced by the 3 kg mass was 60 N. **[2]**
   c State the force experienced by the 6 kg mass. **[1]**
   d Determine whether the collision was elastic, inelastic or super-elastic. **[3]**

13 **A car and a truck, both travelling at the same speed of 60 km h⁻¹ but in opposite directions, collide head on. The truck has twice the mass of the car.**
   a During the collision, how does the force experienced by the truck compare to the force experienced by the car? Explain your answer using one of Newton's laws of motion. **[2]**
   b If the two vehicles become entangled during the collision, calculate the speed of the vehicles immediately after the collision. **[2]**
   c Show that the total kinetic energy before the collision can be written as 5400 *M*, where *M* is the mass of the car. **[2]**
   d Show that the collision was inelastic. **[2]**
   e Suggest what may have happened to some of the 'lost' kinetic energy. **[2]**

14 **Figure 2.15 shows how the momentum of a 3.0 kg mass changes with time.**

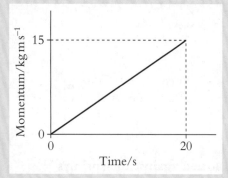

Figure 2.15

Use the graph to determine the:
   a average force being experienced by the object **[2]**
   b change in kinetic energy of the object during the 20 second period. **[2]**

Thermal physics 3

Chapter outline

In this chapter, you will:
- Describe the particle model of solids, liquids and gases.
- Convert between temperatures measured in celsius and in kelvin, understand the concept of internal energy and be able to link this with absolute temperature.
- Solve problems involving specific heat capacity and specific latent heat.
- Understand the concept of phase changes in terms of atomic and/or molecular behaviour and be able to sketch and interpret graphs of *temperature* and *energy* agasinst *time*.
- Use the equation of state for an ideal gas, the concept of a mole, molar mass and the Avogadro constant and understand the assumptions necessary to describe an ideal gas.
- Use and interpret graphs of pressure–volume, pressure–temperature and volume–temperature and demonstrate the gas laws experimentally.

KEY TERMS

Internal energy: The sum of the kinetic energies and the potential energies of all the particles in a sample of a substance.

Specific heat capacity: The amount of energy required to raise the temperature of 1 kg of a substance by one kelvin.

Specific latent heat of fusion/vaporisation: The amount of energy required to change the state of 1 kg of a substance from solid/liquid to liquid/gas without a change in temperature.

Boyle's law: For a fixed amount of gas at a constant temperature, the pressure of the gas is inversely proportional to its volume; $P \propto \dfrac{1}{V}$.

Charles's law: For a fixed amount of gas at a constant pressure, the volume of the gas is proportional to its absolute temperature; $V \propto T$.

The pressure law: For a fixed amount of gas at a constant volume, the pressure of the gas is proportional to its absolute temperature; $P \propto T$.

Ideal gas: A gas that can be considered to have no potential energy in its atoms. In practice this is not possible, but it can be approximated by a gas at a low pressure and temperature.

Mole: One of the SI base units, defined as the amount of a substance that has the same number of particles as there are atoms in 12 gramme of $^{12}_{6}C$.

Ideal gas equation: There are several ways of expressing this important equation:
$PV = \dfrac{1}{3} N\, m\overline{c^2}$, $PV = n\,R\,T$, and $P = \dfrac{1}{3}\rho\,\overline{c^2}$.

Kinetic energy and temperature: $\dfrac{3}{2}kT = \dfrac{1}{2}m\overline{c^2}$, where the Boltzmann constant, $k = 1.38 \times 10^{-23}\,\mathrm{J\,K^{-1}}$.

Exercise 3.1 – Thermal concepts

1   Describe the arrangement of atoms and molecules in a solid.

2   Describe a model that could be used to illustrate the atomic arrangement in a solid.

3   Describe the arrangement of atoms and molecules in a liquid.

4   Describe a model that could be used to illustrate the atomic arrangement in a liquid.

5   Describe the arrangement of atoms and molecules in a gas.

6   Describe a model that could be used to illustrate the atomic arrangement in a gas.

7   Convert the following temperatures from °C to K (show clearly your calculations):
   a   −273 °C
   b   −173 °C
   c   0 °C
   d   27 °C
   e   100 °C
   f   273 °C

8   Convert the following temperatures from K to °C (show clearly your calculations):
   a   0 K
   b   50 K
   c   173 K
   d   273 K
   e   323 K
   f   600 K

9   Explain what is meant by the *internal energy* of a sample of a substance.

10   Explain why it is practically impossible for a gas consisting of molecules to be an *ideal* gas.

11   Explain why adding energy to an ideal gas, with no other changes to its thermodynamic state, must increase its temperature.

12   Describe two ways in which the internal energy of a sample of a substance can be increased.

13   The internal energy of 10 g of steam at 100 °C is greater than the internal energy of 10 g of boiling water at the same temperature.
   a   Explain why this is so.
   b   Suggest why a burn from steam coming out of the kettle may be more harmful than a burn from an equivalent mass of boiling water.

14   Define the terms *specific heat capacity* and *heat capacity*.

15   300 J of energy is added to an object. Its temperature increases by 0.5 °C. What is the heat capacity of the object?

16 A sample of a substance has a heat capacity of 450 J °C^{-1}. If 3.6 kJ of energy are added to the object, calculate the change in temperature of the object.

17 Object A has a heat capacity of 375 J °C^{-1}. Object B has a heat capacity of 500 J °C^{-1}. If both objects are given the same amount of energy, which object's temperature will increase the most?

18 The specific heat capacity, SHC, of liquid water is 4200 J kg^{-1} °C^{-1}. Calculate the following, showing your calculations clearly:
   a The temperature rise of 1.5 kg of water when supplied with 20 kJ of energy.
   b The energy required by 300 g of water to raise its temperature from 20 °C to 100 °C.
   c The mass of water per second that can be heated from 25 °C to 60 °C by a 3 kW water heater.
   d The final temperature of 2.5 kg of water, initially at 20 °C, if 80 kJ of energy are removed from it.
   e The amount of energy required to warm up 2.5 litres of water from 10 °C to 70 °C.

19 A 400 g lump of aluminium, of SHC 900 J kg^{-1} °C^{-1} at a temperature of 800 °C, is added to 2.5 kg of water at 20 °C. After a short time, the aluminium and the water are in thermal equilibrium.
   a Write an equation for how much energy the aluminium loses. Call the final temperature of the aluminium, T_{final}.
   b Write an equation for how much energy the water has to gain. Call the final temperature of the water T_{final}.
   c Calculate the final temperature of the water/aluminium.
   d What assumption has been made in this question?

20 The SHC of iron is 420 J kg^{-1} °C^{-1}. Calculate the amount of energy required to heat 5000 kg of iron from a temperature of 15 °C to its melting temperature of 1540 °C. Give your answer in standard form.

21 A squash ball (made of rubber) of mass 50 g is heated from an initial temperature of 15 °C to a higher, working temperature. If the amount of energy given to the ball is 2.5 kJ, calculate the final temperature of the squash ball. (The SHC of rubber is 1600 J kg^{-1} °C^{-1}.)

22 The specific latent heat of vaporisation (SLHV) of water is about 2.3×10^6 J kg^{-1}. Calculate the amount of energy required to change the state of 1.5 litres of water from liquid to gas at a temperature of 100 °C.

23 In a kettle, there are 1.5 litres of water at an initial temperature of 15 °C. The kettle is supplied with energy at a rate of 1.5 kW. Given that the SHC of water is 4.2 kJ °C^{-1} kg^{-1} and the SLHV of water is 2.3 MJ kg^{-1}, calculate the time it takes for all the water to have boiled away, so that there is no water left in the kettle. You may assume that no energy is lost to the kettle itself or to the surroundings.

24 A glass of 250 cm^3 of water at 12 °C is cooled by inserting an ice cube of mass 50 g at a temperature of −18 °C. The SHC of ice is 2100 J kg^{-1} °C^{-1}. The specific latent heat of fusion of ice is 3.3×10^5 J kg^{-1}. Calculate the final temperature of the glass of water.

25 Marathon des Sables is the world's toughest race. Competitors have to run across more than 150 miles of desert. They must carry all their supplies while running – and they have to do it in five days. The average daily temperature is more than 40 °C.

    a Outline the problems that runners face in trying to maintain a working body temperature (37 °C).

    b Suggest how they are able to prevent themselves from overheating.

Exercise 3.2 – Modelling a gas

1 Outline what is meant by the term *ideal gas*.

2 Under what conditions might a real gas behave like an ideal gas?

3 Outline how the molecules of a gas exert a pressure on their container.

4 State Boyle's law as applied to an ideal gas.

5 Outline an experiment that could verify Boyle's law. Make sure you include:
- the equipment required
- the measurements you would make (and the instruments you would use to make them)
- how you would manipulate the data to show Boyle's law.

6 20 cm³ of an ideal gas at an initial pressure of 100 kPa is compressed slowly to a new volume of 4 cm³. Use Boyle's law to calculate the new pressure of the gas.

7 When a SCUBA diver breathes out under the water, they small bubbles of used air are expelled from the diver's breathing equipment. As the bubbles rise towards the surface of the water, their volume increases. Use your knowledge of Boyle's law to explain why this occurs. State any assumptions you have made.

8 The relationship between the pressure of a fixed volume of ideal gas and its absolute temperature is often called 'the Pressure law'. State what the Pressure law is.

9 Outline how a demonstration of the Pressure law could be used to find a value for absolute zero.

10 Explain why a gas cannot exert a pressure at a temperature of 0 K.

11 A fixed-volume container holds 250 cm³ of air at an initial temperature of 10 °C and pressure of 1.01×10^5 Pa. The container is cooled to a temperature of −60 °C by immersing it for a short time in a bucket of liquid nitrogen at a temperature of −196 °C. Calculate the pressure of the cooled air in the container.

12 The relationship between the temperature of some gas and the volume of the gas at a constant pressure is called Charles's law. State what this relationship is.

13 Outline an experiment that could verify Charles's law. Make sure you include:
- the equipment required
- the measurements you would make (and the instruments you would use to make them)
- how you would manipulate the data to show Charles's law.

14 Outline how you could use the experiment in question **13** to find a value for absolute zero.

15 An ideal gas at constant pressure is heated so that its volume quadruples.
   a What will happen to its absolute temperature?
   b What has happened to the average speed of the molecules?

16 150 cm^3 of air, kept at a constant pressure, is heated from an initial temperature of 20 °C until its volume has become 300 cm^3. Use Charles's law to calculate the final temperature of the gas.

17 a How is a mole defined?
   b How many atoms of hydrogen are there in 2 g of atomic hydrogen?

18 Calculate the number of atoms in 20 g of:
   a ^{56}Fe
   b ^{235}U
   c water.

19 Explain what is meant by the term *molar mass*.

20 The molar mass of air is about 29 g mole^{-1} and the density of air at standard temperature and pressure (STP) is about 1.3 kg m^{-3}.
   a Calculate how many moles of air there are in 1 kg of air.
   b Calculate how many molecules of air there are in 1 kg of air.
   c Calculate how many molecules of air there are in 1 m^3 of air.

21 The molar mass of ^{12}C is 12 g.
   a Calculate the mass of one atom of ^{12}C.
   b The unified atomic mass unit, u, is defined as $\frac{1}{12}$ of the mass of a ^{12}C atom. Show that the value for u is 1.66×10^{-27} kg.

22 One form of the equation of state for an ideal gas is:

$$pV = \frac{1}{3} N m \overline{c^2}$$

   a What do the letters in the equation represent, and what units are they measured in?
   b $N m = M$ (the total mass of all the atoms in the gas). Show that the ideal gas equation can also be written as:

   $p = \frac{1}{3} \rho \overline{c^2}$, where ρ is the density of the gas.

   c Explain why it is necessary for physicists to use the expression $\overline{c^2}$ when dealing with a large number of atoms of gas.

23 The atmospheric pressure at ground level is about 1.01×10^5 Pa. If the density of air is about 1.3 kg m^{-3}, calculate the typical speed at which a molecule of air moves.

24 If an atom of hydrogen (atomic mass = 1 u) moves at a speed of 1000 m s^{-1} at a temperature of T K, how fast would you expect an atom of oxygen (atomic mass = 16 u) to move at the same temperature? Explain your answer.

25 A sample of gas occupies a volume of 5.0×10^{-3} m^3 and exerts a pressure of 100 kPa at a temperature of 20 °C. Calculate the number of:
   a moles of gas present
   b molecules of gas present.

26 The average kinetic energy of a molecule of a gas is 5.0×10^{-21} J. Calculate the temperature of the gas.

? Exam-style questions

1. **Which of the following statements about temperature scales is false?**

   A The smallest value on the Celsius temperature scale is −273 °C.

   B The difference between −65 °C and −64 °C is not the same as the difference between 280 K and 281 K.

   C The smallest value on the Kelvin temperature scale is 0 K.

   D It is not possible to have a temperature of −300 °C.

2. **Which of the following is the best description of absolute temperature?**

   A A measure of how hot a substance is.

   B A measure of how much energy a substance has.

   C A measure of the total kinetic energy the atoms and molecules in a substance have.

   D A measure of the average kinetic energy the atoms and molecules in a substance have.

3. **When a liquid boils, it changes its state from liquid to gas. Which one of the following combinations correctly describes the changes to the average kinetic energy and the potential energy of the molecules during the boiling process?**

   A Average kinetic energy = stays the same; Potential energy = stays the same

   B Average kinetic energy = stays the same; Potential energy = increases

   C Average kinetic energy = increases; Potential energy = stays the same

   D Average kinetic energy = increases; Potential energy = increases

4. **Which one of the statements about an ideal gas is *incorrect*?**

   A Atoms always collide elastically.

   B No forces exist between atoms.

   C All atoms move about in random directions at the same speed.

   D The time it takes for an atom to collide to collide is small compared with the time between one collision and the next.

5. **Two objects next to each other are at the same temperature. Which of the following statements is false?**

   A Both objects are exchanging energy with each other.

   B There is no net transfer of energy from one object to the other.

   C Both objects have the same internal energy.

   D The average kinetic energy of the atoms in each object is the same.

6 A teacher places a 600 g piece of lead into a sealed card 80 cm cylinder. At one end of the cylinder there is a small rubber nozzle, where a sensitive thermometer can be placed to measure the temperature of the lead. At the start of the demonstration, the temperature of the lead is 20 °C. The specific heat capacity of the lead is 160 J kg^{-1} K^{-1}.

The teacher holds the cylinder vertically and flips it end to end, so that the lead falls to the bottom of the cylinder each time it is flipped. At the end of the demonstration, the teacher measures the temperature of the lead.

  a Calculate the heat capacity of the sample of lead in the cylinder. **[2]**

  b Calculate the amount of gravitational potential energy that the lead loses each time the cylinder is flipped. ($g = 10$ N kg^{-1}) **[2]**

  c Outline the energy transformation that takes place each time the lead comes to rest at the bottom of the cylinder. **[2]**

  d If the teacher flips the cylinder 50 times, determine the final temperature of the lead. **[3]**

7 This question is about water changing state from liquid to water vapour.

A teacher sits a beaker of water on a set of electronic scales. The scales read 175 g. After leaving the beaker untouched for 24 hours, the teacher notices that the reading on the scales is 163 g. The teacher explains to her class that some of the water has evaporated and changed state into water vapour.

Explain why:

  a some of the water can change into water vapour without the water needing to be at its boiling temperature **[2]**

  b the water cools when some of it evaporates away. **[2]**

The teacher notes that the temperature of the water is 20 °C. She places a small electrical heater inside the beaker and switches it on. The heater is rated at 200 W and the specific heat capacity of water is 4.2 kJ kg^{-1} °C^{-1}.

  c Calculate the time it takes for the water to reach its boiling temperature. **[2]**

  d As soon as the class is convinced that the water is boiling, the teacher makes a note of the reading on the scales and starts a stopwatch. If the specific latent heat of vaporisation of water is 2.26×10^6 J kg^{-1}, determine the reading on the scales after five minutes. **[2]**

8 This question is about heating up a block of aluminium.

A student places a cylindrical block of aluminium of mass 1.0 kg on a protective pad on a desk. The block has two holes, 3 cm apart: the student places a thin electrical heater, rated at 50 W, into one hole and a thermometer into the other. The student switches on the heater and makes these observations:

• **Temperature of aluminium block before switching on the heater: 20 °C.**

• **There is no change in the value on the thermometer for two minutes.**

• **After six minutes, the reading on the thermometer is rising by 3.3 °C min^{-1}.**

• **After 25 minutes, the reading on the thermometer is 92 °C.**

  a Explain why there is no change in the reading on the thermometer for the first two minutes of heating. **[2]**

  b Show that the specific heat capacity of aluminium is 900 J kg^{-1} °C^{-1}. **[3]**

  c Explain why the reading on the thermometer after 25 minutes of heating is not 103 °C. **[3]**

9   This question is about changing the state of water.

0.5 kg of ice at its melting temperature are changed into liquid water by the continuous addition of thermal energy. The specific latent heat of fusion of water is $3.3 \times 10^5 \text{ J kg}^{-1}$.

a   The thermal energy is supplied by an electrical heater rated at 100 W. Calculate the time required to melt all of the ice. [2]

b   The liquid water is now heated until it reaches its boiling temperature. If the same heater is used, calculate the time it takes for the water to boil. The specific heat capacity of water is $4.2 \text{ kJ kg}^{-1} \text{ K}^{-1}$. [2]

c   When the water reaches its boiling temperature, the heater continues to supply energy until all of the water has changed state into water vapour. Calculate the time it takes for all of the water to change into water vapour. You can assume that *all* of the energy supplied by the heater is used to change the state of the water. The specific latent heat of vaporisation of water is $2.26 \times 10^6 \text{ J kg}^{-1}$. [1]

10   This question is about compressing an ideal gas.

A constant amount of ideal gas is held in a syringe, one end of which is sealed. The gas is then compressed by pushing the other end of the syringe slowly inwards so that the volume occupied by the gas is halved.

a   Before compression, the pressure inside the syringe was 1.0×10^5 Pa. Calculate the pressure inside the syringe after the gas was compressed. [2]

b   Use your knowledge of kinetic theory to explain how the atoms of an ideal gas exert a pressure on the syringe walls. [3]

c   Outline why it is necessary to compress the ideal gas slowly. [2]

d   If the gas was compressed quickly, suggest and explain how the pressure inside the syringe would compare with the value you calculated in part **a**. [3]

Waves 4

Chapter outline

In this chapter, you will:

- Understand the basic concepts of simple harmonic motion, including conditions necessary for an object to oscillate in simple harmonic motion, the meanings of period, frequency, amplitude, displacement and phase difference.
- Use graphs to describe simple harmonic motion and be able to identify the energy transformations that occur.
- Describe a travelling wave, use graphs of displacement against time and displacement against distance to identify wavelength, frequency and period.
- Perform calculations involving wavelength, frequency, period and wave speed and be able to describe the motion of a particle in a medium through which a wave is travelling.
- Understand and classify waves as transverse or longitudinal, describe the nature of a sound wave and understand and use the concept of an inverse square law to solve problems involving intensity and amplitude.
- Apply ideas of superposition to pulses and waves in order to describe the diffraction of waves through a single slit and around objects and to describe and interpret the interference of waves from two sources.
- Interpret diagrams of incident, reflected and transmitted beams using ideas of polarisation and be able to use Malus's law to solve problems with polarisation.
- Understand what happens when waves are incident on a boundary between two different media in order to use Snell's law to solve problems with refraction, critical angle and total internal reflection.
- Use the concept of superposition of two waves to explain the formation of standing waves and be able to discuss the differences between standing waves and travelling waves.
- Describe nodes and antinodes on a standing wave and be able to draw and interpret diagrams involving standing waves on strings and in pipes.
- Understand the three boundary conditions for standing waves on strings and in pipes and be able to solve problems about standing waves involving harmonics and their frequencies, the speed of the wave and the length of the standing wave.

KEY TERMS

Simple harmonic motion: A periodic motion in which the restoring force is proportional to the displacement from the equilibrium position.

Malus's law: For a polariser, $I = I_0 \cos^2 \theta$, where I is the transmitted intensity, I_0 the incident intensity and θ is the angle between the transmission axis of the polariser and the electric vector of the incident wave.

Refractive index, n: A value that gives the ratio of the speed of an electromagnetic wave in a vacuum to the speed of the same wave in a different medium, $n = \dfrac{v_{\text{vacuum}}}{v_{\text{medium}}} = \dfrac{c}{v}$

Snell's law: $_1n_2 = \dfrac{\sin\theta_1}{\sin\theta_2}$

Critical angle, θ_c: The angle at which the refracted ray (from a more dense medium to a less dense medium) travels along the boundary between the two media; $\theta_c = \sin^{-1}\left(\dfrac{1}{_1n_2}\right)$

Young double-slit equation: $s\,d = \lambda D$, where s is the fringe spacing, d is the slit separation, l is the wavelength of the waves and D is the distance from the two slits to the screen on which the interference pattern is observed.

Exercise 4.1 – Oscillations

1 Explain what is meant by:
   a time period of an oscillator
   b frequency
   c amplitude
   d equilibrium position
   e displacement.

2 Figure 4.1 shows the displacement of an oscillating body about its equilibrium position.

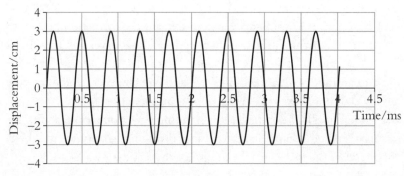

Figure 4.1

Use Figure 4.1 to find:
   a the period of the oscillations
   b the amplitude of the oscillations.

3 a With reference to Figure 4.1, outline how to identify on the graph where:
   i the speed of the oscillating body is a maximum
   ii the speed of the oscillating body is zero.
   b What feature of this graph can be used to find the velocity of the oscillating body?

4   Calculate the frequency of these oscillations:
    a   A small child in a baby bouncer making ten oscillations in 25 s.
    b   A hydrogen atom in a water molecule that oscillates about the oxygen atom once in 4×10^{-7} s.
    c   A pulsar with radio wave emissions that vary in intensity 26 times every 20 seconds.

5   Calculate the time period of the following oscillations:
    a   An electron in an alternating current of frequency 50 Hz.
    b   A simple pendulum that makes 50 oscillations in a minute.
    c   A caesium atom that makes 9.19×10^9 oscillations in one second.

6   Explain what is meant by the term *isochronous*.

7   Convert these angles from degrees into radians:
    a   360°
    b   90°
    c   30°
    d $\dfrac{360°}{2\pi}$ (What is this calculation showing you?)

8   Convert these angles from radians into degrees:
    a 2π
    b $\dfrac{\pi}{4}$
    c $\dfrac{2\pi}{360}$ (What is this calculation showing you?)

9   This question is about using a spreadsheet package to demonstrate a useful mathematical rule.
    Set up a spreadsheet book (such as in Microsoft Excel®) with two columns: x and $\sin x$. (Make sure your spreadsheet calculates sines and cosine using angles that are in radians.) Allow your value of x to begin at $x = 1 \times 10^{-2}$ and increases it incrementally until it has reached the value $x = 1$.
    Now compare your values of x with your values of $\sin x$.
    a   What do you notice when x is a very small value?
    b   At what value of x is $\sin x$ no longer the same value?
    c   What useful mathematical rule has this shown?

10 What two conditions are necessary for an object to oscillate in simple harmonic motion?

11 Consider a simple pendulum oscillating from side-to-side. Outline the energy transformations that take place during oscillations.

12 A mass is attached to two springs; neither spring has been stretched beyond its normal length. The mass is pulled to one side and released. The mass oscillates from side-to-side in simple harmonic motion, with no appreciable friction force between the mass and the surface it is on.
    a   Outline the energy transformations that are taking place during the oscillation.
    b   Use your answer to part **a** to confirm where the mass is when its velocity is a maximum.

13 Figure 4.2 shows how the displacement of an oscillator performing simple harmonic motion varies with time.

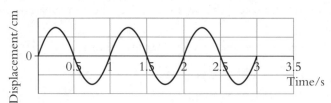

Figure 4.2

    a Sketch how the velocity of the oscillator varies with time.
    b Sketch how the acceleration of the oscillator varies with time.
    c Explain how your sketches support the definition of *simple harmonic motion*.

14 Consider an oscillator performing simple harmonic motion oscillations with an angular frequency, ω. Write an equation for the speed of the oscillator that could describe the simple harmonic motion for:
    a oscillations in which the speed at $t = 0$ is zero
    b oscillations in which the speed at $t = 0$ is a maximum, v_{max}.
(In each case, you may assume that the amplitude and angular frequency of your oscillations are the same.)

15 Figure 4.3 shows an oscillator performing simple harmonic motion.

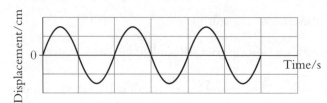

Figure 4.3

    a Mark two places where the oscillator is in phase. Label them P.
    b Mark two places where the oscillator is out of phase. Label them O.
    c Mark two places where there is a phase difference of $\frac{\pi}{2}$ radians. Label them D.

Exercise 4.2 – Travelling waves

1 Describe what is meant by:
    a wavelength, λ
    b frequency, f
    c time period, T
    d amplitude, A.

2 What is the difference between a *transverse wave* and a *longitudinal wave*? Think about the direction in which oscillations occur, and the direction in which the wave is moving.

3 Figure 4.4 shows how the displacement of a fishing float varies with time during the passing of a transverse water wave.

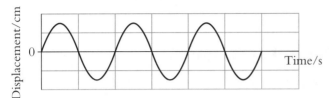

Figure 4.4

   a Mark where the float is at a crest of the wave. Label this C.
   b Mark where the float is at a trough of the wave. Label this T.
   c What is the phase difference between a crest and the next trough?

4 a What is the reflection of a sound wave called?
   b A student shouts 'yes!' in the middle of the school playing field. He hears the word 'yes' 0.5 seconds later due to a reflection from a large wall at the edge of the field. Calculate how far the wall is from the student. (The speed of sound in air is 330 m s^{-1}.)

5 Outline an experiment that could measure the speed of sound in air. (Do not use the idea from question **4**.) Make sure you include:
- the equipment required
- the measurements you need to make (and the instruments you would use to make them)
- the uncertainty you would expect in each measurement
- how you would manipulate the data to calculate the speed of sound in air
- how you will find the uncertainty in your value for the speed of sound in air.

6 Electromagnetic waves are transverse. They travel through air at almost 3×10^8 m s^{-1}. Calculate the frequency of the following electromagnetic waves:
   a A radio wave; $\lambda = 200$ m.
   b A gamma ray; $\lambda = 5 \times 10^{-18}$ m.
   c Green light; $\lambda = 530$ nm.

7 List all types of waves in the electromagnetic spectrum, in decreasing value of wavelength.

8 Geostationary satellites, like those used for satellite television, require electromagnetic waves of wavelength less than about 10 m in order to avoid absorption by the ionosphere.
   a What kind of electromagnetic waves are used for transmissions?
   b What is the minimum frequency at which satellites can communicate with the ground?
   c Astra 2e is a satellite used for the transmission of television signals by the BBC. Most of its television programmes are broadcast at frequencies of about 11 GHz. Show that these signals are not absorbed by the ionosphere.

9 Medical practitioners, dentists and security officers in airports use X-rays to examine the inside of objects. Describe how X-rays are able to reveal information about the inside of objects.

Exercise 4.3 – Wave characteristics

1 When talking about waves, explain what is meant by *wavefront* and *ray*.

2 For a travelling wave, how is a wavefront related to a ray?

3 Draw a suitable diagram to show how a series of closely-spaced Huygens secondary wavelet sources can produce a plane wavefront.

4 A source emits waves with *intensity, I*, 1 m from the source.
   a Explain what is meant by the term *intensity*.
   b What is the intensity of the waves 2 m from the source?
   c The original waves are replaced by waves with an amplitude that is five times larger. What is the intensity of the waves 1 m from the source?

5 A small, spherical loudspeaker emits sound waves in all directions. The output power of the loudspeaker is 20 W.
   a What will the intensity of the sound be at a distance:
      i 1 m away?
      ii 3 m away?
   b Sketch graphs to show how the intensity of the sound varies with:
      i distance from the speaker
      ii amplitude of the waves.

6 The intensity of solar radiation measured from the Earth is 1370 W m^{-2}. The Earth is 1.5×10^{11} m from the Sun. Calculate:
   a the output power of the Sun
   b the intensity of the solar radiation at the surface of Mercury, which is 5.7×10^{10} m from the Sun.

7 Figure 4.5 shows two pulses travelling towards each other.

Figure 4.5

Sketch a diagram to show what happens when the two pulses *superpose* (in other words, when they arrive in the same place at the same time). What physics phrase can be used to describe what is happening?

8 Figure 4.6 shows two more pulses travelling towards each other.

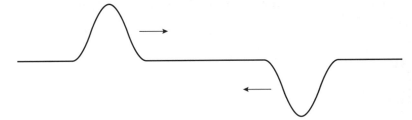

Figure 4.6

a What will happen when the two pulses superpose?
b What physics phrase can be used to describe what is happening?

9 The superposition of two (or more) waves can be thought of as the *addition of the displacements of each wave for each position along the waves' paths*. You might like to explore this phenomenon further by using a spreadsheet package (such as Microsoft Excel®). Here are some ideas:

a Draw a simple sine wave by computing the values of sine and using the graph wizard.
b Draw a different sine wave (change the amplitude, or the frequency, or the phase).
c Add the two sine waves together and see what the result is.
d Add (or subtract) several different waves to see what you can produce. You may even be able to produce a square wave (like a digital signal).

10 Explain what is meant by the term *unpolarised*, when applied to some transverse waves.

11 Consider an unpolarised electromagnetic wave approaching a thin, vertical metal rod.

a Some of the waves will have their electric force vector in the vertical direction. What will these waves do to the free electrons in the metal rod?
b How do you know that the free electrons in the rod have absorbed energy from the wave?
c Some of the waves will have their electric force vector in the horizontal direction. What will these waves do to the free electrons in the metal rod?
d Have the free electrons in the rod absorbed energy from the wave?
e How does the number of waves with their electric force vectors in the *vertical* direction compare before and after the waves have passed through the rod?
f How does the number of waves with their electric force vectors in the horizontal direction compare before and after the waves have passed through the rod?
g Having passed the metal rod, in which direction are the waves likely to have their electric force vectors?
h In which direction is the *transmission axis*?

12 Polarising material is made up of a large number of parallel, complex, long-chain polymer molecules that act like a row of electrical conductors (see Figure 4.7). It can be used to polarise light.

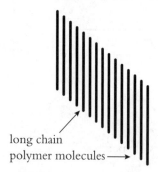

long chain polymer molecules ⟶

Figure 4.7

  a Add a double-headed arrow to Figure 4.7, to show the direction in which the electric vector of light waves will be when the light waves have passed through the polarising material.

  b The intensity of the unpolarised light before passing through the polarising material is I. What is the intensity of the polarised light *after* passing through the polarising material?

13 **a** State Malus's law for polarised light.

  b The angle between a plane of polarisation of light and the transmission axis of a polarising filter is θ. Sketch a graph to show how the intensity of transmitted light varies with θ.

14 Some materials, such as transparent sticky tape, can rotate the plane of polarisation of light. They are 'optically active' materials. Figure 4.8 shows two polarising filters and a piece of glass. Two perpendicular pieces of sticky tape are stuck to the glass.

strips of sticky tape

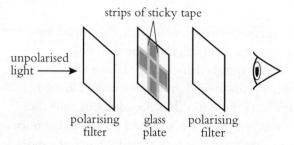

unpolarised light ⟶

polarising filter   glass plate   polarising filter

Figure 4.8

Suggest what you expect to observe when initially unpolarised light passes through to the eye.

Exercise 4.4 – Wave behaviour

1 Figure 4.9 shows a ray that is incident on a plane mirror.

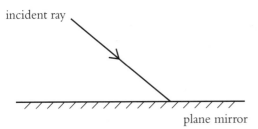

incident ray

plane mirror

Figure 4.9

  a Add to the diagram:
    i the normal
    ii the angle of incidence, i
    iii the reflected ray
    iv the angle of reflection, r.

  b How is the angle of incidence related to the angle of reflection?

2 Figure 4.10 shows a ray of light incident on the boundary between the air and some water.

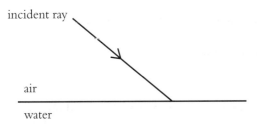

incident ray

air

water

Figure 4.10

  a Add to the diagram:
    i the normal
    ii the reflected ray
    iii the refracted ray.

  b How is the angle of refraction, r, related to the angle of incidence, i? (You may take the refractive index of air to be 1.0.)
  c What is the name of this law?

3 Define the *refractive index*, n, of a substance.

4 A ray of light, frequency 6×10^{14} Hz, is incident on a piece of glass at an angle of incidence of 40°. The refractive index of glass is 1.5.
  a Calculate the angle of refraction of the light.
  b Calculate the speed of the light in the glass. (The speed of light in air is 3×10^8 m s^{-1}.)
  c Calculate the wavelength of the light in air.
  d Calculate the wavelength of the light in the glass.
  e What colour is the light in air?
  f What colour is the light in the glass?

5   The refractive index of a transparent material, X, is n_x. The refractive index of another transparent material, Y, is n_y. What is the ratio of the speed of light in X to the speed of light in Y: $\frac{v_x}{v_y}$?

6   Figure 4.11 shows a ray of light incident on the boundary between water ($n = 1.33$) and air ($n = 1.0$) at an angle of incidence called the critical angle.

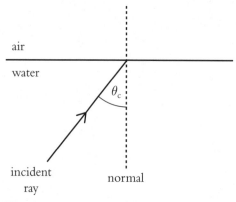

Figure 4.11

a   Complete the diagram to show what happens to the ray of light.
b   Derive the relationship between the critical angle, θ_c, and the refractive index of the water.
c   What happens to the ray of light if the angle of incidence is greater than θ_c?

7   Outline an experiment that could find the refractive index of a rectangular block of glass. Make sure you include:
   • the equipment required
   • the measurements you need to make (and the instruments you would use to make them)
   • how you would manipulate the data to obtain a reliable value for n.

8   a   Use a diagram to help describe how an optical fibre can transmit light.
    b   Suggest some possible uses for optical fibres.

9   Explain what is meant by *diffraction*.

10 What physics process, characteristic of the behaviour of waves, is responsible for producing the single slit diffraction pattern?

11 Coherent green light is incident on a pair of thin slits, as shown in Figure 4.12.

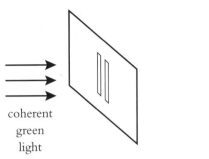 

coherent
green
light

distant
screen

Figure 4.12

a At point B, there is a bright spot of light. Explain how it is produced.
b At point D, there is no light on the screen. Explain why.
c What would you expect to see at point C, which is directly opposite the two slits? Explain your answer.

12 Two speakers are placed 1 m apart, and connected to an amplifier. They produce a coherent pair of sound waves (same frequency, amplitude and phase).
A student walks in a line 4 m away, parallel to the two speakers.
She notices that the sound from the speakers is loud when she is directly opposite them. It becomes quieter a little further along the path, and then loud again.
The wavelength of the sound waves is 0.5 m. How far apart are the loud sounds?

13 Explain what is meant by the term *path difference*.

14 What would you expect to observe from a pair of coherent wave sources when the path difference between the two sources is:
a $n\lambda$, where n is an integer?
b $(n + \frac{1}{2})\lambda$?

15 You will need to use your knowledge of path differences and interference to help answer this question. Explain what would happen to food if it was cooked in a microwave oven without a turntable.

16 Outline an experiment that could find the wavelength of light, using a pair of Young slits. Make sure you include:
• the equipment required
• the measurements you need to make (and the instruments you would use to make them)
• the uncertainty you would expect in each measurement
• how you would manipulate the data to calculate the wavelength of light
• how you will find the uncertainty in your value for the wavelength of light.

17 When Thomas Young performed his experiments in the early 1800s, he did not have a laser to produce a source of coherent light. Explain how Young was able to ensure that it was coherent light that was incident on his pair of slits.

18 A pair of parallel thin slits, 0.15 mm apart, is used to produce an interference pattern on a screen 8 m from the slits.

    a Coherent light of wavelength 450 nm is used. Calculate the separation of the bright fringes on the screen.

    b Without re-doing the calculation completely, how far apart would the bright fringes be if red light of wavelength 675 nm were used?

Exercise 4.5 – Standing waves

1   What is the difference between a progressive wave and a standing wave? Think about the transfer of energy,

2   Describe how a standing wave is formed.

3   An elastic string of length l is held firmly at one end and made to oscillate at the other end. A standing wave is produced in the fundamental (first harmonic) mode.

    a What is the wavelength of the standing wave for the first harmonic?

    b The string is oscillated at a higher frequency. A standing wave is observed when the standing wave is in the second harmonic mode. Sketch a diagram to show what the string will look like with this second harmonic standing wave present. State the wavelength of the second harmonic standing wave.

    c Sketch diagrams for the third and the fourth harmonics. Give the wavelength of both standing waves.

    d The harmonic number is given as n. Derive an equation for the possible wavelengths for standing waves on the string, in terms of l and n .

4   An empty pipe of length l, open at both ends, can produce standing waves of sound with an antinode at each end.

    a What is the wavelength of the standing wave for the first harmonic?

    b Sketch diagrams to show the second, third and fourth harmonics.

    c The harmonic number is given as n. Derive an equation for the possible wavelengths for standing waves on the open pipe, in terms of l and n.

5   Referring back to questions **3** and **4**:

    a If the pipe in question **4** was closed at one end and open at the other end, would your equation for the possible wavelengths of standing waves be different? If so, how?

    b If the string in question **3** had antinodes at both ends, would your equation for the possible wavelengths of standing waves be different? If so, how?

    c Are your equations for wavelengths of standing waves with the same boundary conditions the same for strings and pipes?

    d Are your equations for wavelengths of standing waves with antinodes at each end of the pipe or string the same as for standing waves with nodes at each end?

Exam-style questions

1 **Which of the following statements about a body oscillating in simple harmonic motion is true?**

   A At its maximum displacement from the equilibrium position, its velocity is a maximum.

   B At its maximum displacement from the equilibrium position, its velocity is zero.

   C At its maximum displacement from the equilibrium position, its acceleration is zero.

   D At its maximum displacement from the equilibrium position, its kinetic energy is a maximum.

2 **Which of the following is the best estimate of the frequency of a microwave of wavelength 3 cm?**

   A 10 Hz

   B 10 kHz

   C 10 MHz

   D 10 GHz

3 **Unpolarised light is incident on a horizontal reflective surface. The reflected light will be ...**

   A unpolarised with the same intensity as the incident light.

   B partially plane polarised with the electric vector vertical.

   C partially plane polarised with the electric vector horizontal.

   D unpolarised with a small intensity than the incident light.

4 **An oscillator makes 25 oscillations in a time of 0.5 s. The frequency of the oscillations is ...**

   A 0.02 Hz

   B 0.08 Hz

   C 12.5 Hz

   D 50 Hz

5 **A mass oscillates vertically on a spring with an amplitude of 5.0 cm. If the mass undergoes 50 oscillations, the total displacement of the mass will be ...**

   A 0 cm

   B 20 cm

   C 250 cm

   D 500 cm

6 **Red light, of wavelength 600 nm, is shone on a single narrow slit of width, b. A diffraction pattern is observed on a screen nearby with the angle to the first minimum of 9×10^{-3} radians. If the red light is replaced by purple light of wavelength 400 nm, the angle to the first maximum will be ...**

   A 3×10^{-3} radians

   B 4×10^{-3} radians

   C 6×10^{-3} radians

   D 1.35×10^{-2} radians

7   **When applied to two sources of waves, the term** *coherent* **means…**
    A that they both have the same wavelength.
    B that they both have the same amplitude.
    C that they have a constant phase relationship.
    D that they are both plane polarised.

8   **This question is about a sound wave.**
    Figure 4.13 shows the position of some molecules of air when a sound wave is
    passing through the air. The direction of motion of the sound wave is shown.
    Underneath the diagram is a set of axes, with the same *x*-axis of distance, to enable
    the plotting of the air pressure to be carried out.

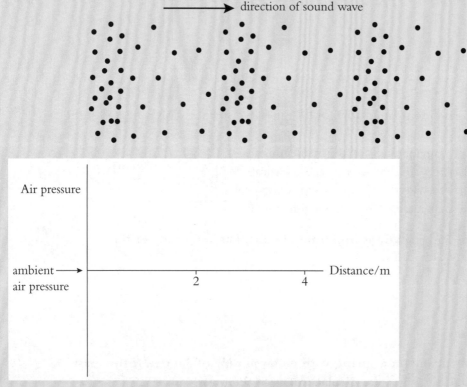

Figure 4.13

a   Indicate on the diagram where the air pressure is:
    •   a maximum; label this P_{max}
    •   a minimum; label this P_{min}
    •   ambient (in other words, when there is no sound wave present); label this P_{amb}. **[3]**
b   Sketch the graph, using the axes provided, to show how the air pressure varies with
    distance. **[3]**
c   Draw a double-headed arrow on one of the air molecules, to show the direction in which
    the air molecule oscillates when the sound wave is present. **[1]**
d   The speed of sound in air is 330 m s^{-1}. Use the diagram (or your graph) to calculate the
    frequency of the sound wave. **[3]**

9   Figure 4.14 shows a representation of a stationary sound wave in a pipe of
    length 3 m.

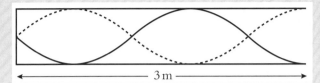

Figure 4.14

Use the diagram to calculate:
a the wavelength of the standing wave [2]
b the frequency of the standing wave. (Speed of sound in air = 330 m s^{-1}) [2]

10 A string is attached to a fixed point at one end. It is made to oscillate up and
    down from the other end, forming a standing wave. The string exhibits *nodes* and
    antinodes. Two consecutive nodes are found to be 8 cm apart.
    a Explain what is meant by the terms *node* and *antinode*. [2]
    b State the wavelength of the waves on the string. [1]
    c The string is made to oscillate with a higher frequency, again forming a standing wave.
       Suggest what would happen to the separation of the nodes and antinodes. [1]

11 Dolphins can communicate by emitting sound waves that travel through water at
    1.5 km s^{-1}. The speed of sound waves in air is 330 m s^{-1}.
    a Suggest why sound waves travel faster through water than through air. [2]
    b If the frequency of a dolphin's sound waves is 200 kHz, calculate:
       i   the wavelength of the sound waves in the water
       ii the wavelength of the sound waves in the air. [3]
    c Is it possible for a human to hear these sound waves? Explain your answer. [2]

12 Plane waves of red light are incident normally on a thin slit. A screen placed
    several metres away from the slit shows an intensity pattern characteristic of single
    slit diffraction.
    a Sketch a diagram to show how this intensity pattern varies on the screen. [3]
    b Suggest how this intensity pattern would be different if blue light was used instead of
       red. [2]
    c In what **two** ways would this intensity pattern be different if the width of the slit
       were smaller? [2]

5 Electricity and magnetism

Chapter outline

In this chapter, you will:

- Recognise two forms of charge and the direction of the electrical force between them.
- Understand the concept of an electric field and be able to solve problems involving electric fields and Coulomb's law and calculate the work done in electric fields, measured in both joules and electronvolts.
- Identify the nature of charge carriers in a metal and identify and calculate the drift speed of charge carriers in a conductor using the drift speed equation (Drude's theory).
- Understand the concepts of potential difference, current and charge and construct and interpret circuit diagrams.
- Identify ohmic and non-ohmic conductors from their V–I graphs.
- Use Kirchhoff's laws to solve problems involving circuits.
- Use the concepts of resistance and resistivity and solve problems involving resistors in series and in parallel.
- Understand and describe ideal ammeters and voltmeters and describe the practical uses of potential divider circuits and demonstrate the ability to investigate experimentally one or more of the factors that affect the resistance of a component.
- Distinguish between primary and secondary cells and identify the direction of a current necessary to recharge a secondary cell.
- Evaluate the internal resistance of a cell experimentally and understand the concept of electromotive force (emf) and use it to solve problems involving internal resistance, current and voltage.
- Determine the size and direction of a force on a current carrying wire in a magnetic field and on a charged particle moving in magnetic field.
- Identify, draw and interpret simple magnetic field patterns of bar magnets, solenoids and long straight conductors carrying a current.
- Recognise the direction of the magnetic field around a current and be able to solve problems involving magnetic fields, currents, charges and the forces occurring.

KEY TERMS

Coulomb's law: $F = k \dfrac{Qq}{r^2}$, where, for a vacuum, $k = \dfrac{1}{4\pi\varepsilon_o}$.

Electric field strength, E: The amount of force acting on a unit positive test charge in the field, $E = \dfrac{F}{q} = k \dfrac{Q}{r^2}$

Flow equation (Drude's theory): $I = nAvq$, where n is the charge carrier number density, A is the cross sectional area of the conductor, v is the drift speed of the charge carriers and q is the charge on each charge carrier.

Electronvolt, eV: The amount of energy gained by an electron that has been accelerated through a potential difference of 1 V, equal to 1.6×10^{-19} J.

Resistance, R: Defined as the value of the voltage across an component divided by the value of the current flowing through the component, $R = \dfrac{V}{I}$.

Resistivity, ρ: The resistance of a sample of material with a cross-sectional area of 1 m^2 and a length of 1 m. This leads to the equation, $R = \rho \dfrac{l}{A}$

Resistors in series and in parallel: In series, $R_{total} = R_1 + R_2 + R_3$

$$\text{In parallel, } \frac{1}{R_{total}} = \frac{1}{R_1} + \frac{1}{R_2} + \frac{1}{R_3}$$

Kirchhoff's laws of circuital theory:

First law – the sum of all currents flowing into a junction equals the sum of all currents flowing out of the junction; sometimes this is written as $\sum I = 0$.

Second law – the sum of all voltages in a simple circuit loop equals the emf supplied to that loop; sometimes written as $\varepsilon = \sum IR$

Magnetic force: $F_m = BIl \sin \theta$ for a conductor of length, l, carrying a current, I at an angle, θ to the magnetic field, B. $F_m = Bqv \sin \theta$ for a charge q moving with a velocity, v at an angle θ to the magnetic field, B.

Magnetic field strength, B: This is given as the magnetic force experienced by a conductor of length 1 m carrying a current of 1 A; $B = \dfrac{F_m}{Il}$. It can be thought of as the number of magnetic field lines passing perpendicularly through an area of 1 m^2.

Exercise 5.1 – Electric fields

1 If you rub a Perspex® ruler on your woollen sweater, the ruler will become positively charged.
  a Explain how the ruler has become positively charged.
  b What has happened to your woollen sweater?

2 If you comb your hair with a plastic comb, the plastic comb will become negatively charged.
  a Explain how the plastic comb has become negatively charged
  b What has happened to your hair?

3 a What kind of charge does an electron have?
  b How much charge does an electron have?
  c The S.I. unit of charge is the coulomb. How many electrons make up one coulomb of charge?

4 Figure 5.1 shows a positively charged Perspex® rod attracting some small pieces of tissue paper. The tissue paper is not charged.

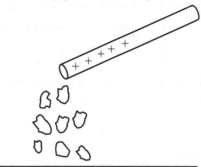

Figure 5.1

Explain how the Perspex® rod is able to attract the pieces of tissue paper.

5 Figure 5.2 shows a toy doll sitting on top of a charged sphere. Explain why the toy doll's hair sticks up in all directions, as shown in the illustration.

Figure 5.2

6 a Explain the term *electrical conductor*.
  b Describe how an electrical insulator is different from an electrical conductor.

7 Explain why metals are good electrical conductors.

8 The SI unit for charge is not a fundamental unit.
  a Explain the term *fundamental unit*.
  b How is a coulomb defined in terms of its base units?
  c What are the SI base units for a coulomb?

9 Figure 5.3 shows a small, positively charged sphere. In the region around the sphere three positions are labelled X, Y and Z.

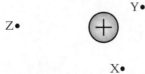

Figure 5.3

a Draw three arrows on Figure 5.3 to represent the force that one coulomb of charge would experience if it were positioned at X, Y and Z. The length of your arrow should represent the magnitude of the force. The direction should represent the direction of the force on the coulomb of charge.

b How does the magnitude of the force experienced by the coulomb of charge vary with its distance from the charged sphere?

10 Two small, charged, spheres, A and B, are separated by a distance, x.
When the charge on A is $+50$ mC and the charge on B is -50 mC, sphere A experiences a force, F.

a In which direction is this force?

b Does sphere B experience a force? If so, how big and in which direction is this force?

c Which of Newton's laws of motion has helped you to answer part **b**?

d Copy and complete Table 5.1.

Charge on A	Charge on B	Distance between A and B	Force experienced by A	Force experienced by B
+50 mC	−50 mC	x	F	
+50 mC	+50 mC	x		
+50 mC	−200 mC	x		
+100 mC	−100 mC	x		
+50 mC	−50 mC	$2x$		
+100 mC	+100 mC	$\dfrac{x}{3}$		

Table 5.1

11 The region of space around a charged object is called an electric field. This electric field exerts a force on any charged particle in it. How does this force depend on:

a the amount of charge on the charged particle in the field?

b the amount of charge that the object creating the field has?

c the distance between the charged object creating the field and the charged particle in the field?

12 Explain what is meant by the term *inverse square law*.

13 State Coulomb's law.

14 The constant in Coulomb's law (usually called the Coulomb constant) has the value 9×10^9 N m^2 C^{-2} if the space occupied by an electric field is a vacuum. Calculate the force between:

a a charge of $+50$ nC and another charge of -20 nC that are 30 cm apart in air

b a charge of $+30$ μC and another charge of $+20$ μC that are 5 mm apart in air

c an electron and a proton that are 100 pm apart in a vacuum

d an alpha particle of charge 6.4×10^{-19} C and a gold nucleus of charge 1.26×10^{-17} C that are 3 fm apart in a vacuum.

15 Calculate the force between two protons separated by a distance of 2 nm in water that has a permittivity of 7.8×10^{-10} C^2 N^{-1} m^{-2}.

16 **a** Using Coulomb's law, calculate the force experienced by a +50 mC charge and a +20 mC charge that are 2 mm apart in air. Is this force an attractive force or a repulsive force?

   b Calculate the force between a −50 mC charge and a +20 mC charge that are 2 mm apart. Is this force an attractive force or a repulsive force?

   c How does physics convention describe whether a force is attractive or repulsive?

17 Figure 5.4 shows an electric field pattern produced around a small charged sphere.

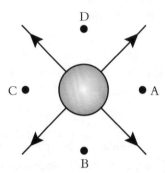

Figure 5.4

   a Is the sphere charged positively or negatively?

   b In which direction would a charge of 1 C experience a force if it were placed at:

   i position A in the diagram?

   ii position B in the diagram?

   c In which direction would an electron experience a force if it were placed at:

   i position C in the diagram?

   ii position D in the diagram?

18 Copy Figure 5.5 and draw the electric field pattern.

Figure 5.5

19 The magnitude of the force experienced by a charged particle of charge q is proportional to q. So, physicists use the term 'field strength' of an electric field, since this is independent of the amount of charge a particle has within the field.

   a How is electric field strength defined?

   b What units does electric field strength have?

   c How is electric field strength related to the force experienced by a charge, q, in the field?

20 Table 5.2 show calculated field strengths in a vacuum. Complete the table.

Charge on object creating the field / C	Distance from charge / m	Field strength / N C^{-1}
40×10^{-6}	3×10^{-2}	
1.6×10^{-19}	1.1×10^{-10}	
6.4×10^{-19}	3×10^{-14}	
-3×10^{-3}	1.5×10^{-2}	

Table 5.2

21 **a** Calculate the electric field strength at a distance of 7×10^{-10} m from a nucleus of carbon.

  b Calculate the force experienced by an electron at a distance of 7×10^{-10} m from a nucleus of carbon.

  c If the mass of the electron is 9.1×10^{-31} kg, calculate the acceleration of the electron.

22 Explain why we would expect free electrons in a metal to be equally spaced.

23 Consider a hollow charged sphere, as shown in Figure 5.6.

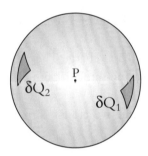

Figure 5.6

  a Draw an arrow on Figure 5.6 to show the electric field caused by δQ_1 only at point P. Label this arrow 1.

  b Draw an arrow on Figure 5.6 to show the electric field caused by δQ_2 only at point P. Label this arrow 2.

  c Imagine you drew more arrows, for all possible places around the surface of the charged sphere. What could you conclude about the electric field strength at point P caused by *all* of the charge on *all* of the surface of the sphere?

  d Imagine you changed the position of P to any other place within the hollow sphere, and repeated parts **a**, **b** and **c**. What could you conclude about the electric field strength inside a hollow charged sphere?

24 Imagine Figure 5.6 showed a solid charged sphere, rather than a hollow charged sphere. If you followed the same steps as question **23** – but this time drawing arrows at small *volume* sections within the sphere – what would you be able to conclude about the electric field strength inside a solid charged sphere?

25 Figure 5.7 shows two small charged spheres, X and Y, 2 cm apart. Each sphere has a charge of +50 μC.

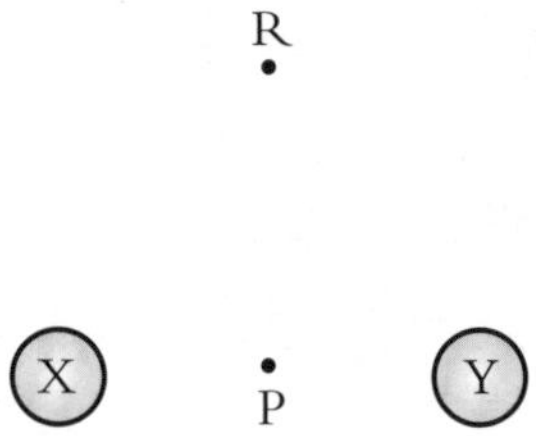

R
•

 •
P

Figure 5.7

a Draw an arrow on Figure 5.7 to show the direction of force on a particle, placed at point P, mid-way between X and Y, that has a charge of +1 C due to:
  - charged sphere X only; label this F_X
  - charged sphere Y only; label this F_Y.
b State the resultant force on the 1 C charged particle at P
c Repeat parts **a** and **b** for a 1 C charged particle at point R, where R is 2 cm from X and 2 cm from Y, making an equilateral triangle with X and Y.

26 Calculate the magnitude and direction of the electric field strength at point P for the following situations:
a Point P is mid-way between a charge of −20 μC and a charge of +40 μC. It is 3 cm away from each charge.
b Point P is 6 cm from a −20 C charge and 3 cm from a +5 C charge. The −20 C charge is 3 cm from the +5 C charge along the line passing through both charges and point P.
c Point P is at one corner of a square of length 3 cm. At the two closest corners to P there are two +4 C charges.

27 Charge X, of +5 μC, sits 15 cm from Charge Y, of +12 μC. Calculate how far from charge X, in a line joining X and Y, the electric field strength is zero.

28 Suppose that an electric field exists such that the electric field strength, E, is a constant in all places.
a What is the relationship between:
  - the force, F, that a charge, q, experiences in the field, and
  - electric field strength?
b Suppose that a charge, q, within the field, experiences this force. It moves a distance, x, in the direction of the force. How much energy has been used to make the charge move this distance?
c We can think of this energy as *work done*. Calculate the work done when a charge of 3 mC sitting in an electric field of field strength, $E = 2 \times 10^{-7}$ N C^{-1}, moves a distance of 5 cm in the direction of the force.

29 An alpha particle of charge 3.2×10^{-19} C and mass 4 u sits in a uniform electric field of field strength 4×10^8 N C^{-1}. Calculate:
a the force experienced by the alpha particle
b the resulting acceleration of the alpha particle.

30 Figure 5.8 shows how the force, F, on a unit test charge, q, varies with distance, x, from a small charged sphere.

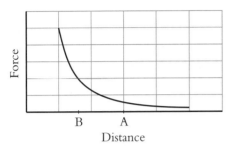

Figure 5.8

  a Indicate how you could use Figure 5.8 to find the work done in moving a unit test charge from A to B.

  b How can you express mathematically what you have shown in part **a**?

31 **a** How much work is done if an electron is moved through a potential difference of 1 V?

  b Physicists express this work done in units of electronvolts, eV.
  1 eV = 1.6×10^{-19} J. Calculate the electronvolts equivalent of:
  i 6.4×10^{-19} J
  ii 3.2×10^{-13} J
  iii 2×10^{-15} J.

32 Calculate the energy equivalents, in joules, of:

  a 3 eV

  b 200 keV

  c 7.4 M eV.

33 Calculate the energy transferred when:

  a 4.8×10^{-19} C of charge move through a potential difference of 200 V

  b a current of 2.5 A flows through a potential difference of 4 V for one minute

  c a current of 40 mA flows through a potential difference of 240 V for one hour.

34 Figure 5.9 represents the inside of a wire when a current is flowing. The wire has a cross-sectional area, A.

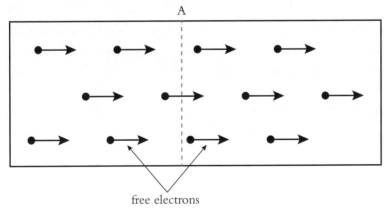

Figure 5.9

  a If all of the electrons are moving at a speed of v (this is the *drift speed*) what volume of electrons within the wire will move past point X in one second?

b There are n electrons per metre-cubed in the wire (this is the *free electron number density*). If each electron has a charge, e, how much charge passes point X in one second?

c Current can be described as charge flowing per second. Write an equation for the current, I, in the wire as a function of electron number density, n, cross-sectional area, A, speed of the electrons, v, and the charge on each electron, e.

35 Table 5.3 shows currents flowing in a copper wire. Complete the table.

Electron number density	Cross-sectional area	Drift speed	Charge on charge carrier	Current
1.6×10^{29} m^{-3}	1.0×10^{-6} m^2	1.5×10^{-5} m s^{-1}	1.6×10^{-19} C	
1.6×10^{29} m^{-3}	4.0×10^{-6} m^2		1.6×10^{-19} C	0.5 A
1.6×10^{29} m^{-3}		2.5×10^{-4} m s^{-1}	1.6×10^{-19} C	80 mA

Table 5.3

36 This question shows you how to find the free electron number density for copper. By substituting values of molar mass, density and how many electrons each atom allows to be free for other metals, you can find the free electron density for any metal.

a The molar mass of copper is 63.5 g mol^{-1}. How many moles of copper atoms are there in 1 kg of copper?

b Calculate how many atoms of copper there are in 1 kg. (Avogadro's number is 6.02×10^{23} mol^{-1}.)

c The density of copper is 8900 kg m^{-3}. Calculate how many atoms of copper there are in 1 m^3 of copper.

d If each atom of copper donates two electrons to the conduction band (in other words, there are two free electrons for each copper atom) calculate the free electron number density for copper.

37 Table 5.4 shows some data about some metals.

Metal	Molar mass / g mole^{-1}	Density / kg m^{-3}	Free electrons per atom
Aluminium	27	2700	1
Gold	197	19 300	1
Iron	56	7850	1

Table 5.4

Calculate the free electron density for:

a aluminium

b gold

c iron.

38 A simple circuit contains a power supply, a light bulb and two 0.8 m leads.

    a Calculate the drift speed of electrons in a wire where:
       $I = 100$ mA; $A = 1 \times 10^{-6}$ m^2; $n = 1.6 \times 10^{29}$ m^{-3} and $e = 1.6 \times 10^{-19}$ C.

    b Calculate how much time it would take for an electron to move from the power supply to the light bulb.

    c As soon as a circuit is switched on, the light bulb produces light. Explain why.

39 Use $I = \dfrac{dQ}{dt}$ to calculate:

    a I, when 4.0 mC flows in 50 s

    b Q, when a current of 30 mA flows for one minute

    c how much time it takes for a current of 25 μA to transfer 1 mC of charge.

40 A 250 mA current flows through a resistor for one minute. The potential difference across the resistor is 6.0 V.

    a Calculate how much charge flows through the resistor.

    b As the current flows through the resistor, there is an energy transfer. Suggest what the main energy transfer in the resistor is.

    c Calculate how much energy is transferred by the current during this time.

    d Calculate the power dissipated by the resistor.

Exercise 5.2 – Heating effect of electric currents

1 A student plans to set up a circuit to investigate how the voltage across a resistor varies when the current flowing through the resistor changes. The student has a cell (emf 6 V; negligible internal resistance), a fixed resistor, an ammeter, a voltmeter, some electrical leads and a variable resistor.

    a What is the independent variable in the student's experiment?

    b Another student plans to investigate how the current flowing through a component varies when the voltage across the component is varied. What would be the independent variable in this student's experiment?

    c Draw a circuit diagram that the student could use.

    d If the student uses another cell of emf 6 V and negligible internal resistance, explain how it is now possible to provide a voltage across the component that varies from 0 V to 6 V.

2 **a** Define *resistance* and state the units it is measured in.

    b State the SI base units for resistance.

3 Calculate the resistance of the following resistors:

    a Current flowing through = 250 mA; voltage across resistor = 0.5 V

    b Current flowing through = 50 μA; voltage across resistor = 5 V

    c Current flowing through = 30 mA; voltage across resistor = 120 V

4 A cube is made from 12 identical resistors, each of resistance R. Calculate the resistance of the cube if current flows into one corner and out of the opposite corner of the cube.

5 **a** Define *resistivity*.

    b A resistor is 1 cm long, has a cross-sectional area of 2.0×10^{-6} m^2, and is made from a material of resistivity 4×10^{-8} Ω m. Calculate its resistance.

6 1 m^3 of copper has a resistance of $1.7 \times 10^{-8} \ \Omega$.

    a How much resistance would 1 cm^3 of copper have?

    b 1 m^3 of copper is stretched into a rod of cross-sectional area 1 cm^2. What is the copper rod's:

      i length?

      ii resistance?

7 A cylindrical $2.2 \text{ k}\Omega$ resistor is 2 cm long with a radius of 1.2 mm. Calculate the resistivity of the material it is made from.

8 A $100 \ \Omega$ resistor is 3 cm long. It is made of a material of resistivity $4 \times 10^{-4} \ \Omega \text{ m}$. Calculate its cross-sectional area.

9 Consider two cylindrical resistors made from the same material. Resistor A is twice as long and twice the diameter of resistor B.

    a The resistance of A is $100 \ \Omega$. Calculate the resistance B.

    b Resistor A is passed through rollers, reducing its radius to $\frac{1}{2}$ its original. What will its new resistance be?

10 **a** State Ohm's law.

    b Explain why it is not possible for a filament light bulb to obey Ohm's law.

    c Sketch the electrical characteristic (the graph of *voltage* against *current*) for a filament light bulb.

    d i How does the resistance of a filament light bulb change as the current flowing through it increases?

      ii Suggest why the resistance varies in this way. Your answer should refer to the microscopic behaviour within the resistor.

11 A semiconductor is an electrical component whose resistance can change because it can change the free electron number density. It does this in one of two ways:

    • by making the atoms of the semiconductor vibrate so violently that they shake off some of their electrons

    • by bombarding the atoms of the semiconductor with photons of light, so that some of the atoms' electrons absorb the energy from the photons and break free of the atom.

    What are the two types of semiconductor called?

12 Figure 5.10 shows three identical Ohmic resistors in an electrical circuit. The current flowing through resistor X is 0.4 mA.

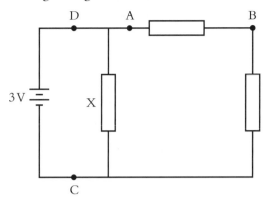

Figure 5.10

a Calculate the resistance of resistor X.
b What is the current flowing at points A, B, C and D?
c Show that the total resistance of the three resistors in parallel is 5 kΩ.

13 Three resistors, rated 3.0 Ω, 5.2 Ω and 0.3 Ω, are placed in series in a circuit. Calculate the total resistance of the three resistors.

14 Two resistors, rated 3 Ω and 6 Ω, are placed in parallel in a circuit. Calculate the total resistance of the two resistors.

15 You are supplied with four identical 10 Ω resistors. Explore how many different total resistances you can make using some or all of the resistors.

16 Look at Figure 5.11 and calculate the current flowing through the:
a 1 Ω resistor
b 6 Ω resistor
c 3 Ω resistor.

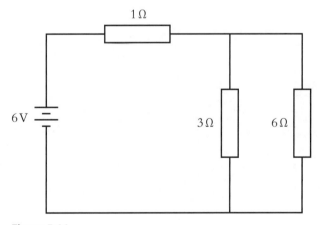

Figure 5.11

17 Determine the reading on the ammeter in Figure 5.12.

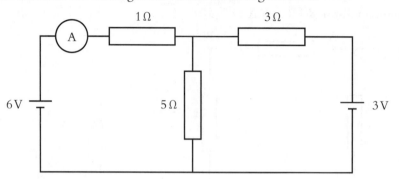

Figure 5.12

18 Look at Figure 5.13.

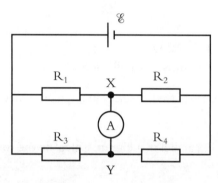

Figure 5.13

  a What is this circuit arrangement of resistors called?
  b Write an algebraic expression for the voltage across resistor R_2.
  c Write an algebraic expression for the voltage across resistor R_4.
  d If the ammeter reads zero, determine how the resistances of R_1, R_2, R_3 and R_4 are related.

19 Figure 5.14 shows a bridge circuit.

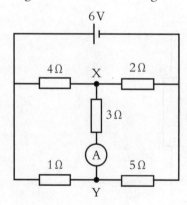

Figure 5.14

  a Determine the reading on the ammeter.
  b Does current flow from X to Y or from Y to X?

20 **a** State Kirchhoff's two laws of circuital theory.

    b Look at Figure 5.15 and use Kirchhoff's laws to show that:

        i the current flowing through the 2 Ω resistor is 1 A

        ii there is no current flowing through the 3 Ω resistor.

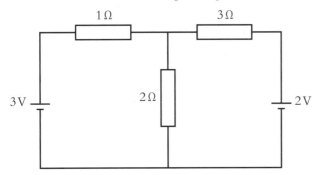

Figure 5.15

21 A student sets up a circuit with two 1 kΩ resistors in series with a 6 V emf source of negligible internal resistance. The student is trying to measure the voltage across one of the two 1 kΩ resistors using a voltmeter in the usual way.

    a What will the voltmeter read if the resistance of the voltmeter is:

        i 1 kΩ?

        ii 100 kΩ?

    b Explain why the resistance of an ideal voltmeter is infinite.

    c In practice, it is not possible to have a voltmeter with an infinite resistance. Suggest how the resistance of a voltmeter should compare with the value of the resistor, across which it is trying to measure the voltage.

22 The energy from a single flash of light from a small strobe lamp is 0.8 J. The voltage across the lamp is 230 V.

    a If the flash of light lasts 10 ms, what is the average current flowing through the lamp?

    b It likely that the actual current flowing through the lamp while the light is flashing is not constant. Explain why.

    c Calculate the average power of the lamp.

23 In a commercial laser radar system, a neodymium-YAG laser produces pulses of light that each last 15 ns.

    a One pulse of light contains 1.0 J of energy. Calculate the effective power of the laser as it produced light.

    b Suggest why the laser produces light in short pulses, rather than continuously.

Exercise 5.3 – Electric cells

1 When a simple cell is placed in a circuit and the circuit is switched on, an energy transformation takes place within the cell.

    a Outline what this energy transformation is.

    b Is this energy transformation likely to occur with 100% efficiency? Explain your answer.

2　a　When a resistor is placed in a circuit and the circuit is switched on, an energy transformation occurs. Outline what this energy transformation is.

　　b　Suggest why real cells are considered to have an internal resistance.

3　Outline the difference between a primary cell and a secondary cell.

4　A primary cell is rated as 1200 mA-hours. In its normal usage, the cell delivers a current of 1.6 mA. Calculate how long it will take to stop delivering a current.

5　A cell used in a circuit has an emf of 1.5 V and an internal resistance of 0.4 Ω.

　　a　Explain what emf means.

　　b　If the cell is connected in series with a resistor of resistance 5.6 Ω, calculate the current that will flow in the circuit.

　　c　What will the voltage across the terminals of the cell be?

　　d　What will happen to the terminal voltage of the cell if the resistor is replaced by one of resistance 0.6 Ω?

6　A cell of internal resistance, r, is connected in series with a variable resistor and an ideal ammeter.

　　a　Sketch a graph to show how the terminal voltage of the cell varies with the current flowing in the circuit.

　　b　How can you use your graph to find the value for the internal resistance of the cell, r?

　　c　What does the terminal voltage of the cell when no current is flowing tell you?

7　Outline an experiment that could find the emf, ε, and internal resistance, r, of a cell. Make sure you include:

　　• the equipment required (and how to set it up)

　　• the measurements you need to make

　　• how you would manipulate the data to calculate ε and r.

8　A cell of emf 6.0 V and internal resistance 1.0 Ω is connected in series to a 5.0 Ω resistor. Calculate the:

　　a　current flowing in the circuit

　　b　terminal voltage of the cell

　　c　power dissipated in the 5.0 Ω resistor.

9　A cell of emf 5 V and internal resistance 3.0 Ω is connected in series with a variable resistor.

　　a　Complete Table 5.5 to show how the power dissipated in the variable resistor varies when the resistance of the variable resistor is varied.

Resistance of variable resistor / Ω	Current in circuit / A	Power dissipated in variable resistor / W
1.0	1.25	1.56
2.0		
3.0		
4.0		
5.0		

Table 5.5

　　b　What can you conclude about the power dissipated in the resistor?

Exercise 5.4 – Magnetic effect of electric currents

1 Sketch the magnetic field pattern around a bar magnet.

2 One of the effects of a current flowing in a conductor is that a magnetic field is produced around the conductor.
   a Sketch a diagram to show the shape of a magnetic field, produced by a current, around a conductor.
   b How can you know which direction the magnetic field is in?
   c If the current flowing in a conductor is increased, how will your sketch of the magnetic field pattern around the conductor change?
   d There is no magnetic field around a conductor through which no current is flowing. Suggest a likely relationship between the strength of a magnetic field caused by a current and the size of the current.
   e Suggest a relationship between the strength of the magnetic field caused by a current flowing in a conductor and the perpendicular distance away from the conductor.

3 Consider two similar bar magnets, separated by a small distance, with opposite poles facing each other.
   a Sketch a diagram to show the magnetic field pattern between the two poles of the magnets.
   b In the region immediately between the two poles, how is this magnetic field pattern usually described?
   c In which units do physicists measure the strength of a magnetic field?

4 Figure 5.16 shows the opposite poles of two magnets. There is a perpendicular conductor carrying a current between the magnets.

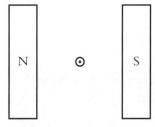

Figure 5.16

   a Copy Figure 5.16 and draw the resulting magnetic field pattern produced by the interaction of the magnetic field from the magnets and the magnetic field from the conductor.
   b What is this kind of magnetic field usually called?
   c What effect does this resultant magnetic field have on the conductor?
   d What *aide memoire* can you use to help you remember this?
   e Suggest three ways in which this effect could be made larger.

5 A conductor of length 5 cm sits perpendicularly in a magnetic field of strength 4.0×10^{-5} T.

    a A current of 250 mA flows in the conductor. Calculate the force experienced by the conductor.

    b The wire is moved slightly so the direction of the current makes an angle of 30° to the magnetic field. Calculate the force experienced by the wire.

6 Outline an investigation to find out how the force on a current-carrying conductor varies with the current flowing in the conductor. Make sure you include:
- what your variables are
- which variables are control variables
- how you will control the control your variables.

7 Consider a current-carrying conductor of length, l, in a magnetic field such that the direction of the current makes an angle, θ, to the magnetic field. If the magnetic field strength is B and the current is I, state how the force experienced by the conductor varies with:

    a B

    b I

    c l

    d θ

8 How is the magnetic field strength, B, defined?

9 A copper wire of diameter 2.0 mm and length 8.0 cm is positioned horizontally in a uniform magnetic field of strength 0.2 T perpendicular to the wire. The density of copper is 8900 kg m^{-3}. Calculate the current that needs to flow through the wire so that it is suspended in mid-air. ($g = 9.8$ N kg^{-1})

10 Two parallel wires, separated by a small distance, each carry a current.

    a If the currents in the two wires are in the same direction, what would you expect to happen to the two wires? Explain your answer.

    b If the currents in the two wires were in opposite directions, what would you expect to happen to the two wires? Explain your answer.

    c How are your answers to parts **a** and **b** relevant to the way in which the SI unit of current is defined?

11 Consider a long coil of wire (a solenoid) in which a current flows.

    a Sketch a diagram to show the magnetic field pattern produced by the current flowing in the solenoid.

    b What would happen to the strength of the magnetic field if the coil:

        i had more turns per metre length

        ii carried a larger current

        iii had a smaller cross-sectional area?

12 A solenoid is another name for a long coil of wire. A solenoid of length 20 cm consists
    of 150 turns of thin wire wrapped around a hollow paper tube. If the solenoid carries
    a current of 30 mA, calculate the strength of the magnetic field produced at the:
    a centre of the solenoid along the central axis
    b edge of the solenoid along the central axis.

13 Suppose a charged particle of charge, q, moves through a distance, l, with a speed, v,
    in a direction that is perpendicular to a uniform magnetic field of strength, B.
    a What will the time it takes for the particle to travel the distance, l, be?
    b What is the current caused by the moving charged particle?
    c Since this current occurs over a length, l, show that the force on the moving
       charged particle in the magnetic field is given by $F = B\,q\,v$.

14 An electron moves in a plane that is perpendicular to a uniform magnetic field of
    strength 0.5 T.
    a If the electron moves with a speed of 2×10^6 m s^{-1}, calculate the magnetic force
       that the electron experiences.
    b What can you say about the direction of this force?
    c What will be the subsequent path of the electron?

15 An electron and a proton both travel at the same speed in a direction that is
    perpendicular to a uniform magnetic field. Suggest:
    a what the subsequent paths of the two particles have in common
    b how the two paths will differ.

? Exam-style questions

1   Two electrodes separated by a distance, d, are maintained at a constant potential
    difference, V. When an electron moves from one of the electrodes to the other, its
    gain in kinetic energy is E.
    The distance between the two electrodes is increased to $2d$. When an electron moves
    from one of the electrodes to the other, what will its gain in kinetic energy be?
    A $\dfrac{E}{4}$
    B $\dfrac{E}{2}$
    C E
    D $2E$

2   A simple electrical circuit is set up with a resistance, R, in series with an emf
    source of negligible internal resistance. The power dissipated is P. If the resistance
    is replaced by a new resistance of $3R$, the power dissipated will be:
    A $\dfrac{P}{9}$
    B $\dfrac{P}{3}$
    C P
    D $3P$

3 Which of the following descriptions best describes the electrical field strength inside a hollow sphere?

A The electrical field strength is zero everywhere inside.

B The electric field strength is proportional to the radial distance from the centre of the sphere.

C The electrical field strength is a non-zero constant everywhere inside the sphere.

D The electrical field strength is inversely proportional to the square of the distance from the centre of the sphere.

4 A copper wire of cross-sectional area 1×10^{-6} m^2 carries a current of 1 A. The free electron number density of copper is about 10^{29} m^{-3}. The charge on an electron is of the order of 10^{-19} C. What is the best estimate for the speed at which the electrons move along the wire?

A 10^{-4} m s^{-1}

B 1 m s^{-1}

C 100 m s^{-1}

D 10^4 m s^{-1}

5 This question is about the motion of an electron in a magnetic field and in an electric field. An electron enters a magnetic field so that its velocity is perpendicular to the direction of the magnetic field. Another electron with the same initial velocity enters a uniform electric field so that its velocity is perpendicular to the direction of the electric field. Which of the following combinations describes the shape of the path followed by the electrons in the two fields?

A Shape of path in the magnetic field = circular; Shape of path in the electric field = circular

B Shape of path in the magnetic field = circular; Shape of path in the electric field = parabolic

C Shape of path in the magnetic field = parabolic; Shape of path in the electric field = circular

D Shape of path in the magnetic field = parabolic; Shape of path in the electric field = parabolic

6 Figure 5.17 shows a length of an electrical conductor connected to a power supply. The two ends of the conductor have a potential difference of 6 V across them.

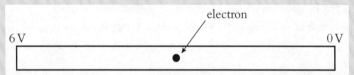

Figure 5.17

a Draw an arrow on Figure 5.17 to show the direction of the conventional current that will flow through the conductor. Label this arrow I. **[1]**

b Draw another arrow on Figure 5.17 to show the direction in which the free electrons within the conductor will move. Label this e. **[1]**

c If the length of the conductor is 20 cm, show that the electric field strength, E, within the conductor is 30 V m^{-1}. **[2]**

d Calculate the acceleration of the electron shown. **[2]**

e Calculate the time it would take for the electron to move from its present position (half-way along the conductor) to the other end of the conductor. **[2]**

f In fact, it takes an electron much longer to travel this distance through the conductor. Suggest why. **[2]**

7   A student plans to set up a circuit to investigate how the voltage across a resistor varies when the current flowing through the resistor changes. The student has a cell (emf 6V; negligible internal resistance), a fixed resistor, an ammeter, a voltmeter, some electrical leads and a variable resistor.

a   Draw a circuit diagram to show how the student should set up the circuit. **[3]**

b   The student conducts the experiment. The graph of results is shown in Figure 5.18.

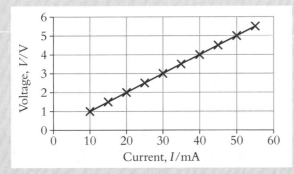

Figure 5.18

The student says the resistor is an Ohmic device. Suggest why the graph supports this suggestion. **[2]**

c   Using the graph, calculate the resistance of the resistor. **[2]**

d   Suggest why the student was not able to plot points on the graph for voltages across the resistor of 0 V and 6 V. **[2]**

8   **This question is about ammeters and voltmeters.**

a   Complete Table 5.6 by inserting a tick in the appropriate box to show how ammeters and voltmeters are connected in a circuit. **[2]**

Type of meter	Connected in series	Connected in parallel
Ammeter		
Voltmeter		

Table 5.6

b   A student has set up an incorrect circuit, as shown in Figure 5.19.

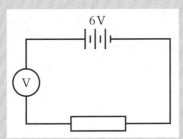

Figure 5.19

What value will the voltmeter read? Explain your thinking. **[2]**

c Another student has set up a circuit incorrectly, as shown in Figure 5.20.

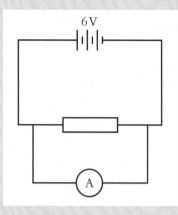

Figure 5.20

Explain why the ammeter is likely to read a value that is much larger than the actual current flowing through the resistor. **[2]**

9 **A cell rated as 6 V, and with negligible internal resistance, is to be connected to four identical resistors.**

  a Sketch circuit diagrams to show how the circuit should be arranged so that each resistor has a voltage of:

   i 1.5 V across it

   ii 3 V across it

   iii 6 V across it. **[3]**

  b In which of your three circuits will the cell continue to work for the longest time? Explain your answer. **[2]**

10 **This question is about the power dissipation in resistors.**

  Figure 5.21 shows three resistors and a cell of negligible internal resistance in a circuit.

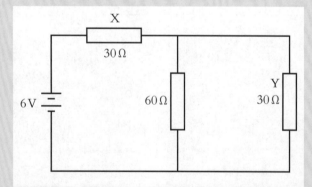

Figure 5.21

  a Calculate the total resistance in the circuit. **[2]**

  b Calculate the current flowing through resistor X. **[2]**

  c Calculate the ratio of the powers P_X and P_Y dissipated in resistors X and Y, $\dfrac{P_X}{P_Y}$. **[2]**

  d Calculate how much energy the cell uses if it is switched on for one hour. **[2]**

11 **A 5 V cell is used to power a 6 mW laser.**
   a What is the value of the current flowing in the laser? **[2]**
   b If the cell powers the laser for 30 minutes, how much charge will have flowed through the laser? **[1]**
   c How much energy will the cell have transformed? **[2]**
   d In fact, the cell will transform more than your answer to part **c**. Suggest a reason for this. **[2]**

12 **The superconducting coils that form the bending magnets at CERN have to produce a magnetic field of strength 8.3 T. The solenoids are 14.3 m long and carry a current of 11 850 A.**
   a Show that the number of turns on each coil is about 8000. **[2]**
   b Calculate the diameter of the conducting wire from which the coils are made. **[2]**
   c Suggest how it is possible for a wire so thin to carry a current of 11 850 A. **[2]**

13 **Look at Figure 5.22. The ammeter reads 0 A. Determine the emf, ε, of the right-hand cell. [3]**

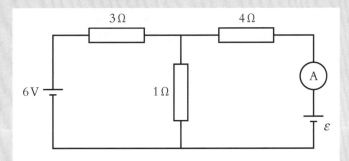

Figure 5.22

14 **Look at Figure 5.23. Calculate the reading on the ammeter. [3]**

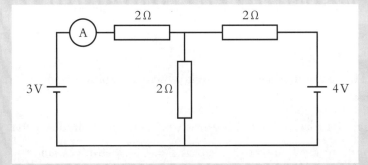

Figure 5.23

6 Circular motion and gravitation

Chapter outline

In this chapter, you will:

- Understand that circular motion requires an unbalanced force – the centripetal force which produces a centripetal acceleration, and identify the forces that provide this centripetal force (such as tension, friction, gravitational force, electrical force and magnetic force).
- Solve problems involving centripetal force, centripetal acceleration, time period, frequency, angular displacement, angular speed and linear speed.
- Describe, qualitatively and quantitatively, examples of circular motion in the horizontal and in the vertical planes.
- Understand Newton's law of gravitation, and apply it to the orbit of a mass around another mass.
- Understand the idea of gravitational field strength and solve problems involving gravitational field strength, orbital speed and period, and determine the combined gravitational field strength due to two masses.

KEY TERMS

Time period, T: The time it takes for an orbiting object to make one complete orbit.

Frequency, f: The number of complete orbits made in one second.

Angular displacement: The angle through which an object has moved during its circular motion/orbit.

Angular speed: The amount of angle through which an orbiting body has moved in a time of 1 second.

Centripetal force: The force, directed towards the centre of a circular orbit, necessary for a body to move in orbit; given as $F = \dfrac{mv^2}{r} = mr\omega^2 = mv\omega$

Centripetal acceleration: The rate of change of velocity of a body in orbit; given as $a = \dfrac{\Delta v}{\Delta t} = \dfrac{v^2}{r} = r\omega^2 = v\omega$ and is directed towards the centre of the circular orbit.

Newton's law of gravitation: $F = -G\dfrac{Mm}{r^2}$

Gravitational field strength, g: The gravitational force that acts on a unit point mass in the gravitational field; given as $g = \dfrac{F}{m} = -G\dfrac{M}{r^2}$

Exercise 6.1 – Circular motion

1   Define *time period* of an object in circular motion.

2   What is the time period of these examples of circular motion?
    a   The second hand of a wrist watch.
    b   The hour hand of a wrist watch.
    c   The Earth in its orbit around the Sun.

3   The wheel of a bicycle makes 400 complete rotations in three minutes. Calculate the time period of the circular motion of the wheel.

4   How many radians does the minute hand of a clock turn through in 15 minutes?

5   Calculate the angular displacement in 20 minutes of the:
    a   second hand of a clock
    b   minute hand of a clock
    c   hour hand of a clock.

6   The fan blade of a popular modern hair drier makes 110 000 rotations in one minute. Calculate the:
    a   time period of one rotation
    b   angular displacement of the blade in one second.

7   The angular displacement made in one second is also called the angular speed, ω.
    a   Write the equation to show how ω is related to the time period, T, of rotation.
    b   Write the equation to show how ω is related to the frequency, f, of the rotations.

8   Calculate the angular speed, ω, of:
    a   the Earth in its orbit around the Sun
    b   a children's carousel that makes one rotation in one minute
    c   the Moon that makes 13 rotations of the Earth in one year.

9   The Singapore Flyer is a large Ferris wheel of radius 75 m, with observation pods for spectators on the circumference. It takes 30 minutes to make one complete rotation. Calculate the:
    a   frequency of the Singapore Flyer's rotation
    b   angular speed of the Singapore Flyer
    c   linear speed at which one of the observation pods travels.

10 Calculate the linear speed of the Earth in its orbit around the Sun. (The radius of the Earth's orbit is 1.5×10^{11} m.)

11 The blades of a helicopter have to rotate so that the tip of the rotor blades travel slower than the speed of sound (speed of sound in air = 330 m s^{-1}). If the blades can rotate at 250 rotations per minute, what is the maximum length that the rotor blades can be?

12 Astra 3B is a communications satellite that provides satellite television to most of Europe. It orbits the Earth at a radius of 42 Mm. Calculate:
a the angular speed of the satellite in its orbit
b its linear speed through space.

13 Any body that is performing circular motion is accelerating. Explain why this statement must be true.

14 Figure 6.1 shows an object making anticlockwise circular motion about its centre of rotation.

Figure 6.1

Copy the diagram and add arrows to show the:
a instantaneous linear velocity of the object
b acceleration of the object.

15 a When a body is rotating in circular motion, in which direction **must** there be an unbalanced force?
b What is the name of this unbalanced force that produces circular motion?

16 Sketch graphs to show how the acceleration of a body in circular motion depends on the:
a body's mass, m
b body's linear speed, v
c radius of the circle in which it is moving.

17 Sketch graphs to show how the force on a body undergoing circular motion varies with the:
a body's mass
b body's linear speed
c radius of the circle in which the body is moving.

18 Write the equation for the necessary force, F, required for a body to make circular motion. Be sure to note what each of the terms in the equation mean.

19 The necessary centripetal force has to be provided by a real force occurring in the motion of an object. For each of the following examples, outline what the real force is that is providing the necessary centripetal force for circular motion:
a The Moon in its orbit around the Earth.
b An electron in its orbit around a nucleus.
c A proton in its orbit around the Large Hadron Collider at CERN.
d A car moving on an arc of a circle on a bend in a road.
e A ball attached to light string being rotated in a horizontal plane.

20 The mass of the Earth is given as M_E, the mass of the Sun is given as M_S and the radius of the Earth's orbit is given as R.

    a Write the equation for the:

        i gravitational force between the Sun and the Earth

        ii centripetal force required for the Earth to make its motion around the Sun.

    b The radius of the Earth's orbit around the Sun is 1.5×10^{11} m. Show that the mass of the Sun, M_S, is about 2×10^{30} kg.

21 In one model of a hydrogen atom, the electron is considered to orbit the nucleus at a distance of 5.29×10^{-11} m.

    a Calculate the electrical force exerted on the electron by the proton in the hydrogen atom.

    b The mass of the electron is 9.1×10^{-31} kg. Calculate the speed of the electron in its orbit around the proton.

22 Consider a car travelling on a circular road at a constant speed.

    a How does the friction force between the road and the car's tyres depend on the car's mass?

    b Derive an expression for the maximum speed of the car around the circular road. Show that this must apply to all cars, large or small.

    c Explain why the maximum speed at which a car can travel safely on a circular road is likely to be slower when the road is wet or icy.

23 The exit road from a major motorway is usually an arc of a circle. The speed limit on this part of the road is always clearly shown as a motorist leaves the motorway.

    a Explain why the speed limit on the exit road of the motorway is always smaller than the speed limit on the carriageway of the motorway.

    b If the average coefficient of friction between the exit road and a car's tyres is 0.75, and the radius of the circular arc is 80 m, calculate the maximum speed at which a car can travel safely on the exit road without skidding.

24 The tyres of a car are worn. This has halved the coefficient of static friction between the road and the car's tyres. How has the maximum speed at which the car can travel safely around a bend changed?

25 A student attaches a small ball of mass 100 g to the end of a string of length 60 cm. The student makes the ball execute circular motion in the horizontal plane with a frequency of 2.5 Hz.

    a Calculate the:

        i linear speed of the ball

        ii tension in the string.

    b In fact, it is not possible for anyone to make a ball on the end of a string execute circular motion in an exactly horizontal plane.

        i Explain why this must be the case

        ii Draw a free body force diagram for such a ball on the end of a string being rotated.

    c Must the actual tension in the string be smaller, the same or larger than when the string is perfectly horizontal?

    d Which component of the tension is acting as the centripetal force?

    e What is the other component of the tension force doing?

26 Consider a cyclist on a banked section of a circular track.

    a Draw a free body force diagram for the cyclist. (You do not need to think about the friction force between the cycle's tyres and the track.)

    b Use your free body force diagram to derive an expression for the angle, θ, of the banked track in terms of the speed of the cyclist, v, and the radius of the circular track, r.

    c Explain why the angle of banking for an Olympic cyclist track is likely to be larger than that for an amateur cyclist track.

27 Figure 6.2 shows the path of a mass, m, which is being swung around by a light string in a vertical circle of radius, r.

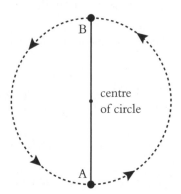

Figure 6.2

    a Copy the diagram and add arrows to show the forces acting on the mass at position A.

    b Derive an expression for the tension, T, in the string at position A.

    c Derive an expression for the tension in the string at position B.

    d What do you notice about the tension in the string as the mass moves in a vertical circle?

    e How much work is done by the centripetal force on the mass as it moves in its circular path?

    f Explain your answer to part **e**.

    g How much gravitational potential energy does the mass gain when it moves from position A to position B?

    h If the total energy of the mass is constant during its motion through the vertical circle, how do you explain the increase in gravitational potential energy that the mass gains when moving from A to B?

Exercise 6.2 – Newton's law of gravitation

1 Outline what is meant by *gravitational field*.

2 Newton's universal law of gravitation is usually written as: $F = -G\dfrac{Mm}{R^2}$

    a What does each term represent, and what units are they measured in?

    b What is the purpose of the minus sign in this equation?

3 Calculate the gravitational force between:

    a the Earth and the Sun ($M_{Earth} = 6 \times 10^{24}$ kg; $M_{Sun} = 2 \times 10^{30}$ kg; $R = 1.5 \times 10^{11}$ m kg; $G = 6.67 \times 10^{-11}$ N m^2 kg^{-2})

    b two protons of mass 1.7×10^{-27} kg, 2×10^{-15} m apart

    c two students, 60 kg and 70 kg, sitting 1 m apart in a classroom.

4   **a** Explain what is meant by *gravitational field strength*.
     b How is gravitational field strength related to gravitational force?

5   The Earth has a mass of 6×10^{24} kg. Its average radius is 6.4×10^6 m.
     a Calculate the gravitational field strength at the surface of the Earth.
     b Explain why this gravitational field strength is usually quoted as a *globally averaged* value.
     c Is the gravitational field strength of the Earth largest at the equator or at the poles? Explain your answer.

6   Show that the units for gravitational field strength are the same as those for acceleration.

7   How do physicists usually describe the gravitational force acting on a mass?

8   The mass of the Moon is 7.3×10^{22} kg. Its radius is 1.6×10^6 m. Show that the ratio of the surface gravitational field strength of the Earth to that of the Moon is about 5:1.

9   The gravitational field strength at the surface of Mars is 0.38 of that of the Earth. The radius of Mars is 3400 km. Calculate the mass of Mars.

10   **a** Calculate the gravitational field strength of the Sun ($M_{Sun} = 2 \times 10^{30}$ kg) at a distance of 1 AU . (1 AU is the average radial distance of the Earth from the Sun = 1.5×10^{11} m.)
      b Calculate the gravitational field strength of the Moon at a distance equal to the average orbital radius of the moon around the Earth.
         (Moon's orbital radius = 3.8×10^8 m.)
      c By comparing your answers to parts **a** and **b**, explain why the Moon – and not the Sun – is responsible for the oceans' tides on the Earth's surface.

11   The gravitational field strength, g, for the Earth is given by: $g = G\dfrac{M}{R^2}$
     a Assuming that the Earth has a constant density, ρ:
        i   show that the gravitational field strength **inside** the Earth is proportional to distance from the centre of the Earth
        ii sketch a graph to show how g varies with distance from the centre of the Earth outwards to about three Earth radii
        iii show that G can be expressed as: $G = \dfrac{3\,g}{4\,\pi\,R\,\rho}$
     b The average density of the Earth is 5.5×10^3 kg m^{-3}. Calculate the percentage difference between the value of G calculated using $G = \dfrac{3\,g}{4\pi\,R\,\rho}$ and the currently accepted value of 6.67×10^{-11} N m^2 kg^{-2}.

12   The Earth orbits the Sun because of the gravitational force of the Sun acting on the Earth.
     a Using your knowledge of centripetal force, write an equation to express this.

     b Show that the speed at which the Earth moves in its orbit is given by the expression, $v = \sqrt{\dfrac{G\,M_{Sun}}{R}}$, where R is the radius of the Earth's orbit.
     c Calculate the linear speed of the Earth in its orbit.

13 Figure 6.3 shows the Earth and the Moon (not to scale). They are 3.8×10^8 m apart.

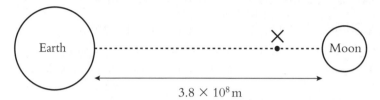

Figure 6.3

a The Earth's mass is 6×10^{24} kg and the Moon's mass is 7.3×10^{22} kg. At point X, the gravitational field strength is zero. Calculate how far X is from the Earth.

b Sketch a graph to show how the gravitational field strength varies with distance between the Earth and the Sun.

14 $\dfrac{M_{Earth}\, v^2}{R} = G\dfrac{M_{Sun}\, M_{Earth}}{R^2}$ and $v = \dfrac{2\pi R}{T}$, where T is the time period of one orbit of the Earth.

a Show that, for the Sun–Earth system, $T^2 \propto R^3$ (Kepler's third law).

b If $T =$ one year and $R = 1.5 \times 10^{11}$ m, show that the mass of the Sun is about 2×10^{30} kg.

c Jupiter also orbits about the Sun. Its orbital period is 11.86 years. Calculate Jupiter's orbital radius.

15 The radius of the Moon's orbit about the Earth is 3.8×10^8 m. Its orbital period is 27.3 days. Show that the mass of the Earth is about 6×10^{24} kg.

❓ Exam-style questions

1 Which value is the best estimate for the angular speed of the Earth in its orbit around the Sun?

A 10^{-1} radians s^{-1}

B 10^{-3} radians s^{-1}

C 10^{-5} radians s^{-1}

D 10^{-7} radians s^{-1}

2 A child swings a small mass attached to a length of string round in a circle. The child applies a pull of F on the string, of length, l, which makes the mass move with a speed, v. If the child now applies the same force, F, but halves the length of the string, what will the new speed of the mass will be?

A $\dfrac{v}{\sqrt{2}}$

B $\dfrac{v}{2}$

C $\sqrt{2}v$

D $2v$

3 A car of mass, m, is driving at a speed, v, over a bridge. The bridge is the arc of a circle of radius, r, as shown in Figure 6.4.

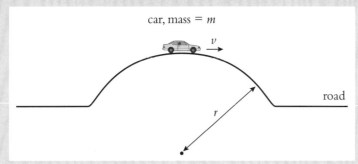

Figure 6.4

Which of the following expressions gives the maximum value of v for which the car will remain in contact with the road?

A $r\,g$

B $m\,r\,g$

C $\sqrt{r\,g}$

D $\sqrt{m\,r\,g}$

4 The mass of the Sun is about 3.3×10^5 times the mass of the Earth. The distance from the Earth to the Sun is 1.5×10^{11} m. If the gravitational force exerted by the Earth on the Sun is F, what is the gravitational force exerted by the Sun on the Earth?

A $\dfrac{F}{3.3 \times 10^5}$

B $-F$

C F

D $3.3 \times 10^5\,F$

5 The gravitational field strength of the Earth at a distance equal to the orbital radius of the Moon is very nearly the same value as the orbital centripetal acceleration of the Moon. Which of the following is not a part of the explanation for this?

A The Moon's orbit is not circular.

B The centre of rotation of the Moon's orbit is not at the centre of the Earth.

C The Moon's mass is significantly smaller than the mass of the Earth.

D The Earth does not remain motionless during an orbit of the Moon.

6   An object placed at a distance of twice the Earth's radius, $2R_E$, from the Earth is allowed to fall to the ground. The mass of the Earth is M. In the absence of any frictional forces, which of the following gives the speed at which the object will hit the Earth's surface?

A $\sqrt{\dfrac{GM}{2R_E}}$

B $\sqrt{\dfrac{GM}{R_E}}$

C $2\sqrt{\dfrac{2GM}{R_E}}$

D $2\sqrt{\dfrac{GM}{R_E}}$

7   Table 6.1 shows some data for Jupiter's four innermost moons.

Name of moon	Orbital radius / Mm	Time period of orbit / s
Io	422	1.53×10^5
Europa	671	3.07×10^5
Ganymede	1070	6.19×10^5
Callisto	1883	1.44×10^6

Table 6.1

a Draw the graph of *(orbital radius)*^{3} against *(time period of orbit)*^{2} for these moons of Jupiter. [4]

b Use your graph to estimate the mass of Jupiter. [3]

8   Sometimes, in competition ice skating, a male skater swings his partner around in a circle. If the skater's arm makes an angle of 30° with the horizontal, and his 60 kg partner rotates around a circle of radius 2.2m, calculate:

a the tension in the male skater's arm [3]

b the angular speed of his partner. [2]

Atomic, nuclear and particle physics 7

Chapter outline

In this chapter, you will:
- Describe the discrete nature of electron energy levels in atoms and how these give rise to emission and absorption spectra.
- Solve problems involving changes of electron energy levels, including calculating the wavelength of absorbed or emitted photons.
- Describe alpha, beta and gamma decay by the use of decay equations, including the presence of neutrinos and anti-neutrinos, and understand that isotopes are evidence for the existence of neutrons and identify the major contributors to background radiation.
- Understand the concept of a radioactive half-life and be able to determine half-lives experimentally and from decay graphs; solve problems involving integral numbers of half-lives.
- Identify the absorption characteristics of alpha, beta and gamma emissions,
- Understand and be able to use the unified atomic mass unit in calculations involving mass defect and nuclear binding energy.
- Solve problems involving the energy released in radioactive decay, nuclear fission and nuclear fusion and know and be able interpret the graph of *binding energy per nucleon against nucleon number*.
- Describe and explain the significance of the alpha particle scattering experiment conducted by Geiger and Marsden under the leadership of Rutherford.
- Identify the four fundamental forces of nature, their properties, range and relative strength and their associated exchange particles.
- Identify the three families of fundamental particles: quarks, leptons and bosons and know the general quark structure of baryons and mesons as members of the hadron family, including the quark structure of protons and neutrons.
- Use the conservation laws (charge, lepton number, strangeness, baryon number) to verify various nuclear and particle interactions and how to construct and interpret simple Feynman diagrams to illustrate them.
- Understand the concept of quark confinement and be able to describe the role of the Higgs boson and its association with the concept of mass.

KEY TERMS

Photon energy: $E = hf = \dfrac{hc}{\lambda}$

Electronvolt: The energy gained by an electron that has been accelerated through a potential difference of 1 volt; $1 \text{ eV} = 1.6 \times 10^{-19}$ J

Half-life, $t_{\frac{1}{2}}$: The average time it takes for half of the undecayed nuclei to decay. Alternatively, the half-life can be considered to be the average time it takes for the activity of a given sample of radioactive material to halve.

Unified atomic mass unit, u: This is a unit of mass used in atomic and particle Physics. It is defined as $\frac{1}{12}$ of the mass of a $^{12}_{6}$C atom; u = 1.661 × 10^{-27} kg.

Mass defect, Δ*m*: The difference in mass between the sum of the masses of the protons and neutrons that make up a nucleus and the actual mass of the nucleus: $\Delta m = ZM_\text{p} + (A - Z)M_\text{n} - M_\text{nucleus}$

Binding energy: The amount of energy required to completely separate all of the protons and neutrons in a nucleus.

Quark confinement: A feature of the theory of quantum chromodynamics that says that quarks cannot exist on their own; they can only exist as combinations in mesons and baryons.

Conservation rules: A simple set of rules that have to be obeyed if an interaction is viable: charge, lepton number, baryon number and, sometimes, strangeness.

Boson or exchange particle: The particle that is responsible for the action of a force: gluon and meson for the strong nuclear force, W^-, W^+ and Z^0 for the weak nuclear force, photon for the electromagnetic force and (it is proposed) graviton for the gravitational force.

Feynman diagram: A specialised diagram that represents an interaction between particles.

Higgs boson: The exchange particle responsible for the physical effect of mass.

Exercise 7.1 – Discrete energy and radioactivity

1 **a** Explain what is meant by *emission spectrum* when applied to a container of gas at a low pressure.

   b Describe how a student may observe such an emission spectrum in the laboratory.

2 Explain how the emission spectrum from a gas provides empirical evidence for the existence of discrete energy levels of atoms.

3 Consider an electron in an atom of hydrogen.

   a Describe how the planetary model of the atom helps us to visualise the electron in the atom.

   b i What force keeps the electron in the atom orbiting around the nucleus?

     ii In which direction is this force on the electron acting?

     iii In the planetary model of the atom, is the electron in the hydrogen atom accelerating? Explain your answer.

   c Suggest a reason why modern physicists find the planetary model of the atom flawed.

4 Figure 7.1 shows some of the energy levels possible for a hydrogen atom.

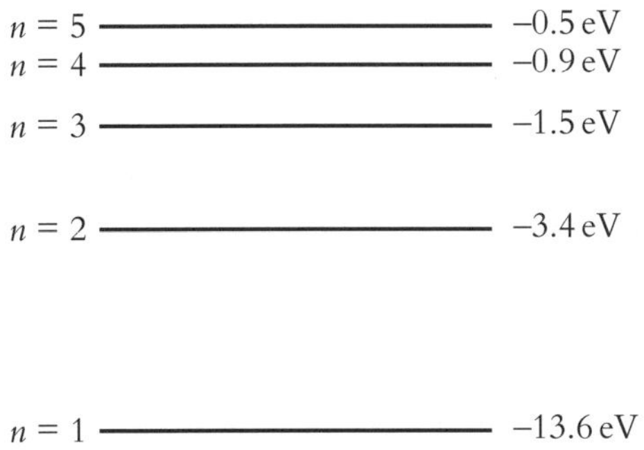

$n = 5$ ———————————— $-0.5\,\text{eV}$
$n = 4$ ———————————— $-0.9\,\text{eV}$
$n = 3$ ———————————— $-1.5\,\text{eV}$

$n = 2$ ———————————— $-3.4\,\text{eV}$

$n = 1$ ———————————— $-13.6\,\text{eV}$

Figure 7.1

a Why are all the electron energy levels given negative energy values?
b Which energy level is usually described as the *ground state*?
c In a container of hydrogen gas at room temperature, in which energy level would you expect to find most of the electrons in the hydrogen atoms?
d If an electron in the ground state were to gain 10.2 eV, what would you expect the electron to do?
e What name would you give to the process occurring in part **d**?

5 This question is also about the energy levels in a hydrogen atom.
a For a container of hydrogen gas at a moderate to high temperature, in which energy level(s) might you expect to find electrons in the hydrogen atoms?
b Explain what is meant by *excited* when applied to electrons in atoms.
c An excited electron in a hydrogen atom is unlikely to remain excited for more than about 10^{-18} s. What is such an excited electron likely to do?
d What is the name given to the process in part **c**?
e As a result of this process, what has happened to the energy of the atom?

6 Bohr showed that the electron energy levels in a hydrogen atom should be given by:
$$E_n = \frac{-13.6\ \text{eV}}{n^2}$$
Calculate the total energy that an electron has in level:
a $n = 2$
b $n = 3$
c $n = 4$

7 a Draw an electron energy level diagram for a hydrogen atom.
b Add all possible electron energy level transitions for the electron in energy level $n = 4$.
c Which of the transitions for the electron in energy level $n = 4$ will produce the:
  i highest frequency emission
  ii lowest frequency emission?

8 The visible emission spectrum from a hydrogen atom shows four lines.
a Which transitions do these four lines correspond to?
b The red line in the emission spectrum of hydrogen is called the hydrogen alpha line. Its wavelength is 656.3 nm. Show that photons of this wavelength have an energy of 1.9 eV.
c Which colour emission line is caused by the transition from $n = 4$ to $n = 2$, a change in energy of 2.55 eV?

9 Calculate the energy of the following photons; give your answer in joules and in eV.
   a A red photon of wavelength 630 nm.
   b A green photon of wavelength 532 nm.
   c A blue photon of wavelength 430 nm.

10 Calculate the number of photons emitted per second from a 60 W light bulb. The average wavelength of the emitted radiation is 500 nm.

11 Which energy level do electrons fall to in the Balmer series of emissions from a hydrogen atom?

12 In which part of the electromagnetic spectrum do all of the emissions in the Lyman series occur?

13 Describe how the emission spectrum from a filament light bulb is different to the emission spectrum of a gas, such as hydrogen.

14 The emission spectrum of sodium is dominated by two emission lines at 589.0 and 589.6 nm.
   a If these emission lines are the result of transitions from electron energy levels $n = 2$ to $n = 1$, calculate the average energy difference between the electron energy level $n = 2$ and the electron energy level $n = 1$
   b Suggest a reason why there are two emission lines, at two slightly different wavelengths, from this transition.

15 A typical He–Ne laser in a CD player emits light with a wavelength of 632.8 nm.
   a What colour is this light?
   b This light is the result of electron energy level transitions in the neon atom. Calculate the energy difference between these two levels in:
      i joules
      ii eV.

16 A blue laser pointer emits 1.0 mW of power at a wavelength of 450 nm. Calculate how many photons are emitted by the laser per second.

17 One kind of X-ray has a frequency of 3.20×10^{17} Hz.
   a Calculate the wavelength of this X-ray.
   b Calculate the energy required to produce a photon of this X-ray.
   c If this photon is produced by the rapid deceleration of a fast moving electron (as it collides with a heavy nucleus and subsequently stops), calculate the initial speed of the electron. (The mass of an electron is 9.1×10^{-31} kg.)

18 Figure 7.2 shows a hypothetical electron energy level diagram for an atom.

$n = 5$ ——————————————— $-0.1\,\text{eV}$
$n = 4$ ——————————————— $-0.3\,\text{eV}$
$n = 3$ ——————————————— $-1.4\,\text{eV}$

$n = 2$ ——————————————— $-3.1\,\text{eV}$

$n = 1$ ——————————————— $-5.6\,\text{eV}$

Figure 7.2

a Copy and complete Figure 7.2 to show all possible electron energy level transitions that will give rise to an emitted photon.

b Draw another diagram to show what the emission spectrum from this atom would look like if observed using a spectrometer.

c By calculating the wavelength of each of the transitions, which of the emission lines would you be able to see? (In other words, which of the transitions have wavelengths between 400 nm and 700 nm?)

19 Explain what is meant by the following terms:
a nucleon
b isotope
c nuclide.

20 Complete Table 7.1.

Isotope	Number of protons in the nucleus	Number of neutrons in the nucleus
$_{2}^{3}\text{He}$		
$_{6}^{12}\text{C}$		
$_{6}^{13}\text{C}$		
$_{26}^{56}\text{Fe}$		
$_{11}^{21}\text{Na}$		

Table 7.1

21 a Generally, why do some nuclei undergo beta-minus (β^-) decay?
b Generally, why do some nuclei undergo beta-plus (β^+) decay?

22 Complete the following nuclear decay equations.

a $_{6}^{13}\text{C} \rightarrow$ _____ $+ \beta^- + \bar{\nu}_e$

b $_{90}^{234}\text{Th} \rightarrow \,_{91}^{234}\text{Pa} +$ _____ $+$ _____

c $_{11}^{21}\text{Na} \rightarrow$ _____ $+ \beta^+ + \nu_e$

d $_{6}^{11}\text{C} \rightarrow \,_{5}^{11}\text{B} +$ _____ $+$ _____

23 The accepted way of showing the nucleon number (the sum of the protons and neutrons in the nucleus) is to use the letter A. The number of protons in the nucleus (the atomic number) is given the letter Z.

Use A for the nucleon number, Z for the atomic number, and X and Y for nuclides to write the decay equation for the:

a alpha decay of nuclide X

b beta-minus decay of nuclide X

c beta plus decay of nuclide X

d gamma decay of nuclide X.

24 A beta-minus particle is often referred to as a fast-moving electron that has come from an unstable nucleus. How could you refer to:

a an alpha particle

b a beta–plus particle?

25 In what way(s) are a beta-minus particle and a beta-plus particle:

a similar

b different?

26 When the emissions from unstable nuclei pass through other atoms, they are able to *ionise* some of the atoms.

a Explain the term *ionise*.

b Suggest three reasons why alpha particles are good ionisers.

c Suggest three reasons why beta-minus particles are worse ionisers than alpha particles.

27 For an alpha particle to cause an ionisation event, the alpha particle must lose energy. Suppose an alpha particle emitted by an unstable nucleus had 5.0 MeV of energy and it required about 30 eV to ionise an atom.

Estimate how many ion pairs the alpha particle could produce.

28 For an emission from a radioactive nucleus, how are the ionisation ability and the penetration through matter ability related?

29 Complete Table 7.2 to show what is required to stop an emission from an unstable nucleus.

Emission type	What stops the emission?
α particle	
β⁻ particle	
γ ray	

Table 7.2

30 A single piece of paper is about 8×10^{-5} m thick. The diameter of an atom is about 10^{-10} m. Atoms in a solid are about 10^{-10} m apart. An alpha particle has, typically, about 5 MeV kinetic energy. Each time an alpha particle causes an ionising event, it loses about 30 eV of kinetic energy.

a Use this information to calculate how many:

i atoms thick a typical piece of paper is

ii ionising events a typical alpha particle can cause.

b Show why alpha particles are stopped by a piece of paper.

31 a When an alpha particle has lost all of its energy, what is likely to happen to it?

  b How does your answer to part **a** confirm how Rutherford and Royds, in 1909, were able to demonstrate that alpha particles were the same thing as helium nuclei?

32 Explain how gamma decay provides evidence for nuclei to have energy levels in a similar way to atoms having energy levels for their electrons.

33 Figure 7.3 shows how the intensity of γ-radiation passing through a slab of lead varies with the distance through the lead.

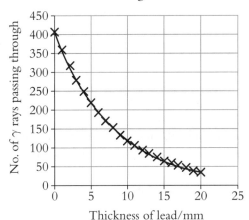

Figure 7.3

  a By taking suitable values from the graph, show that the variation of intensity with distance is exponential. Hint: Use the constant ratio rule.

  b Use the graph to find the thickness of lead required to:

   i halve the intensity

   ii reduce the intensity by a factor of 1/e.

34 Explain what is meant by:

  a half-life

  b activity.

35 You are carrying out a probability experiment. You have a number, N, of dice.

  a You roll one die. What is the probability that it will show a six?

  b You throw three dice. What is the probability that one or more of them will show a six?

  c How many sixes might you expect to see if you throw all N dice?

36 a In a sample of N radioactive nuclei, the probability of any one nucleus decaying within the next second is λ. How many radioactive nuclei might you expect to decay within one second?

  b Sketch a graph of the number of undecayed nuclei as a function of time, for the nuclei in part **a**.

  c Show how you would be able to find the half-life of the radioactive nuclei.

  d What does the gradient of your graph tell you?

37 A sample of radioactive nuclei has a mass of 160 g. If the half-life of the radioactive isotope is 6 minutes, what mass of radioactive nuclei will remain after:
a 6 minutes?
b 12 minutes?
c 24 minutes?

38 **a** Explain what is meant by *background radiation*.
b Give three likely sources of background radiation.
c Explain what is meant by *corrected count*.

39 Outline an experiment to find the half-life of a sample of radioactive material. You know its half-life is between 10 and 20 minutes. Make sure you include:
• the equipment required
• your method
• the measurements you need to make
• how you would manipulate the data to find the half-life.

40 In the medical treatment of abnormal thyroid glands, doctors administer a solution of radioactive sodium iodide. It has an activity of 5×10^5 Bq. The atoms of iodine are radioactive; they have a half-life of about 13 hours.
a Suggest why a radioactive isotope with a half-life of about 13 hours is appropriate for a medical procedure.
b Calculate how many atoms of iodine are required to produce an activity of 5×10^5 Bq.

41 **a** Outline how scientists are able to use radioactive carbon-14 to find the age of fossilised organic material.
b A sample of 1 g of a growing oak tree will produce a corrected count of 144 in a time of ten minutes.
i What uncertainty is there is this corrected count?
ii The half-life of $^{14}_{6}C$ is 5700 years. How old would a fossilised piece of oak tree be if the corrected count in 10 minutes from it was 18?

42 **a** Write the four fundamental forces of nature.
b Which of the forces has/have an infinite range?
c Which of the forces has the shortest range?

43 Which of the four fundamental forces is responsible for:
a β^- decay?
b a black hole not emitting any light?
c the movement of a speaker cone?
d two protons existing in a nucleus of helium?

44 **a** By considering the different forces that act on nucleons, explain how it is possible for most nuclei to hold their nucleons within the nucleus.
b With reference to the forces acting in a nucleus, suggest a reason why some nuclei are able to decay by alpha decay.

45 In the early 1900s, Ernest Rutherford observed alpha particles being deflected by the nuclei of gold atoms.

   a At low energies, the alpha particles were repelled by the gold nuclei. Use your knowledge of the four fundamental forces to explain why we now expect this to happen.

   b If the energy of the alpha particles had been substantially higher, the alpha particles may have been absorbed by the gold nuclei. Use your knowledge of the fundamental forces to explain why this can happen.

Exercise 7.2 – Nuclear reactions

1 Define the term *unified atomic mass unit*.

2 Complete Table 7.3 showing masses of some sub-atomic particles.

Name of particle	Mass / u	Mass / kg
proton	1.007 276	
neutron	1.008 665	
electron		9.11×10^{-31}

Table 7.3

3 **a** Using $E = mc^2$, show that the energy equivalence of one unified atomic mass unit is about 931 MeV.

   b Many data books give the energy equivalence of u as ~931.5 MeV. Suggest why there is a discrepancy between your answer in part **a** and the data books.

4 **a** The mass of an alpha particle is given as 4.002 604 u. Calculate the mass of an alpha particle in kg.

   b Calculate the total mass of the particles that make up an alpha particle. Give your answer in u.

   c How do your answers to parts **a** and **b** compare?

   d Calculate the difference between the mass of the particles that make up the alpha particle and the actual mass of the alpha particle.

   e Calculate the energy equivalence, in MeV, of the mass defect of the alpha particle.

5 Calculate the mass defect of a nucleus of $^{15}_{6}C$ (nuclear mass: 15.01060 u). Give your answer in MeV c^{-2}.

6 To heat up 1 kg of water by 1 °C you have to give the water 4200 J of energy. What percentage increase in mass is there in 1 kg of water that has been heated by 20 °C?

7 Define the term *binding energy*.

8 $^{12}_{6}C$ and $^{13}_{6}C$ are two nuclides of carbon. Which has the largest binding energy? Explain your answer.

9 **a** Calculate the energy equivalence of the mass of an electron.
  b Calculate the kinetic energy of an electron travelling at a speed of 5×10^6 m s^{-1}
  c What do you notice about your answers to parts **a** and **b**?

10 The mass of a nucleus of $^{24}_{11}$Na is 23.990 96 u. Calculate the binding energy per nucleon of this nucleus.

11 The mass of a nucleus of $^{56}_{26}$Fe is 55.934 939 u. Calculate the binding energy per nucleon for $^{56}_{26}$Fe.

12 **a** Sketch a graph to show how the binding energy per nucleon varies with nucleon number.
  b How can you use your graph to indicate which nuclei are the most stable?
  c Indicate the region where nuclear **fusion** can occur to produce energy.
  d Indicate the region where nuclear **fission** can occur to produce energy.

13 **a** Outline what is meant by *nuclear fusion*.
  b Outline what is meant by *nuclear fission*.

14 **a** Calculate the number of atoms of $^{235}_{92}$U in 1 kg of uranium-235.
  b If every fission of $^{235}_{92}$U produces 173 Mev, calculate the specific energy available from uranium-235. Give your answer in joules.

15 In a nuclear power station, outline the role of the:
  a moderator
  b control rods.

Exercise 7.3 – The structure of matter

1 **a** J. J. Thomson first suggested the *plum pudding* model of the atom in the late 1870s. Outline the model's main features.
  b Outline Geiger and Marsden's experiment that led to the demise of the plum pudding model.

2 In the now-famous alpha particle scattering experiment of 1909, two major observations were made (see Table 7.4). For each observation, state the conclusions made (which led to the Rutherford model of the atom).

Experimental observation	Conclusion
The vast majority of alpha particles passed through the gold foil undeflected.	
Some alpha particles were deflected through such large angles that they bounced backwards.	

Table 7.4

3   The Standard Model distinguishes between particles that are fundamental and those that are not.
    a   Explain what is meant by a fundamental particle.
    b   The Standard Model arranges all fundamental particles into three groups. Name the three groups.

4   The standard model explains many features of the physical universe, but it has one major flaw. What is this flaw?

5   Copy and complete Table 7.5 showing the family of quarks and some of their properties. Charge is given in units relative to that of a proton.

Generation	Name of quark	Symbol	Charge	Baryon number
First				
Second				
Third				

Table 7.5

6   Copy and complete Table 7.6 showing the family of leptons and some of their properties. Charge is given in units relative to that of a proton.

Generation	Name of lepton	Symbol	Charge	Lepton number
First				
Second				
Third				

Table 7.6

7   a   Explain what is meant by *hadron*.
    b   What is the difference between a baryon and a meson?
    c   What is the quark structure of:
        i   a proton?
        ii   a neutron?
        iii an anti-proton?
        iv   a π^+ meson?
    d   Explain what is meant by *quark confinement* and its consequence for experimental physics.

8   Three of the conservation laws are obeyed in any particle interaction are:
      • conservation of charge
      • conservation of baryon number
      • conservation of electron lepton number.
      By applying these three conservation laws, determine whether the following particle interactions are possible.

      a $^1_1\text{p} + ^{\,0}_{-1}\text{e} \rightarrow ^1_0\text{n}$

      b $^1_1\text{p} + ^1_1\text{p} \rightarrow ^1_1\text{p} + ^1_1\text{p} + ^1_0\text{n}$

      c $^1_1\text{p} + ^1_1\text{p} \rightarrow ^1_1\text{p} + ^1_1\text{p} + ^{\,0}_{-1}\text{e} + ^0_0\overline{\nu}$

9   For each of the following particle interactions, apply the conservation laws to see if the interaction is possible.

      a $^1_1\text{p} + ^1_1\text{p} \rightarrow ^1_1\text{p} + ^1_1\text{p} + \pi^0$

      b $\pi^- + ^1_1\text{p} \rightarrow ^1_0\text{n} + \pi^0$

      c $^1_1\text{p} + ^1_0\text{n} \rightarrow \pi^+ + \pi^0$

10   **a** How much *strangeness* does a strange quark have?
      b Is the conservation of strangeness a universal rule, in the same way as the other three conservation laws? Explain your answer.
      c A neutral kaon has quark composition: $\text{d}\overline{\text{s}}$. What is its strangeness?

11   A neutral kaon particle is seen to decay into a positive pion and a negative pion. The equation for this, in terms of quarks, is: $\text{d}\overline{\text{s}} \rightarrow \text{u}\overline{\text{d}} + \overline{\text{u}}\text{d}$
      By applying the conservation laws appropriate to a weak interaction, show that this decay process is viable.

12   Complete Table 7.7 showing the four fundamental forces of nature and some of their features.

Force	Range	Relative strength	Acts on	Exchange particle
Strong nuclear				
Electromagnetic				
Weak nuclear				
Gravitational				

Table 7.7

13   The Higgs boson has been established within the Standard Model as an attempt to explain the concept of mass. Particles gain mass as a consequence of interacting with the Higgs field that occupies all of space.
      a Which two particles in the Standard Model particularly required the existence of the Higgs boson to explain their mass?
      b Suggest a way in which the Higgs boson differs from the other exchange particles in the Standard Model.

14 Figure 7.4 shows a Feynman diagram for an interaction.

Figure 7.4

    a Describe what is happening in this interaction.
    b Which of the four fundamental forces is responsible for this?

15 Sketch a Feynman diagram to show the β^- decay of a neutron. Label each of the particles involved.

16 Figure 7.5 shows a Feynman diagram for an example of the weak interaction.

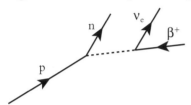

Figure 7.5

    a Identify which weak interaction is occurring.
    b Which exchange particle is responsible?

17 **a** Sketch a Feynman diagram for electron capture by a proton.
    b Which exchange boson is responsible for this interaction?

18 Figure 7.6 shows the interaction of a neutron with an electron neutrino.

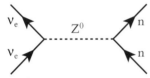

Figure 7.6

    a The exchange particle involved in this interaction is the Z^0 particle. Suggest why this kind of interaction is sometimes referred to as a *neutral current* interaction.
    b It is possible for the interaction of a neutron with an electron neutrino to be mediated by a W^+ boson. Sketch the Feynman diagram for such an interaction.
    c Suggest why the interaction in part **b** is sometimes referred to as a *charged current* interaction.

1 **Which of the following combinations of protons and neutrons is the correct composition of the nucleus, $^{63}_{29}\text{Cu}$?**
   A protons = 29; neutrons = 63
   B protons = 34; neutrons = 29
   C protons = 29; neutrons = 34
   D protons = 63; neutrons = 29

2 **Monochromatic light is incident on a metal plate. Electrons are emitted from the metal plate's surface. If the intensity of the incident light is increased, which of the following combinations describes the new rate at which electrons are emitted and the maximum kinetic energy of the electrons?**
   A new rate = same as before; maximum KE = same as before
   B new rate = same as before; maximum KE = increased
   C new rate = increased; maximum KE = same as before
   D new rate = increased; maximum KE = increased

3 **The following particle interaction is not observed:**
   p + p ⟶ p + p + n
   What is the main reason for this?
   A The initial two protons cannot contain enough energy to form an extra neutron.
   B The conservation of lepton number is disobeyed.
   C The conservation of charge is disobeyed.
   D The conservation of baryon number is disobeyed.

4 **Figure 7.7 shows four possible emission spectra from radioactive nuclei.**

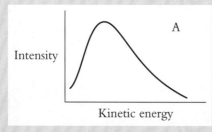
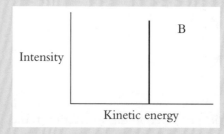
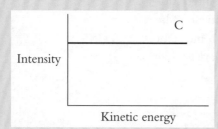
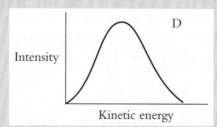

Figure 7.7

   a Which of the spectra best describes α-decay?
   b Which of the spectra best describes β⁻ decay?

5 **A continuous spectrum of light is incident on a cloud of hydrogen gas. After passing through the gas, it is observed using a spectrometer.**

   a Explain why the light observed contains dark lines in the continuous spectrum. **[2]**

   b One of the dark lines in the spectrum has a wavelength of 434 nm. Calculate the energy of a photon of light with this wavelength. Give your answer in eV. **[3]**

   c State which electron energy level transition is responsible for this dark line. **[1]**

   d Outline how astronomers can use their observations of the dark lines in the spectra from stars to find information about the composition of the stars. **[2]**

6 **The mass of a nucleus of $^{3}_{2}$He is 3.01603 u.**

   a Outline the composition of this nucleus. **[1]**

   b The mass of a proton is given as 1.007276 u and the mass of a neutron is 1.008665 u. Calculate the binding energy per nucleon, in MeV, of this nucleus. **[3]**

   c This kind of nucleus is produced in stars, such as our Sun, by the process of nuclear fusion. Complete the nuclear equation for this fusion process:

   $^{2}_{1}D + ^{2}_{1}D \rightarrow ^{3}_{2}He +$ _____ **[2]**

   d Suggest why the production of $^{3}_{2}$He generates energy. **[1]**

7 **$^{233}_{92}$U is an unstable nuclide of uranium that decays by α-emission.**

   a Write a nuclear decay equation for this decay. **[2]**

   b The mass difference between the $^{233}_{92}$U nucleus and the daughter nucleus it decays into is 4.00787 u. The mass of an alpha particle is 4.00260 u. Calculate how much energy, in MeV, is available for the α-particle to transform into KE. **[2]**

   c In fact, the α particle carries away only 4.82 MeV. Suggest what has happened to the remainder of the energy. **[1]**

8 **The following radioactive decay process is observed to occur:**

   $^{220}_{86}Rn \rightarrow ^{216}_{84}Po + ^{4}_{2}\alpha$

   a The mass of a $^{220}_{86}$Rn nucleus is 220.01140 u. The mass of a $^{216}_{84}$Po nucleus is 216.00192 u. The mass of an alpha particle is 4.002604 u. Calculate the mass available to be converted into KE during the α-decay process. **[1]**

   b Calculate the ratio of the KE of the α-particle to the KE of the Po nucleus after the decay. **[2]**

   c Calculate the KE of the α-particle. **[2]**

9 **The mass of a nucleus of $^{14}_{6}$C is 14.003241 u. The mass of a nucleus of $^{14}_{7}$N is 13.999231 u. $^{14}_{6}$C decays by β^{-} decay.**

   a State the nuclear decay equation for the β^{-} decay of $^{14}_{6}$C. **[2]**

   b Calculate the maximum possible KE of the β^{-} particle. **[2]**

   c With reference to your decay equation, explain why β^{-} particles from the decay of $^{14}_{6}$C are never observed with this amount of KE. **[1]**

10 This equation shows a nuclear process:

$$^{235}_{92}U + ^{1}_{0}n \rightarrow ^{236}_{92}U \rightarrow ^{144}_{56}Ba + ^{89}_{36}Kr + 3\,^{1}_{0}n$$

The masses of the various particles are:

$^{236}_{92}U = 236.0526$ u; $^{144}_{56}Ba = 143.92292$ u; $^{89}_{36}Kr = 88.91781$ u; $^{1}_{0}n = 1.008665$ u

a State which kind of nuclear process is represented by the equation. [1]

b Calculate the energy released during this process. Give your answer in MeV. [3]

c State the form in which the energy released. [1]

11 This equation shows a nuclear process:

$$^{2}_{1}D + ^{3}_{1}T \rightarrow ^{4}_{2}H + ^{1}_{0}n$$

The masses of the particles involved are:

$^{2}_{1}D = 2.014102$ u; $^{3}_{1}T = 3.016050$ u; $^{4}_{2}He = 4.002604$ u; $^{1}_{0}n = 1.008665$ u

a State which kind of nuclear process is represented by the equation. [1]

b Calculate the energy released during this process. [3]

c State the form in which the energy released. [1]

Energy production 8

Chapter outline

In this chapter, you will:
- Understand the concept of primary and secondary energy sources, the terms specific energy and energy density and be able to solve problems involving them.
- Sketch and interpret Sankey diagrams.
- Describe the basic features of and solve problems involving the energy transformations in fossil-fuelled power stations, nuclear fission power stations, wind generators, pumped storage hydroelectric power stations and solar power cells.
- Understand and be able to discuss the risks and safety issues involved in nuclear power stations.
- Distinguish between photovoltaic cells and solar heating cells.
- Understand the processes of conduction, convection and radiation and be able to sketch and interpret graphs showing the intensity against wavelength for radiating bodies at different temperatures.
- Solve problems associated with Wien's displacement law and the Stefan–Boltzmann law.
- Describe the effect of the Earth's atmosphere on its mean surface temperature and the role of the greenhouse effect.
- Understand the terms emissivity, albedo and the solar constant, and be able to recall the contribution to the greenhouse effect of methane, water vapour, carbon dioxide and nitrous oxide.
- Solve problems associated with albedo, emissivity, the solar constant and the average temperature of the Earth's surface.

KEY TERMS

Specific energy: The energy available from 1 kg of a substance.

Energy density: The amount of energy available from 1 m^3 of a substance.

Wien's displacement law: The wavelength of emitted radiation that occurs most is inversely proportional to the absolute temperature of the emitter:
$$\lambda_{max} = \frac{2.9 \times 10^{-3}}{T}$$

Stefan–Boltzmann law: The total power emitted by a black body is proportional to the body's surface area and to its absolute temperature to the fourth power: $P = \sigma A T^4$, where σ is the Stefan–Boltzmann constant equal to $5.7 \times 10^{-8} \text{ W m}^{-2} \text{ K}^{-4}$

Solar constant: The amount of energy, across all wavelengths, per second and per unit area arriving at the top of the Earth's atmosphere from the Sun – about 1400 W m^{-2}.

Albedo: The fraction of energy incident on a surface that is reflected.

Exercise 8.1 – Energy sources

1   Explain what is meant by the following terms, and give an example of each one.
   a Primary energy source.
   b Secondary energy source.

2   Explain what is meant by the following terms, and give the units for each one.
   a Specific energy.
   b Energy density.

3   Look at this list of energy sources:
   natural gas; coal; uranium-235; petrol
   Rank the energy sources, 1–4, where 1 has the highest specific energy and 4 has the lowest specific energy.

4   **a** How are *specific energy* and *energy density* related?
   b The specific energy of $^{235}_{92}$U is about 7.0×10^{13} J kg^{-1}. The density of $^{235}_{92}$U is 1.9×10^4 kg m^{-3}, calculate the energy density of $^{235}_{92}$U.

5   Explain what is meant by the terms:
   a renewable energy source
   b non-renewable energy source.

6   Table 8.1 lists some energy sources and ways of producing energy. Copy and complete the table. There may be more than one advantage/disadvantage for each source of energy.

Energy source	Advantages	Disadvantages
Fossil fuels		
Nuclear fuels		
Solar energy		
Wind energy		
Hydroelectric energy		

Table 8.1

7   Explain what is meant by *degraded energy*.

8   Figure 8.1 shows a typical Sankey diagram for a coal-fired power station.

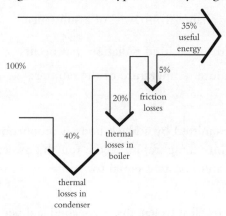

Figure 8.1

Use the diagram to determine the efficiency of the power station.

9 A 1 kW kettle is switched on for 2 minutes to boil some water. It loses 20 kJ of thermal energy to the surroundings and 10 kJ of energy in heating up the internal parts of the kettle.

    a Draw a Sankey diagram for the kettle while boiling the water.

    b Calculate the efficiency of the kettle.

    c The water started at 20 °C. Calculate the mass of water boiled.
       (SHC of water = 4200 J kg^{-1} °C^{-1}.)

10 For a typical family car, 12% of energy from fuel is wasted in exhaust fumes, 30% is wasted as mechanical energy in moving parts and 25% is wasted as thermal energy. Determine the efficiency of the car.

11 In a hydroelectric power station, 25% of the available energy from the water is lost due to friction in the water pipes. 17% is lost due to friction in the mechanical moving parts of the turbines and generators. 4% is lost as thermal energy in the electrical cables. Determine the efficiency of the hydroelectric power station.

12 Outline the energy transformations that take place in a fossil-fuelled power station. Assume that the energy in the fossil fuels is chemical energy, and the secondary energy produced by the power station is electrical energy.

13 Name the energy transformation that takes place in the following parts of a coal-fired power station.

    a The furnace.

    b The turbine.

    c The generator.

14 In a typical nuclear power station, the following nuclear process occurs:
$$^{235}_{92}U + X \rightarrow A + B + nX$$

    a What type of nuclear process is this?

    b Identify the particles labelled X.

    c What form of energy does this process produce?

15 Uranium mined for power stations contains about 0.6% of the isotope $^{235}_{92}U$; the rest is mostly $^{238}_{92}U$.

    a Suggest why most of the energy production comes from the isotope $^{235}_{92}U$.

    b The specific energy for isotope $^{235}_{92}U$ is about 8.0×10^{13} J kg^{-1}. How much energy is available from 1 kg of natural uranium?

    c How does your answer to part **b** compare with the specific energy of fossil fuels such as coal or oil?

    d Modern nuclear power stations use *enriched nuclear fuel*. Explain what the term *enriched nuclear fuel* means and explain how it aids overall efficiency of the power station.

16 The energy produced in a single fission of a $^{235}_{92}U$ nucleus is about 200 MeV. Show that the specific energy of $^{235}_{92}U$ is about 8×10^{13} J kg^{-1}.

17 Outline the energy transformations that take place in a nuclear power station. Begin with the energy form at the start of the process, and end with secondary energy in the form of electrical energy.

18 In a nuclear power station, outline the main functions of, and the material used for, the:
  a moderator
  b control rods
  c heat exchanger(s).

19 What would you expect to happen to the output of a nuclear power station if you removed the:
  a moderator?
  b control rods?

20 Outline the problems disposing of nuclear waste from a nuclear power station.

21 Outline the energy transformations in the production of electrical energy from wind.

22 Consider the air flow past a wind-turbine. Derive the equation: $P_{max} = \frac{1}{2} \rho \pi r^2 v^3$, to show the maximum power available from the turbine, where ρ is the density of the air in the wind, r is the radius of the wind turbine blades, and v is the speed of the air in the wind.

23 A wind turbine has 15 m rotor blades and an overall efficiency of 30%. The ideal wind speed for its generator is between 5 m s^{-1} and 15 m s^{-1}.
  a Calculate the maximum power available from the generator.
    (Density of air = 1.3 kg m^{-3}.)
  b By what factor is the power output of the wind turbine different when the wind is blowing at 15 m s^{-1} compared to when it blows at 5 m s^{-1}?
  c Suggest why the output from a wind-powered generator is so variable.

24 Outline the energy transformations that take place during the operation of a hydroelectric power station. Begin with the energy form at the start of the process, and end with electrical energy.

25 This question is about deriving and using an expression for the available power output of a hydroelectric power station.
  a A volume of water, V, sits in a reservoir at height, h, above a hydroelectric power station. Show that the gravitational potential energy (GPE) of the water can be expressed as: GPE = $V\rho gh$
  b The volume of water flowing through the power station from the reservoir in a time, t, is Q (the *volume flow rate*). The overall efficiency of the power station is ε. Derive an expression for the power output of the power station.
  c The Three Gorges Dam in the Hubei province of China has an efficiency of 52% and a maximum output power of 22 GW. If the height of the reservoir is 110 m above the turbines and generators, calculate the expected volume flow rate, Q, of the power station during its operation.

26 A pumped storage system power station retains some water that has flowed through its turbines in a secondary reservoir. Electrically operated pumps then pump some of the water back to the higher reservoir to be used again. Suggest why this is more a useful way of producing energy than hydroelectric systems that allow 'used' water to flow away.

27 Outline the energy transformations occurring in a:
  a solar heating panel
  b photovoltaic cell.

28 A house in Thailand has 30 m² of 30% efficient solar panels. The infrared radiation incident on the panels is 650 W m⁻². What volume of water can the solar panels heat, per second, from 25 °C to 35 °C? Is this enough for a hot shower?

29 A photovoltaic cell, with an efficiency of about 20%, operates as an emf source of about 1 V.
  a Suggest why several photovoltaic cells are usually connected in series in a solar cell.
  b Suggest why several series of photovoltaic cells are connected in parallel in a solar cell.

Exercise 8.2 – Thermal energy transfer

1 Describe what is meant by *heat*.

2 This question is about conduction.
  a Explain why conduction is more effective in solid materials than in liquids or gases.
  b Explain why it takes a long time for thermal energy to be transferred by the process of conduction.
  c Explain why metals are good thermal conductors.

3 **a** Outline how the process of thermal conduction is similar to the process of electrical conduction.
  b If the electrical resistance of a resistor is given by $R = \rho \dfrac{l}{A}$, what would be the corresponding equation for a thermal resistor?

4 Explain how convection transfers thermal energy at a faster rate than conduction.

5 Blowing gently on a hot drink to cool it down is an example of *forced convection*. Explain how forced convection creates an accelerated cooling.

6 Explain what is meant by a *convection current* and explain the origin of an onshore breeze during a sunny day at the beach.

7 **a** How is the transfer of thermal energy by radiation different to the transfer of thermal energy by conduction and convection?
  b Explain how the Earth can receive energy from the Sun, 1.5×10^{11} m away.

8 Explain the term *black body*.

9 **a** What factors does a black body's ability to radiate energy depend upon?
  b State the Stefan–Boltzmann law for a black body.
  c How is the Stefan–Boltzmann law modified if a body is not a black body?

10 Calculate the power emitted by a black body of surface area 4.0×10^{-2} m² at 400 °C.

11 The Sun's luminosity (total power emitted by a star, assumed to be a black body) is given as 3.8×10^{26} W. If the surface temperature of the Sun is 5778 K, calculate the radius of the Sun.

12 A naked, adult human has an average skin temperature of about 32 °C. The surface area of his body is 2.0 m². The emissivity of human skin is 0.85. Calculate the rate at which he is losing energy by radiation.

13 Figure 8.2 shows how the intensity of radiated energy varies with wavelength for a black body.

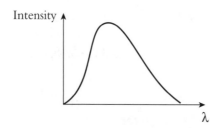

Figure 8.2

  a Explain how the graph can be used to find the temperature of the black body.
  b Add another curve to show how the intensity of radiated energy varies with wavelength for a black body at a lower temperature.
  c Explain how your curve shows that the total energy being radiated by the cooler black body is less than that of the hotter black body.

14 **a** State Wien's displacement law.
  b Calculate the peak wavelength of emitted radiation for a black body at a temperature of:
    i 6000 K
    ii 300 K.
  c How do your answers to part **b** explain why you can see the Sun shining, but you cannot see a person glowing in the dark?

15 **a** A black body has an emission spectrum with a peak wavelength occurring at $\lambda = 5.0 \times 10^{-7}$ m. Use Wien's displacement law to calculate the temperature of the black body.
  b The cosmic microwave background radiation observed from deep space has an emission spectrum with a peak wavelength of 1.063 mm. Use Wien's displacement law to calculate the temperature of deep space.

16 The Sun emits energy at a rate of 3.8×10^{26} W. Calculate the energy arriving on 1 m² of area at a distance of 1.5×10^{11} m from the Sun. (This distance, called an astronomical unit, AU, is the average distance of the Earth from the Sun.)

17 **a** Define the term *solar constant*.
  b In fact, the solar constant is not a constant. Suggest two reasons why the value of the solar constant may vary.

18 **a** Explain the term *albedo*.
  b What would the albedo of a black body be?
  c Suggest two reasons why the albedo has a different value in different places on the Earth's surface.

19 The pattern of atmospheric thermal energy transfer around the world is driven by the fact that equatorial regions are hot and polar regions are cold.

   a Suggest two reasons why the equatorial regions of the Earth are hotter than the polar regions.

   b Which of the three processes of thermal energy transfer is primarily responsible for the Earth's thermal energy circulation via the atmosphere?

20 The solar constant is $1370\ \mathrm{W\ m^{-2}}$. The radius of the Earth is 6.4×10^6 m. The Earth's average albedo is 0.3.

   a Show that the energy absorbed, per second, by 1 $\mathrm{m^2}$ of the Earth's surface is about 250 W.

   b For the Earth to remain in thermal equilibrium, it must radiate $250\ \mathrm{W\ m^{-2}}$. If the Earth is assumed to radiate as a black body, calculate the surface temperature needed to maintain its thermal equilibrium.

   c In fact, the average surface temperature of the Earth is about 288 K. This suggests that not all of the energy radiated from the Earth's surface is lost. Suggest a mechanism that could account for this.

   d Which atmospheric constituents are primarily responsible for reducing the radiative energy loss from the Earth's surface?

   e How are these atmospheric gases usually described?

21 With reference to the Earth's radiation budget, explain what is meant by the:

   a greenhouse effect

   b enhanced greenhouse effect.

22 Greenhouse gases, such as CO_2, CH_4, N_2O and H_2O, are molecules made from atoms held together by covalent bonds. The covalent bonds vibrate at specific frequencies. These frequencies depend in part on the relative atomic masses of the bonded atoms.

   a Suggest a reason why greenhouse gases will absorb radiation at several, discrete, wavelengths.

   b Some of these wavelengths are 2.7 μm, 4.3 μm and 15 μm. If the Earth's surface temperature is 288 K, show that these wavelengths will be present in the radiation emitted by the Earth's surface and so can contribute to the greenhouse effect.

23 **a** Explain the term *global warming*. How is the enhanced greenhouse effect responsible for global warming over the last 250 years or so?

   b Carbon dioxide is one of the gases responsible for global warming.

      i Suggest how the amount of carbon dioxide in the Earth's atmosphere has increased over the last 250 years.

      ii Suggest what natural mechanisms there are for reducing the amount of carbon dioxide in the atmosphere.

      iii Outline how international collaboration between governments attempts to reduce the amount of carbon dioxide in the atmosphere.

? Exam-style questions

1 **In which of the following places on the Earth's surface is the albedo likely to be the largest?**
   A Tropical rain forest
   B Middle of an ocean
   C Middle of a desert
   D Polar cap

2 **A wind turbine produces energy at a rate of P. If the efficiency of the wind turbine remains constant and the wind speed doubles, it will produce energy at a rate of:**
   A P
   B $2P$
   C $4P$
   D $8P$

3 **Deforestation in South America is a major concern for environmental scientists. Select a reason for their concern.**
   A An increased albedo, because the Earth's surface is brighter than that of a forest.
   B An increase in soil erosion, because the roots of trees help to hold the soil together.
   C An increase in carbon-based gases in the atmosphere, because the trees remove carbon from the atmosphere.
   D An increase in the water vapour content of the atmosphere, because the trees absorb water from the atmosphere.

4 **Fossil fuels have energy densities that are similar in magnitude. Which of the following is the best estimate of the ratio of the energy density of a fossil fuel to the energy density of a nuclear fuel, such as $^{235}_{92}\text{U}$?**
   A 10^8
   B 10^4
   C 10^{-4}
   D 10^{-8}

5 **Which of the following is the best estimate of the percentage of the world's energy produced from fossil fuels?**
   A 20%
   B 40%
   C 60%
   D 80%

6 **Black body X has a surface area of A and an absolute temperature of T. Black body Y has a surface area of 2A and a temperature of $\frac{T}{2}$. Which of the following is the best estimate for the ratio of the emitted power of X to Y, $\frac{P_X}{P_Y}$?**
   A 16
   B 8
   C 4
   D 1

7 **A coal-fired power station in India produces energy at a rate of 1.5 GW.**

   a The overall efficiency of the power station is 25%. The specific energy of coal is 4.0×10^7 J kg^{-1}. Calculate the rate at which the power station uses coal. **[3]**

   b A nuclear power station with the same output power and efficiency uses nuclear fuel with a specific energy of 8.0×10^{13} J kg^{-1}. What rate would the power station use its nuclear fuel? **[1]**

8 a What thermodynamic factor has the biggest influence on the efficiency of a fossil-fuelled power station? **[1]**

   b Suggest why the world continues to build fossil fuel power stations despite their poor efficiency. **[3]**

   c Suggest two advantages of natural gas-fuelled power station over a coal-fired power station. **[2]**

9 **For a typical wind-powered generator, 40% of the input energy is lost because of the non-zero velocity of the air passing through the blades, 25% is lost in friction of the rotating parts of the turbine and another 5% is lost in the transfer of the electrical energy produced.**

   a Sketch a Sankey diagram for a typical wind-powered generator. **[3]**

   b Use your diagram to calculate the efficiency of the wind-powered generator. **[2]**

10 **The fission of a $^{235}_{92}$U nucleus produces fast neutrons with about 200 MeV of kinetic energy.**

   a Calculate the effective 'temperature' of these fast neutrons. **[2]**

   b The neutrons' temperature needs to be about 20 °C to sustain a controlled chain reaction. Calculate the energy, in eV, of a 'thermal' electron at 20 °C. **[2]**

   c Each collision between a fast neutron and the moderator causes the neutron to lose 30% of its kinetic energy. Estimate the number of collisions required for a fast neutron to become a thermal neutron, so a chain reaction is produced. **[2]**

11 **This question is about comparing the annual volume of fuel used in a coal-fired power station and a nuclear power station.**

   Suppose there are two power stations, each capable of producing 1 GW of output power and each operating at an efficiency of 30%.

   a The energy density of coal is 7.0×10^{10} J m^{-3}. Calculate the volume of coal required to keep the power station running for one year. **[2]**

   b The energy density of $^{235}_{92}$U is 1.4×10^{18} J m^{-3}. Calculate the volume of $^{235}_{92}$U required to keep the power station running for one year. **[2]**

   c Suggest the environmental and aesthetic advantages of using $^{235}_{92}$U as a nuclear fuel. **[2]**

12 **Nitrogen oxide (N$_2$O), a greenhouse gas, absorbs electromagnetic radiation of frequency 3.5×10^{13} Hz.**

   a Calculate the wavelength of radiation absorbed by N$_2$O molecules. **[2]**

   b The Sun has a surface temperature of 5700 K. Show that solar radiation incident on the atmosphere is not significantly reduced by absorption due to N$_2$O. **[2]**

   c The Earth's surface temperature is about 288 K. Show that N$_2$O molecules play a significant part in the greenhouse effect for the Earth's atmosphere. **[2]**

13 **An important way of 'knowing' is through empirical perception: that is, making an observation of something. Suppose you touch a wooden desk and then its metal legs.**

   a What does your brain tell you about the sensation of touching the two materials? **[1]**

   b Does the sensation of feeling provide accurate information about the temperature of something? **[1]**

   c What does the sensation of feeling tell you about conduction? How do you explain that the desktop and the desk legs are the same temperature, even though what you feel is very different? **[3]**

Wave phenomena 9

Chapter outline

In this chapter, you will:

- Define simple harmonic motion with an equation and solve problems involving acceleration, velocity and displacement during simple harmonic motion (graphically and algebraically).
- Describe the way that kinetic energy and potential energy are transferred during simple harmonic motion, and solve problems associated with energy and its transfers during simple harmonic motion.
- Describe single-slit diffraction and the effect of a varying slit width.
- Determine the position of the first minimum on the single-slit diffraction pattern.
- Describe qualitatively the single-slit diffraction patterns produced by monochromatic light wavelengths and by a white light source, and show how the single-slit diffraction pattern is modified by the introduction of another slit.
- Understand the concept of resolution, the Rayleigh criterion and the role that different aperture sizes plays and solve problems involving the Rayleigh criterion.
- Investigate experimentally the interference pattern produced by a Young's double-slit and sketch and interpret double-slit interference patterns.
- Identify the effect of multiple slits on the intensity off the interference pattern, show how this leads to the concept of a diffraction grating and solve problems involving interference from thin films and solve problems associated with the resolvance of a diffraction grating.
- Solve problems involving the diffraction grating equation.
- Understand the conditions necessary for constructive and destructive interference from thin films, including when a phase change occurs at a boundary between two different refractive index media.
- Understand the Doppler effect for sound and light waves, be able to sketch and interpret diagrams of the Doppler effect involving relative motion between an observer and the source.
- Solve problems involving the change in wavelength or frequency observed during the Doppler effect and its relation to the relative velocity between the observer and the source.

KEY TERMS

Simple harmonic motion equation: Since simple harmonic motion is defined as a periodic motion in which the acceleration is proportional to the displacement from, and directed towards, the equilibrium position, $a = -\omega^2 x$

Velocity and displacement equation: $v = \pm\omega\sqrt{x_0^2 - x^2}$

Period of a simple pendulum and a mass on a spring: $T = 2\pi\sqrt{\dfrac{l}{g}}$ and $T = 2\pi\sqrt{\dfrac{m}{k}}$

Energy in a simple harmonic motion oscillator: $E_{total} = \dfrac{1}{2}m x_0^2 \omega^2$

Single-slit diffraction equation: A minimum occurs when $\lambda = b \sin \theta$, where b is the slit width.

Young's double-slit equation: $s = \dfrac{\lambda D}{d}$

Diffraction grating equation: Maxima occur when $n\lambda = s \sin \theta$, where s is the slit spacing.

Thin film interference: For light reflecting from a thin film of thickness, t, and refractive index, n: $m\lambda = 2tn$ gives the condition for destructive interference. Constructive interference is given by $(m + \frac{1}{2})\lambda = 2tn$.

Rayleigh's criterion: When the first minimum of one diffraction pattern overlaps exactly with the central maximum of another diffraction pattern then the two images are just resolved; in this case, $\theta = 1.22\,\dfrac{\lambda}{b}$, where θ is the angle subtended by the two objects being observed.

Resolvance of a diffraction grating: $R = \dfrac{\lambda}{\Delta \lambda} = Nm$, where m is the order of the maximum in the interference pattern from the diffraction grating and N is the total number of slits illuminated by the incident beam.

Doppler effect equations: For a moving source, $f' = f\,\dfrac{v}{v \pm u_s}$; for a moving observer, $f' = f\,\dfrac{v \pm u_o}{v}$; for EM waves, $\dfrac{\Delta f}{f} = \dfrac{\Delta \lambda}{\lambda} \approx \dfrac{v}{c}$.

Exercise 9.1 – Simple harmonic motion

1   What two conditions are necessary for an object to oscillate in simple harmonic motion?

2   The term *angular frequency* is often used when talking about oscillations. How is the angular frequency, ω, related to the frequency of the oscillations? What units does angular frequency have?

3   Calculate the angular frequency of the following oscillations:
   a   Frequency = 25 Hz
   b   A body oscillates 400 times in one minute.
   c   Frequency = 6×10^{14} Hz

4   The equation that defines simple harmonic motion is: $a = -\omega^2 x$.
   a   Define the terms, a, ω and x in the above equation.
   b   Explain the significance of the minus sign in the equation.

5   A body undergoes simple harmonic motion as described by the equation: $x = 0.4\cos(20t)$.
   a   What is the amplitude, x_0, of this oscillation?
   b   What is the angular frequency, ω, of this oscillation?
   c   What is the frequency, f, of this oscillation?

d What is the time period, T, of this oscillation?

e When $t = 2.0$ s, calculate the:

   i   displacement, x

   ii velocity, v

   iii acceleration, a.

6 In the Science Museum in London there is a pendulum of length 22.45 m which oscillates in simple harmonic motion. Calculate the time period of its oscillations.

7 An oscillator performing simple harmonic motion has an amplitude, A, of 15 cm and a period, T, of 2.0 s. At $t = 0$, its displacement from the equilibrium position is A.

a Calculate the angular frequency of the simple harmonic motion oscillations.

b Write an equation that describes the displacement of the oscillator as a function of time.

c Calculate the displacement from the equilibrium position at:

   i $t = 0.25$ s

   ii $t = 0.50$ s

   iii $t = 1.0$ s

8 A mass is suspended by a light string. When it is disturbed from its equilibrium position, it oscillates in simple harmonic motion.

Explain what would happen to the period of oscillation if the:

a mass were doubled

b string were replaced by a new string of double the length

c initial disturbance were doubled in magnitude

d string and the mass were on the moon.

9 A mass, m, is suspended from a spring of spring constant, k. The mass is pulled down a short distance and released. The mass oscillates up and down in simple harmonic motion with a frequency, f.

Explain what would happen to f if the:

a mass was doubled

b spring was replaced with a new spring of spring constant $2k$

c distance the mass was displaced was doubled.

10 Consider a mass, m, suspended from a spring of spring constant, k. If the mass is displaced downwards by a distance, A, from its equilibrium point and released, the mass will undergo simple harmonic motion oscillations.

a State how the force, F, required to displace the mass downwards from its equilibrium position varies with displacement, x.

b What is the spring constant, k, of a spring?

c Write an equation to show how the elastic potential energy (EPE) in the spring varies with x.

d For the mass–spring system, $\omega^2 = \dfrac{k}{m}$. Write a new equation for EPE in terms of m and ω.

e What will the maximum EPE be?

f Where will the mass be in its oscillation when the EPE is a maximum?

g Where will the mass be when the EPE is a minimum?

h The *total energy* of the system remains constant. When the EPE is zero, what will the maximum kinetic energy, KE, be?

i Show that the maximum speed of the mass is $v_{max} = \omega A$

11 An oscillator performs simple harmonic motion with a period of 0.500 s and an amplitude of 0.400 m. At time $t = 0.00$ s, the displacement of the oscillator from its equilibrium position is zero. Calculate the:

a angular frequency of the oscillations, ω

b maximum speed of the oscillator

c speed of the oscillator at time $t = 0.2$ s

d value of the maximum acceleration of the oscillator.

12 Outline an experiment that could find the value of the Earth's gravitational field strength, g, using a simple pendulum oscillating in simple harmonic motion. Make sure you include:

• the equipment required

• the measurements you need to take (and what their expected uncertainties are likely to be)

• how you would manipulate the data to find g.

13 A mass of 100 g is suspended between two springs. The combined spring constant of the two springs is 400 N m^{-1}. The mass is displaced from its equilibrium position by 15 mm and the subsequent oscillations of the mass undergo simple harmonic motion. Calculate the:

a maximum acceleration of the mass

b frequency at which the mass oscillates

c total energy contained in the mass–spring system.

14 **a** A simple harmonic motion oscillation has a maximum displacement from the equilibrium position, A. Sketch a graph for to show how the kinetic energy of the oscillator varies with displacement from the equilibrium position.

b Add another line to show how the potential energy of the oscillator varies with displacement from the equilibrium position.

c What can you say about the total energy of the oscillator?

Exercise 9.2 – Single-slit diffraction

1   Figure 9.1 shows a series of Huygens secondary wavelet sources (HSWS) modelling the wavefront of a wave as it passes through a single slit. A ray from the first HSWS and a ray from the HSWS that is just past the centre of the slit are heading for a distant place on a screen at an angle of θ to the straight ahead direction, as shown. These two rays are parallel. The path difference between the two rays is indicated.

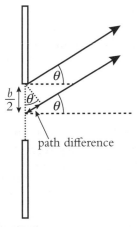

Figure 9.1

   a   Use Figure 9.1, and your knowledge of geometry, to write an equation for the path difference shown.
   b   If the two rays arrive at the screen and produce destructive interference, what is the path difference?
   c   Write an equation that relates the path difference to the condition that this path difference causes destructive interference – this is what physicists call the *single-slit diffraction* equation.

2   Consider some waves of wavelength, λ, incident on a single slit of width, b. How much diffraction would you expect when:
   a $\lambda \ll b$
   b $\lambda \geq b$.

3   Waves passing through a single slit produce a single-slit diffraction pattern on a distant screen.
   a   Sketch a diagram to show how the intensity of the waves varies with distance on the screen.
   b   What would happen to this diagram if the:
      i   slit width were wider?
      ii wavelength of the waves were larger?

4   In a single-slit diffraction pattern, the width of the central maximum is twice the width of the higher order maxima. Calculate the angular width of the central maximum for light waves of wavelength 600 nm passing through a 0.15 mm slit.

5 A class of students are waiting for their teacher. As he approaches, his shoes squeak on the corridor at a frequency of 300 Hz. The width of the open classroom door is 0.90 m. Using your knowledge of single-slit diffraction, explain why pupils sitting anywhere inside the classroom can hear the teacher approaching. (The speed of sound in air is 330 m s^{-1}.)

6 **a** Microwaves of wavelength 2 cm are incident normally on a gap between two thick metal plates. If the width of the gap is 5 cm, calculate the:
   i angle at which the first minimum of the diffraction pattern will occur
   ii separation of the first-order minimum and the second-order minimum when observed from a distance 1.5 m from the slit.
   b How many minima are there?

7 How wide would the central maximum of a single-slit diffraction pattern be if the width of the slit were infinitesimally thin? (You may assume that there is enough energy passing through the slit to produce an observable pattern on a screen.)

Exercise 9.3 – Interference

1 Explain why the Young double-slit experiment is so important in physics (particularly when studying the properties of waves).

2 When two narrow slits are placed side-by-side with a coherent source of waves incident on the slits, an interference pattern will be observed at some distance from the slits. If the two slits have an infinitesimal width, what can you say about the intensity of the maxima observed?

3 The spacing of the maxima in the double-slit interference pattern can be found from the equation $s = \dfrac{\lambda D}{d}$ Explain what each of the terms in the equation represents.

4 Two speakers are placed 1.2 m apart and emit sound of wavelength 0.8 m. If a person walks past the speakers at a distance of 4 m, how far apart would the person hear the maxima to be?

5 A laser emitting red light of wavelength 630 nm shines normally on a pair of narrow slits that are 1.5×10^{-4} m apart. If the resulting interference pattern is observed on a screen that is 3.0 m away, calculate the spacing of the maxima.

6 **a** Sketch the diffraction pattern that is observed on a screen when light waves of wavelength 500 nm pass through a single slit of width 0.1 mm.
   b Two such slits are brought together so they are separated by a distance of 0.4 mm. Sketch the interference pattern that will be observed on a screen.
   c In what way has the single-slit diffraction pattern *modulated* the double-slit interference pattern?

7   a   In the single-slit diffraction pattern, what does the equation, $n\lambda = b\sin\theta_n$ tell us?
    b   In the double-slit interference pattern, what does the equation, $m\lambda = d\sin\theta_m$ tell us?
    c   In a double-slit interference pattern produced by two slits that are not infinitesimally thin, the value for $\sin\theta_n$ is equal to the value for $\sin\theta_m$. What will the ratio of $\dfrac{d}{b}$ be?
    d   Which order of maximum of the interference pattern is *missing*?
    e   How many of the interference maxima will be inside the central maximum of the diffraction pattern?

8   A Young slits interference pattern is observed on a distant screen when monochromatic light passes through two equally narrow slits.
    a   The two slits are replaced by a large number of slits, each of the same width as the originals and each separated by the same distance as before. Sketch a diagram to show how the observations compare to observations for only two slits.
    b   What has happened to the intensity of the maxima? Explain.
    c   What has happened to the spacing of the maxima? Explain.
    d   What has happened to the width of the maxima? Explain.

9   Describe what is meant by a *diffraction grating*.

10 When monochromatic light of wavelength 590 nm illuminates a diffraction grating, a diffraction pattern is observed on a screen some distance away. The light source is replaced by one with a wavelength 450 nm. Suggest two ways in which the observed diffraction pattern on the screen would differ from the original pattern.

11 Light from a laser of wavelength 630 nm produces an interference pattern when incident on a diffraction grating labelled 600 lines mm^{-1}. Calculate the separation of the central maximum from the first-order maximum on a screen 5 m away.

12 Monochromatic light is incident normally on a diffraction grating labelled 600 lines mm^{-1}, producing an interference pattern on a screen that is 8 m away. If the distance between the second-order maximum and the central maximum is 9.5 m, calculate the wavelength of the light.

13 a   Low-energy X-rays of wavelength 1.0×10^{-10} m are incident on a diffraction grating labelled 600 lines mm^{-1}. Show that the diffraction grating would not produce an interference pattern that could be observed with an X-ray detector.
    b   The same low-energy X-rays are now incident on a thin crystal, where the regular lattice spacing of the atoms in the crystal is about 0.3 nm. Show that an interference pattern could now be observed.
    c   How might such observations as those in part **b** give us useful information about crystals?

14 Consider the ray of light that is incident on a thin rectangular piece of material of refractive index, n, as shown in Figure 9.2.

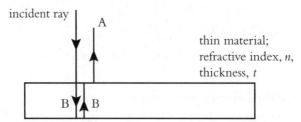

Figure 9.2

   a Some of this ray of light may be reflected from the front surface of the material. This ray is labelled *ray A* in the diagram. What will happen to the phase of this ray?

   b Some of this ray of light will be transmitted through the material, where it will reflect off the far surface of the material. This ray is labelled *ray B* in the diagram. What will happen to the phase of this ray when it reflects from the far side of the material?

   c Ray B will be transmitted back through the material until it reaches the first surface again. How much further has this ray travelled than ray A?

   d What happened to ray B's wavelength while it was in the material? By what factor had its wavelength changed?

   e How much further has ray B travelled than ray A? Use units of smaller wavelengths for your answer; this number is m, the *optical path difference*.

   f When ray B now passes through the first surface and into the air, it can superpose with ray A. What will happen to the phase of ray B as it passes from the material into the air?

   g If this superposition results in destructive interference, what can you say about m?

   h Hence show that for destructive interference, $2tn = m\lambda$, where thickness of the material is t, refractive index of the material is n, wavelength of the light is λ, and the optical path difference is m.

15 Write the equation that would provide constructive interference when rays A and B superpose, for the piece of material in Figure 9.2.

16 Green light of wavelength 500 nm is incident normally on a thin film of refractive index 1.2.

What is the minimum thickness of the film for there to be no reflected light?

17 A simple children's toy consists of a small pot of detergent and a circular ring that the child can hold. The child dips the ring into the detergent and then blows the resulting thin film into a bubble. When the child looks at the bubbles, some coloured patterns can be observed.

   a Explain how these coloured patterns are formed.

   b Explain why the spacing of the coloured patterns changes during the short lifetime of the bubble.

18 Figure 9.3 shows a thin film of refractive index, *n*, sitting on the surface of some glass. Light is incident normally on the surface of the thin film, as shown.

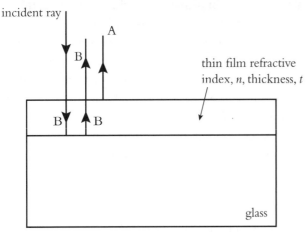

Figure 9.3

a Ray A reflects off the film–air boundary. What phase change occurs for this ray?

b Ray B passes through the film–air boundary and is reflected from the film–glass boundary. The refractive index of glass is more than the refractive index of the film. What phase change occurs for this ray when it reflects from the film–glass boundary?

c Ray B then passes through the film-air surface and is parallel to ray A. If the thin film has a thickness, *t*, what is the optical path difference between the reflected ray A and the reflected ray B?

d If this optical path difference is equal to an odd number of half wavelengths of light, what would you expect to happen to the reflected light?

e Suggest a practical use for the addition of a thin film to some glass.

19 The lenses of high-quality optical equipment, such as those used in photography, are coated with a thin film. This is called lens blooming. The lenses appear reddish-purple. Suggest why. (Think about the range of wavelengths in the visible spectrum and the conditions necessary for destructive interference to occur from a thin film on the surface of some glass.)

20 A thin film of oil (refractive index 1.4) floats on the surface of some water (refractive index 1.5). When viewed from a direction that is nearly normal to the surface of the oil, part of the oil film is green with a wavelength of 520 nm. If the optical path difference is one wavelength, calculate the thickness of the oil film.

Exercise 9.4 – Resolution

1 When waves pass through a circular hole of diameter, b, a single-slit diffraction pattern will be formed on a screen a distance away from the hole.

    a Describe what this single-slit diffraction pattern would look like for monochromatic light passing through a circular pin hole.

    b Using the correction factor for a circular aperture, write an equation for the angle at which the first minimum will occur on the single-slit diffraction pattern. Calculate this angle if $b = 4$ mm and $\lambda = 500$ nm.

    Imagine there are now two sources of light, both illuminating the circular hole. They are a distance, D, away from the circular hole, and are separated by a distance, x.

    c Give an expression for the angle subtended by the two light sources at the circular aperture.

    If this angle is equal to the angle you calculated in part **b**, then the two sources are *just resolved*; they are seen to be two sources, rather than one source. This is called *Rayleigh's criterion for resolution*. If the angle is smaller than your angle in part **b**, then the two sources are not resolved and they will appear as one source.

    d If two sources are 2 cm apart at a distance of 5 m away from the circular aperture, will they be resolved?

2 State, and explain, Rayleigh's criterion for resolution.

3 A tarsier is a small primate with extremely large eyes. The diameter of their eyes is about 1.6 cm.

    a What is the minimum angle subtended by two sources of light that will allow the tarsier to resolve the two sources? (Average wavelength of visible light = 500 nm.)

    b The tarsier is stood 50 m away from two objects. How far apart must the two objects be in order for the tarsier to see them as two objects, rather than one?

4 A telescope just resolves two stars that subtend an angle of 2.5×10^{-7} radians at a wavelength of 550 nm. Calculate the diameter of a telescope.

5 The Hubble telescope has a diameter of 2.4 m.

    a What is the minimum angle that two astronomical objects can subtend for the Hubble telescope to resolve them? (Average wavelength of visible light = 500 nm.)

    b If two such distant objects are just resolved at a distance of four light–years away, how far apart do the two sources appear to be?

6 The diameter of the pupil of a human eye in daylight is about 3 mm.

    a Calculate the minimum angle that two objects must subtend if they are to be resolved by the human eye.

    b If two people are walking, side by side, what is the maximum distance that they could be away from an observer if they are resolved in light of wavelength 500 nm?

    c How does the human eye's ability to resolve change:

      i in blue light, rather than in a mixture of all colours

      ii at night.

7 A diffraction grating is labelled *300 lines mm^{-1}*.
   a Calculate the spacing, s, of the slits on the diffraction grating.
   b Calculate how many slits there will be on the diffraction grating, N, if it is
      1.5 cm wide.
   c What is the resolvance, R, of the diffraction grating in the second-order spectrum?
   d Two spectral lines, one at wavelength 500.0 nm and the other at wavelength
      500.2 nm, are viewed through the diffraction grating. Can the two lines be
      resolved as separate lines in the second-order spectrum?

8 The sodium doublet emission lines occur at $\lambda = 589.0$ nm and $\lambda = 589.6$ nm. If
   viewed through a diffraction grating with a 4 mm beam width, what is the maximum
   separation of the slits on the grating for them to be resolved as two lines, rather than
   one line in the second order?

Exercise 9.5 – Doppler effect

1 A toy car has a horn that emits sound at a frequency of 1.50 kHz.
   a If the toy car has its horn sounding while moving away from an observer, describe
      what the observer will hear.
   b The speed of sound in air is 330 m s^{-1}. What frequency of sound will the
      observer hear if the car moves at a speed of 15.0 m s^{-1}?

2 The speed of the visible edge of the Sun rotates at 1.900 km s^{-1}. When observed in
   a laboratory, the hydrogen-alpha line (the bright red line in the emission spectrum of
   hydrogen) has a wavelength of 656.28 nm.
   a At what percentage of the speed of light does the edge of the Sun rotate?
   b Calculate the change in wavelength of the hydrogen-alpha line observed at the
      Earth from the edge of the Sun as it rotates away from us.
   c State the change in the wavelength of the hydrogen-alpha line observed at the
      Earth from the edge of the Sun as it rotates towards us.

3 In some countries, policemen use a Doppler radar gun to measure the speed of cars
   travelling along the road. Explain how the police are able to get an accurate value for
   the speed of a moving car.

4 A cyclist approaches a vehicle with a siren of frequency 450.0 Hz. The cyclist is
   travelling at 40 km hour^{-1}. Calculate the frequency of the siren that the cyclist hears.
   (Speed of sound in air = 330 m s^{-1}.)

5 A train moving at a constant speed of 60 m s^{-1} approaches a bridge. The train's
   whistle blows as it approaches, passes under the bridge and continues along the track.
   (Speed of sound in air = 330 m s^{-1}.)
   a Describe what a train-spotter stood on the bridge will hear as the train approaches
      and passes the bridge.
   b If the train's whistle emits sound of frequency 800 Hz, calculate the frequency of
      the sound from the train's whistle when the train is:
      i   approaching the bridge
      ii travelling away from the bridge.

6 Light from a distant star is observed using a telescope and a diffraction grating. One spectral line from the star is measured at a wavelength of 580.9 nm, whereas the same spectral line measured in a laboratory has a wavelength of 527.0 nm.

   a What can you say about the relative motion of the distant star and the Earth?

   b Calculate the speed at which the distant star is moving relative to the Earth.

? Exam-style questions

1 **Which of the following statements about simple harmonic motion is *false*?**
  A The period of the oscillation is constant.
  B The amplitude of the oscillations decreases with time.
  C The period of the oscillations is independent of the amplitude.
  D The total energy of the oscillator is constant.

2 **What is the best estimate for the time period of a simple pendulum of length 1 m?**
  A 0.1 s
  B 1 s
  C 10 s
  D 100 s

3 **A mass of 10 kg, attached to a vertical spring of spring constant, k, oscillates in a vertical direction. If the time period of the oscillations is 4 s, what is the best estimate for the spring constant of the spring?**
  A 1 N m^{-1}
  B 8 N m^{-1}
  C 16 N m^{-1}
  D 25 N m^{-1}

4 **When monochromatic light of wavelength, λ, is incident on a thin slit of width, b, a diffraction pattern is observed on a screen. The spacing of the maxima is x. The light is changed to one with wavelength of 2λ and the width of the slit is reduced to $\frac{b}{2}$. What is the spacing of the maxima on the new diffraction pattern?**
  A $\frac{x}{4}$
  B x
  C $2x$
  D $4x$

5 **A pair of binoculars is used to view light of wavelength, λ. What is the best estimate for the thickness of the coating on the surface of a binocular lens?**
  A $\frac{\lambda}{4}$
  B $\frac{\lambda}{2}$
  C λ
  D 2λ

6   Figure 9.4 shows how the acceleration of an oscillator varies with its displacement from the equilibrium position.

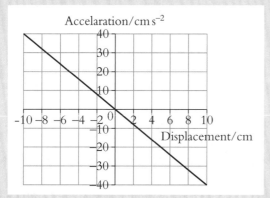

Figure 9.4

a   Explain how the graph shows that the oscillations are simple harmonic. **[2]**
b   Use the graph to calculate the angular frequency, ω. **[2]**
c   Determine the frequency and the time period of the oscillations. **[2]**

7   **A man has legs that are about 0.8 m long.**
a   Assume that the act of walking can be modelled as the simple harmonic motion of each leg swinging back and forth. Calculate the frequency of the leg's oscillations. **[2]**
b   Each step moves the man 1.7 m. Calculate how far he can walk in one hour. **[2]**
c   How does your calculation compare to an accepted walking speed for a human? **[1]**

8   **A mass of 400 g is suspended from a spring of spring constant 25 N m^{-1}. When the mass is displaced downwards by 10 cm and released, the mass oscillates in simple harmonic motion. Determine the:**
a   angular frequency of the oscillations **[2]**
b   maximum speed of the mass **[2]**
c   position of the mass when the KE of the mass and the EPE of the spring are equal. **[2]**

9   **Green light of wavelength 530 nm is incident normally on a single slit of width 0.1 mm. The resulting diffraction pattern is observed on a screen that is 8 m away.**
a   Calculate the width of the central maximum of the diffraction pattern. **[3]**
b   The light is changed for a red light of wavelength 650 nm. What is the width of the central maximum? **[2]**
c   The light is changed for white light. How will the single-slit diffraction pattern on the screen change? **[2]**

10 **A diffraction grating is labelled *300 lines mm^{-1}*.**
a   Calculate the spacing of the slits. **[2]**
b   Orange light of wavelength 590 nm is incident normally on the diffraction grating. Calculate the angle between the central maximum and the first order maximum of the interference pattern produced. **[2]**
c   Determine what other angles would produce maxima. **[2]**

10 Fields

Chapter outline

In this chapter, you will:

- Use appropriate symbols to represent aspects of fields (sources of mass and charge, and field lines).
- Understand the concept of potential and be able to sketch and interpret graphs of potential against radial distance in electric and gravitational fields.
- Describe the relationship between equipotential surfaces and the direction of fields as given by field lines.
- Determine the potential energy of a point mass in a gravitational field and a point charge in an electric field, and solve problems involving potential energy, energy in the circular orbits of charged particles and masses, and forces on charged particles and masses in radial and in uniform fields.
- Determine the potential inside a charged sphere, and solve problems of a mass in orbit around a planet (or star) and the escape speed necessary to escape the gravitational field altogether.

KEY TERMS

Field line: A line showing the direction of the force acting in a field.

Electrical/gravitational potential: The amount of electrical/gravitational potential energy possessed by a unit test charge/mass in an electric/gravitational field. It is defined as the work done to move a unit test charge/mass from infinity to where it is in the electric field. Electrical/gravitational potential is defined to be zero at infinity.

Equipotential: A line or surface on which the value of the potential is the same.

Electrical/gravitational potential difference: The work done in moving a unit charge/mass from one place in the field to another.

Field equations:

$$F_E = k\frac{Qq}{r^2} = Eq = -\frac{d\,(\text{EPE})}{dr}$$

$$F_g = -G\frac{Mm}{r^2} = mg = -\frac{d\,(\text{GPE})}{dr}$$

$$E = k\frac{Q}{r^2} = \frac{F_E}{q} = -\frac{dV_E}{dr}$$

$$g = -G\frac{M}{r^2} = \frac{F_g}{m} = -\frac{dV_g}{dr}$$

$$V_E = k\frac{Q}{r} = -\int E\,dr = \frac{\text{EPE}}{q}$$

$$V_g = -G\frac{M}{r} = -\int g\,dr = \frac{\text{GPE}}{m}$$

$$\text{EPE} = k\frac{Qq}{r} = -\int F_E \, dr = qV_E$$

$$\text{GPE} = -G\frac{Mm}{r} = -\int F_g \, dr = mV_g$$

Charge density, σ: The amount of charge per unit area. For a capacitor, $\sigma = \varepsilon E$.

Escape speed: The initial speed of a vertically projected object necessary for the object to be able to escape from the gravitational field; $v_{esc} = \sqrt{2gR}$.

Exercise 10.1 – Describing fields

1   State what is meant by:
    a   an electric field
    b   a gravitational field
    c   a magnetic field.

2   Explain what is meant by *uniform field*.

3   Explain what is meant by:
    a   electric field strength
    b   gravitational field strength.

4   Calculate the electric force on an electron in a uniform electric field of field strength 4×10^7 N C^{-1}.

5   Calculate the gravitational force on a mass of 3.5×10^4 kg in a gravitational field of field strength 25 N kg^{-1}.

6   Two parallel metal plates are 2.4 cm apart. They are charged, giving a potential difference between the plates of 300 V. Calculate the:
    a   electric field strength between the plates
    b   force that an alpha particle would experience if it were within the field.

7   The gravitational field strength near the surface of the Earth is constant; it has a globally averaged value of 9.81 N kg^{-1}. Calculate the weight of an 80 kg adult standing on the surface of the Earth.

8   The mass of the Earth is 5.97×10^{24} kg. Its radius is 6.38×10^6 m.
    a   Calculate the average density of the Earth.
    b   The gravitational field strength, g, at the surface of the Earth is 9.81 N kg^{-1}. Show that g can be expressed in terms of $G = \dfrac{3g}{4\pi\rho R_E}$, where R_E is the radius of the Earth and r is the average density of the Earth.
    c   Use the expression for G to calculate the average density of the Earth.
    d   Calculate the percentage difference in your answers to parts **a** and **b**.

9   A uniform electric field is set with two parallel plates, 4 cm apart. The top plate is connected to a supply kept at 50 V. The bottom plate is kept at a potential of 10 V.

   a   Suppose a 1 C charge was sitting on the underside surface of the top plate. How much electrical potential energy would it have?

   b   Suppose the 1 C charge sat on the upper side of the bottom plate. How much electrical potential energy would it have?

   c   How much work would have to be done to move the 1 C charge from the bottom plate to the top plate?

   d   In answering part **c** above, was it necessary to consider the *actual* path along which the 1 C charge would move?

10   A small sphere, covered in conducting paint, is held by a thin insulating rod. The sphere is charged by touching it with a supply of +400 V.

   a   Sketch a diagram of the electric field around the sphere.

   b   How do your electric field lines suggest that the electric field strength is decreasing with distance from the sphere?

   c   How far from the sphere will the electric field strength be zero?

   d   How much work would have to be done on a 1 C charge to move it from where the field strength is zero to the surface of the sphere?

   e   Define *electric potential*.

11   Calculate the following potentials.

   a   The electric potential at a distance of 30 cm from a small charged sphere of charge 3.0×10^{-9} C.

   b   The gravitational potential at a distance of 1.5×10^{11} m from a star of mass 2.0×10^{30} kg.

12   a   Sketch the graph of how the gravitational field strength varies from the surface of the Earth outwards into space.

   b   How could you use your graph to find the gravitational potential at the surface of the Earth?

   c   Imagine a 1 kg mass moved away from the surface of the Earth by a distance twice the Earth's radius. How could you use your graph to find the energy needed for the mass to move this distance?

13   a   Calculate the gravitational potential at the surface of the Earth. (The radius of the Earth is 6400 km. Its mass is 6.0×10^{24} kg.)

   b   State the value of the gravitational potential at a distance 12 800 km from the Earth's centre.

   c   How much energy would a 2500 kg spacecraft need to move from the Earth's surface to 12 800 km away from the centre of the Earth?

14   a   Explain what an *electrical equipotential* is.

   b   Explain what a *gravitational equipotential* is.

   c   What is the relationship between an equipotential and a field line? Is this always the case?

15 Figure 10.1 shows two electrical equipotentials in an electric field.

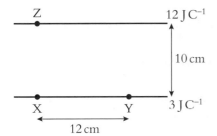

Figure 10.1

How much work must be done to move a 4 μC charge from:
a point X to point Y?
b point X to point Z?
c point Y to point Z?

16 A small sphere is charged to a potential of −200 V.
a Sketch a diagram to show the electric field around the sphere.
b What is the potential at the surface of the sphere?
c How does this potential vary with increasing distance from the sphere?
d Add some equipotential lines to represent your answer to part **c**.
e How does the separation of the equipotential lines relate to the electric field strength?

17 Consider two identically charged spheres separated by a small distance.
a Sketch a diagram to show the electric field lines that define the shape of the electric field between and around the two spheres.
b Complete the diagram to show some equipotentials.
c How does your diagram help you to identify where the electric field strength is smallest?

18 Consider a small, positively charged sphere a small distance above a negatively charged metal plate.
a Sketch a diagram to show the shape of the electric field between the sphere and the plate.
b Add some equipotentials. (It is not necessary to give these equipotentials numerical values.)
c What is the relationship between the orientation of equipotentials and the field lines?

19 Consider two oppositely charged spheres separated by a small distance. The charge on each sphere has the same magnitude, but opposite sign.
a Sketch a diagram to show the electric field lines that define the shape of the electric field between and around the two spheres.
b Using your knowledge of the relationship between electric field lines and equipotentials, add some equipotentials to your diagram from part **a**.
c How does your diagram help you to identify where the electric field strength is greatest?

Exercise 10.2 – Fields at work

1 A hotel has eight floors, each 4 m high. A full elevator at the hotel has a mass of 1000 kg.

   a Calculate the work done by the full elevator when moving from floor four to floor eight.

   b If each floor is represented by a gravitational equipotential, calculate the change in gravitational potential from floor one to floor two.

   c The Earth's gravitational field strength is 9.81 N kg^{-1}. Given that your answer to part **b** occurs over a height difference of 4 m, how might you be able to express g?

2 Figure 10.2 shows a small region of the Earth's surface.

Earth's surface

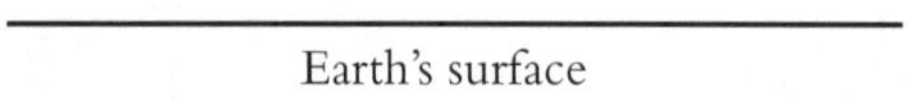

Figure 10.2

   a Add some gravitational field lines to show the shape of the gravitational field.

   b Add some equipotentials.

   c How do your equipotentials show that the gravitational field strength is a constant in this small region of the Earth's surface?

3 The gravitational field strength is 9.81 N kg^{-1} near to the Earth's surface. Calculate the gravitational potential difference between the Earth's surface and the flag at the top of Mount Everest (8.8 km above the Earth's surface).

4 Figure 10.3 shows how the gravitational potential varies with distance from the Earth's surface.

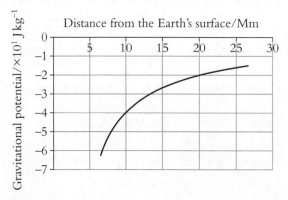

Figure 10.3

   a Use the diagram to determine the gravitational field strength at a distance of:

   i   10 Mm

   ii 20 Mm.

   b Do your answers correspond with the idea that the gravitational field strength follows an inverse-square law?

5 **a** Point X is 5 cm from a small, positively charged sphere of charge 6.0 mC. Point Y is 10 cm from the sphere. Calculate the electrical potential difference between points X and Y.

   b Calculate the work required to move a charge of 2.0 μC from point Y to point X. (Assume that the charged sphere does not move.)

   c Suppose that the 2.0 μC charge has zero kinetic energy when it arrives at point Y. Suggest what will happen to the 2.0 μC charge.

6 In a radial electric field (such as that occurring around a small charged sphere) what is the relationship between the:

   a force, F, acting on a charge, q, and the field strength, E?

   b electrical potential, V_E, and the electrical potential energy, EPE, for a charge, q?

   c electric field strength, E, and the electric potential, V_E?

   d force, F, and the electrical potential energy, EPE?

7 For a gravitational field (such as that around a distant planet or a star) what is the relationship between the:

   a force, F, acting on a mass, m, and the field strength, g?

   b gravitational potential, V_g, and the gravitational potential energy, GPE, for a mass, m?

   c gravitational field strength, g, and the gravitational potential, V_g?

   d force, F, and the gravitational potential energy, GPE?

8 **a** Ignoring the effects of air friction, how much energy would a 1 kg mass need to escape from the surface of the Earth?

   b If this energy was supplied as kinetic energy (firing vertically from a gun, for example), calculate the initial speed of the mass.

9 The Moon has a mass of 7.35×10^{22} kg and a radius of 1.74×10^6 m. Calculate the escape speed for the Moon.

10 The escape speed from a black hole is greater than the speed of light. (That is why the black hole appears black: no radiation is escaping from it for us to observe.)

   a If the mass of a black hole is 2.4 times the mass of our Sun ($M_{Sun} = 2.0 \times 10^{30}$ kg), calculate the distance from the centre of the black hole to where radiation is *just* able to escape from the gravitational field.

   b Is the actual 'size' of the black hole likely to be the value you have calculated in part **a**, or smaller? Explain your answer.

   c What is the name given to the distance you have calculated?

11 **a** Calculate the speed of a polar-orbiting satellite with an orbital radius 400 km above the Earth's surface. (The radius of the Earth is 6400 km.)

   b How many orbits can a polar-orbiting satellite make in one day?

12   a   The speed of a satellite in orbit around the Earth is given by $v = \sqrt{\dfrac{GM_E}{r}}$.

Determine an expression for the kinetic energy of the satellite if the mass of the satellite is m.

   b   State the gravitational potential energy of the satellite in its orbit.

   c   Show that the total energy of the satellite is less than zero.

   d   How does the magnitude of the kinetic energy of the satellite compare with the magnitude of the gravitational potential energy of the satellite?

   e   Express the total energy of the satellite in terms of its KE.

13   The Moon orbits the Earth at a distance of 3.8×10^8 m.

   a   Calculate the speed at which the Moon is travelling in its orbit around the Earth.

   b   Show that the Moon makes about 13 orbits in one year.

14   The mass of the Sun is 2.0×10^{30} kg. The Earth orbits the Sun at a distance of 1.5×10^{11} m.

   a   Calculate the speed at which the Earth moves in its orbit around the Sun.

   b   Show that it takes one year for the Earth to make one orbit.

15   a   State the equation for the electrical force between an electron of charge e and mass m, and the nucleus of charge Q, which it orbits at a radius r.

   b   Show that the kinetic energy of the electron is $KE = \dfrac{kQe}{2r}$.

   c   Show that the total energy of the electron in its orbit around the nucleus is less than zero.

   d   The total energy of an electron in its ground state in a hydrogen atom is -13.6 eV. Calculate the radius of the electron's orbit around the nucleus.

16   An electron in an excited energy level emits a photon and moves to a different orbit around the nucleus.

   a   Has the total energy of the electron increased or decreased?

   b   What has happened to the kinetic energy of the electron?

   c   What has happened to the electrical potential energy of the electron?

   d   Is its new orbit closer to the nucleus or further away from the nucleus?

17   A student conducted an investigation to find out how the intensity of light varies with distance from the light. She used a photographer's light meter which produced a voltage reading.

Her measurements are shown in Table 10.1.

Distance from light source / m	0.5	1.0	1.5	2.0	2.5	3.0
Voltage reading / mV	2440	612	270	153	98	68

Table 10.1

Conduct an arithmetic test to check that the light intensity is inversely proportional to the distance from the light.

? Exam-style questions

1 **Which of the following statements about a charged sphere is true?**
   A The electrical potential inside the sphere is zero everywhere.
   B The electrical potential inside the sphere is a non-zero constant everywhere.
   C The electrical potential inside the sphere varies linearly with distance from the centre of the sphere.
   D The electrical potential inside the sphere varies inversely with distance from the centre of the sphere.

2 **An orbiting satellite is moved into a new orbit further from the Earth. Which one of the following statements about the satellite's energy is true?**
   A Kinetic energy = decreases; Total energy = stays the same
   B Kinetic energy = decreases; Total energy = increases
   C Kinetic energy = increases; Total energy = stays the same
   D Kinetic energy = increases; Total energy = increases

3 **Which of the following statements about equipotentials is *incorrect*?**
   A A charged particle experiences the same force anywhere on an equipotential.
   B An equipotential is always perpendicular to a field line.
   C No work is done against the field when a charged particle moves along an equipotential.
   D A charged particle possesses the same amount of energy anywhere on an equipotential.

4 **Complete this sentence: The gravitational field strength inside a solid sphere is …**
   A …zero.
   B …a constant, non-zero value.
   C …proportional to the distance from the sphere's centre.
   D …inversely proportional to the square of the distance from the sphere's centre.

5 **A test charge is located in the electric field between a pair of oppositely charge metal plates.**
   Which of the following combinations best describes how the force on the test charge and the electrical potential energy (EPE) of the test charge varies with its distance from one of the plates?
   A Force = constant; EPE = constant
   B Force = constant; EPE = proportional to distance from one plate
   C Force = proportional to distance from one plate; EPE = constant
   D Force = proportional to distance from one plate; EPE = proportional to distance from one plate

6 **A satellite is orbiting the Earth. Which of the following combinations best describes its kinetic energy (KE), gravitational potential energy (GPE) and its total energy?**
   A KE = > 0; GPE = > 0; Total energy = > 0
   B KE = < 0; GPE = 0; Total energy = < 0
   C KE = > 0; GPE = < 0; Total energy = 0
   D KE = > 0; GPE = < 0; Total energy = < 0

7   Figure 10.4 shows two charged metal plates, 30 mm apart. The top plate is
    connected to a supply of +300 V. The bottom plate is earthed (its potential is kept
    at 0 V).

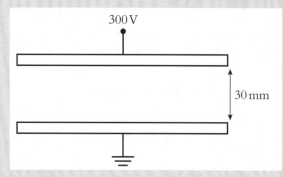

Figure 10.4

   a Calculate the electric field strength between the two plates. [2]
   b Add some electric field lines to show the shape of the electric field between the plates. [1]
   c An electron is placed into the region between the plates. Calculate the force it would
      experience. [2]
   d Which direction would this force be in? [1]
   e Calculate the acceleration of the electron. [2]

8 **This question is about a satellite in orbit around the Earth.**
   a State the force that provides the necessary centripetal force for the circular motion of the
      satellite. [1]
   b Show that the speed of the satellite in its orbit is given by $v = \sqrt{\dfrac{GM_E}{r}}$, where M_E is the

      mass of the Earth and r is the radius of the satellite's orbit. [2]
   c Geostationary satellites orbiting the Earth have an orbital period of one day. Calculate the
      radius of the orbit of a geostationary satellite. [2]

9 **Two parallel metal plates, 20 cm apart, are connected to a power supply. One plate
   is held at a potential of 100 V. The other is held at a potential of 0 V.**
   a Calculate the electric field strength between the two plates. [2]
   b Calculate how much electrical potential energy a charge of 6 μC has if it is positioned:
      i   on the surface of the 100 V plate
      ii   exactly half way between the two plates
      iii on the surface of the 0 V plate. [3]
   c Calculate the electrical force on a charge of 6 μC if it is positioned:
      i   on the surface of the 100 V plate
      ii   exactly half way between the two plates
      iii on the surface of the 0 V plate. [3]
   d Calculate the work done to move the 6 μC charge from the 0 V plate to the 100 V plate. [2]
   e In the uniform electric field between the two plates, what is the relationship between:
      • the force on the charged particle,
      • the distance through which the charged particle moves, and
      • the change in the charged particle's electrical potential energy? [1]

10 **A thin wire has a potential difference of 12 V across is. The wire is 60 cm long.**
   a Calculate the electric field strength in the wire. [2]
   b Calculate how much energy is used by an electron in moving from one end of the wire to another. [2]
   c Outline the energy transformations occurring in the wire as the electron moves from one end of the wire to the other. [3]

11 **Electric field strength, E, and gravitational field strength, g, are both examples of the inverse-square law.**
   a Explain what an inverse-square law is. [2]
   b Suggest a simple arithmetic test to check whether two variables, X and Y, are related by an inverse-square law. [2]
   c Measurements of two variables, X and Y, are shown in Table 10.2.

X	2.0	4.0	6.0	8.0	10.0	12.0
Y	302	76	34	19	12	8

Table 10.2

Carry out an arithmetic test to see if the two variables are related by an inverse-square law. [2]

11 Electromagnetic induction

Chapter outline

In this chapter, you will:

- Understand the concept of electromotive force (emf) and describe the production of an induced emf in terms of a changing magnetic flux, use Faraday's law of electromagnetic induction to solve problems involving magnetic flux and magnetic flux linkage.
- Understand the concept of Lenz's law and describe it in terms of the conservation of energy.
- Explain the principles of operation of a basic alternating current generator (including the effect of a changing frequency), solve problems involving the use of average power and root-mean-square values of current and voltage in an ac circuit.
- Understand the principle of operation of a transformer, distinguish between and solve problems involving step-up and step-down transformers and describe the use of transformers in the distribution of electrical power.
- Investigate, experimentally, the operation of a simple diode rectifier and understand qualitatively half- and full-wave rectification and the uses of adding a capacitor to a diode bridge rectifier.
- Understand the nature of capacitance, describe the effect of different dielectric materials on capacitance and solve problems involving parallel plate capacitors in series and in parallel.
- Determine the energy stored in a charged capacitor and understand and be able to solve problems involving the exponential nature of the discharge of a charged capacitor through a fixed resistance.
- Understand the concept of a time constant in an RC circuit and be able to solve problems involving current and voltage.

KEY TERMS

Electromagnetic induction: When the magnetic flux linked to a conductor changes in any way, an electromotive force (emf) is induced in the conductor.

Faraday's laws of electromagnetic induction: There are two of these, though they are often considered to be two parts of just one concept:

- An induced emf occurs in any conductor linked with a changing magnetic flux.

- The magnitude of the induced emf is proportional to the rate of change of magnetic flux linkage: $\varepsilon \propto N \dfrac{d\Phi}{dt}$

Lenz's law: The direction of the induced emf is such that its effect is to oppose the original flux change. (This shows itself as the minus sign in the equation: $\varepsilon = -N \dfrac{d\Phi}{dt}$.)

Transformer: An electromagnetic device that is able to change an alternating electrical supply from one potential difference to another; a **step-up** transformer produces a larger potential difference than it is supplied with, and a **step-down** transformer produces a smaller potential difference than it is supplied with.

Rectification: The process of changing an alternating supply into a direct supply.

Bridge circuit: An electrical circuit consisting of four components, two parallel branches of two components in series.

Wheatstone bridge: A bridge circuit consisting of four resistors – originally designed to identify the resistance of an unknown resistor.

Capacitor: An electrical device that is able to separate charge and thus provide a potential difference across two electrical conducting surfaces.

Capacitance, C: This is defined as the amount of charge that can be separated per unit potential difference between the two surfaces, $C = \dfrac{Q}{V}$.

Time constant of an RC circuit, τ: The time it takes for the current flowing in an RC circuit to fall to $\dfrac{1}{e}(= 37\%)$ of its initial value. $\tau = RC$.

Exercise 11.1 – Electromagnetic induction

1   A wire, connected to a centre-zero galvanometer, can be moved through a magnetic field, as in Figure 11.1.

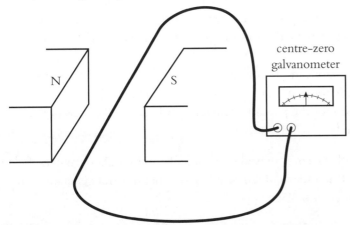

Figure 11.1

  a Describe what you would expect to see on the galvanometer when the wire is moved vertically downwards through the magnetic field.

  b If the wire is moved vertically upwards through the magnetic field, at the same speed as in part **a**, describe what you would see on the galvanometer.

  c Describe what you would expect to see on the galvanometer when the wire is moved horizontally, from left-to-right, in the magnetic field.

  d How will your answers to parts **a** and **b** differ if the wire is moved more quickly?

  e If the wire remains stationary in the magnetic field, what would you expect to see on the galvanometer?

2 A bar magnet can be moved towards or away from a coil of wire that has its ends connected to a centre-zero galvanometer.

    a The bar magnet is moved towards the coil. How would the galvanometer respond?

    b Part **a** is repeated and the magnet is moved faster. How would the galvanometer respond?

    c The bar magnet is moved away from the coil. How would the galvanometer respond?

3 A metal conductor, such as a copper wire, contains a large number of free electrons. The conductor is moved through a magnetic field in a direction perpendicular to the magnetic field lines, as shown in Figure 11.2.

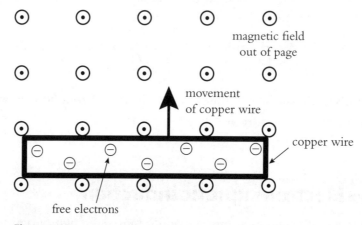

Figure 11.2

    a A force acts on each of the free electrons. In which direction?

    b Since the electrons are free to move, what will happen in the conductor?

    c Will there be an electric field across the ends of the conductor? Explain your answer.

    d When the free electrons in the conductor are in equilibrium, what can you say about the magnetic force and the electrical force acting on them?

    e Derive an equation for the potential difference ΔV across the ends of the conductor, length l.

4 A conductor of length 12 cm is moved perpendicularly through a magnetic field of strength 4.0×10^{-2} T at a speed of 2.0 m s^{-1}. Show that the emf generated across the ends of the conductor is 9.6 mV.

5 Calculate the emf produced when a wire of length 5.0 cm is moved perpendicularly through a magnetic field of strength 0.14 T at a speed of 60 cm s^{-1}.

6 A wire of length 25 cm is moved at a speed of 1.5 m s^{-1} through a magnetic field of strength 0.3 T at an angle θ to the field lines. The emf generated across the ends of the wire is 97 mV. Determine the angle, θ.

7 State what is meant by *magnetic flux* and *magnetic flux linkage*.

8 A single circular coil of wire surrounds an area A in a magnetic field of strength B at an angle θ, as shown in Figure 11.3.

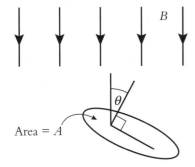

Figure 11.3

   a Give an expression for the magnetic flux linkage associated with the coil of wire.
   b What will θ be for the magnetic flux linkage to be a maximum?
   c What will θ be for the magnetic flux to be zero?

9 At the UK Olympic Hockey Centre in London, a hockey pitch measures $91.4\text{ m} \times 55.0\text{ m}$. The Earth's magnetic field has strength $4.87 \times 10^{-5}\text{ T}$ and is in a direction $24°$ from the vertical. Calculate the value of the magnetic flux linked with the hockey pitch.

10 Faraday's laws of electromagnetic induction may be expressed by the equation:

$$\varepsilon \propto N\frac{d(\Phi)}{dt}$$

   a Explain what each of the terms in this equation are.
   b If $\Phi = BA$, expand the equation so that Faraday's laws have two terms for ε.
   c How does this suggest that there are two ways of inducing an emf? Outline these two ways.

11 When a length of wire, connected to a galvanometer, is allowed to fall perpendicularly through a constant horizontal magnetic field, a current flows in the wire.
   a Explain why there is a current in the wire.
   b Current needs energy to flow. Where does the energy come from?
   c What do you think happened to the speed of the wire's movement when it entered the magnetic field?

12 a How long would it take for a mass of 100 g to fall 2.0 m? ($g = 9.81$ m s^{-2} and air resistance is negligible.)

b A small, strong, 100 g magnet is dropped through a vertical 2.0 m copper tube. It takes about eight seconds for the magnet to pass through the tube. Use Faraday's laws and energy to explain why.

c The same magnet is dropped through another 2.0 m copper tube with a cross-section as shown in Figure 11.4.

Figure 11.4

How will this set-up affect the speed of the magnet? Explain your answer.

13 a State Lenz's law.

b Which of the conservation laws is Lenz's law an example of?

14 A bar magnet moves towards a coil of wire. The ends of the coil of wire are connected to a galvanometer.

a What happens in the coil as the north pole of the magnet approaches it?

b The coil behaves like an electromagnet. Which pole, north or south, will the nearest end of the coil to the north pole of the magnet have? Explain your answer using Lenz's law.

15 A solenoid is connected in series to a resistor, a dc power supply of negligible internal resistance and a simple switch. An oscilloscope is connected across the resistor so that the current flowing through the solenoid/resistor circuit can be observed as a function of time. The trace observed on the oscilloscope screen is shown in Figure 11.5.

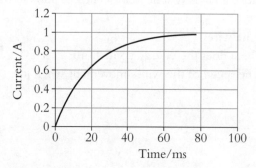

Figure 11.5

a Suggest why the current flowing through the solenoid does not immediately rise to 1.0 A.

b If the solenoid is replaced with another solenoid of similar dimensions but twice the number of turns, what would you expect to see on the oscilloscope trace?

16 The 'jumping ring' demonstration consists of a large coil connected to an ac supply by a push switch. An iron rod passes through the centre of the coil, protruding upwards. A small aluminium ring is placed over the iron rod, as shown in Figure 11.6.

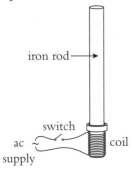

iron rod →

switch

ac ~ coil
supply

Figure 11.6

When the push switch is pressed, the aluminium ring jumps upwards (one or two metres) and leaves the iron rod.

a What happens to the iron rod when the ac supply is switched on?

b What happens in the aluminium ring when the ac supply is switched on?

c What does Lenz's law suggest will happen?

d Explain why the aluminium ring jumps upwards.

e If the aluminium ring is placed over the iron rod *after* the supply has been switched on, the ring floats mid-way along the iron rod rather than jumping upwards. Suggest why this happens.

f If the aluminium ring is not a complete circle (as in Figure 11.4), what would happen when the supply is switched on?

Exercise 11.2 – Power generation and transmission

1 Figure 11.7 shows a single coil of area, A, within a magnetic field of flux density, B. The coil is able to rotate about an axis shown by the dotted line.

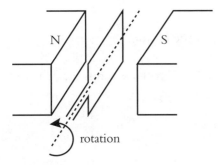

rotation

Figure 11.7

At any time, t, the angle between the normal to the plane of the coil and the magnetic field is ω.

a State an expression for the magnetic flux linkage for the coil.

b If the coil is able to rotate with an angular frequency of ω, state an expression for ω in terms of ω and t.

c Hence state an expression for the magnetic flux linkage for the rotating coil.

d Apply Faraday's and Lenz's laws to derive an expression for the induced emf in the coil as a function of time.

e What is the peak emf?

f What is the phase difference between the induced emf and the magnetic flux linkage?

2 A peak induced emf of 60 V is generated by rotating a 200-turn coil at an angular frequency of 30π radians s^{-1}. What will the peak induced emf be if the coil:

a is rotated at an angular frequency of 60π radians s^{-1}?

b is replaced by a similar dimension coil with 150 turns?

3 The induced emf, ε, from a rotating coil in a magnetic field can be expressed as:

$\varepsilon = \varepsilon_o \sin \omega t$

If the coil provides a complete path for a current to flow, an induced current, I, is given by:

$I = I_0 \sin \omega t$.

a What is the mean voltage being generated?

b What is the mean current flowing?

c Give an expression for the power being generated as a function of time.

d State the mean power being generated.

4 **a** State what is meant by the term *root-mean-square value*, I_{RMS}, of a current, I.

b How is the RMS current, I_{RMS}, related to the peak current, I_0?

c In the UK, the RMS voltage of the mains supply is 240 V. Calculate the peak voltage.

5 In a simple dynamo on a child's bicycle, the peak voltage induced is 5.0 V and the peak current flowing is 600 mA. Calculate the average power dissipated by the dynamo.

6 An ac source of peak voltage 18 V is connected to a small device with a resistance of 12 Ω. Calculate the:

a RMS voltage of the source

b average power dissipated in the circuit.

7 **a** Draw a circuit diagram for a transformer.

b What kind of current is supplied to the primary coil?

c Explain why the core of the transformer is made of iron.

d Explain why the iron core is laminated.

e Outline how the transformer is able to change the voltage across the primary coil into a different voltage across the secondary coil.

8 **a** Explain what is meant by a *step-up transformer*.

b Explain what is meant by a *step-down transformer*.

c Explain what is meant by the term *ideal*, when applied to a transformer.

d Suggest why a transformer might have an equal number of turns on the primary coil as on the secondary coil.

9 An ideal transformer has 360 turns on the primary coil and 45 turns on the secondary coil. The primary coil is supplied with an RMS alternating voltage of 110 V.

a Is the transformer a step-up or a step-down transformer?

b Calculate the voltage across the secondary coil.

c Suggest a possible use for the transformer in your home.

10 An ideal transformer is used on the output of a small coal-fired power station to step-up the voltage from 2 kV to 400 kV.

    a The primary coil of the transformer has 250 turns. How many turns are there on the secondary coil?

    b The current in the primary coil is 150 A. Calculate the:

       i power being generated by the power station

      ii current in the secondary coil.

11 A step-down transformer used in a mobile phone charger is 85% efficient. The supply voltage is 240 V. The power rating of the charger is 20 W. The turns ratio of the transformer is $\dfrac{N_s}{N_p} = 0.05$.

    a Calculate the current in the:

       i primary coil

      ii secondary coil.

    b The mobile phone charges at a constant rate. How much charge will be added in 10 minutes?

12 Explain why power stations use a step-up transformer at the output of the generators to supply the transmission lines with a voltage of about 400 kV.

13 In order to 'convert' an ac supply into a dc supply, it is necessary to rectify the current. This can be done with a half- or full-wave rectifier.

    a Outline what a half-wave rectifier does to an alternating current.

    b Outline what a full-wave rectifier does to an alternating current.

14 **a** Outline the function of a diode in an electrical circuit.

    b Explain what is meant by the term *forward biased* when applied to a circuit containing a diode.

    c Sketch a circuit diagram of an electrical circuit containing a dc power supply, a resistor and a diode in forward bias.

15 Figure 11.8 shows a half-wave rectifier circuit attached to the output of a transformer. There are two voltmeters, V_1 and V_2 in the circuit.

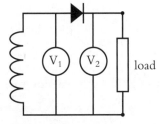

Figure 11.8

    a Sketch a graph to show how the voltage measured by V_1 changes with time.

    b Sketch another graph, with the same time axis, to show how the voltage measured by V_2 varies with time.

    c Why is this circuit called a half-wave rectifier?

16 The output from a half-wave rectifier does not produce a regular voltage (or current). If a device using direct current is attached to a half-wave rectifier, the output from the rectifier needs to be smoothed.

a Add to Figure 11.9 to show how a half-wave rectifier may be adapted to smooth its output.

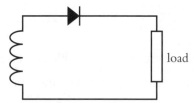

Figure 11.9

b Sketch a diagram to show how the output of the smoothing circuit compares to the output of the half-wave rectifier.

c Explain why the time constant of the smoothing circuit must be longer than half the time period of the alternating voltage from the secondary coil of the transformer.

17 a Figure 11.10 shows a circuit diagram for a full-wave rectifier circuit. Explain how this circuit is able to provide a better rectified current than a half-wave rectifier. (Some parts of the circuit have been labelled to help your explanation.)

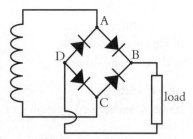

Figure 11.10

b Sketch a graph to show how the output from the full-wave rectifier varies with time.

c i Add to Figure 11.10 to show how the output from the full-wave rectifier can be smoothed.

ii Sketch a new graph of the smoothed output from the full-wave rectifier.

Exercise 11.3 – Capacitance

1 Figure 11.11 shows a capacitor in series with an emf supply of negligible internal resistance and a switch.

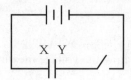

Figure 11.11

a What will happen to capacitor plate X when the switch is closed?
b What will happen to capacitor plate Y when the switch is closed?
c Some people say that a capacitor stores charge. Do you agree?
d What does a charged capacitor store?

2   a Is the material between the two plates of a capacitor an insulator or a conductor? Explain your answer.
     b If the material between the two plates, called the dielectric, has a large value of permittivity, will it help or hinder the build-up of charge on the plates? Explain your answer.
     c In fact, the amount of charge that can build up on each plate is proportional to the permittivity of the dielectric between the two plates. On what three other factors does the amount of charge on each plate depend?
     d Write an equation for how much charge can build up on each plate.
     e If the capacitance, C, is defined as the charge on each plate per unit voltage between the two plates, write an equation for the capacitance of the parallel plate capacitor.

3   An air-cored parallel plate capacitor, whose plates have an area of 5 cm × 1 cm and are 1 mm apart, is connected in a circuit with an emf supply of 12 V. Calculate the capacitance of the capacitor.

4   Commercial capacitors are small. Outline, with reference to your equation for the capacitance of a capacitor, three ways in which a commercial capacitor can have a large capacitance but only be small in size.

5   An industrial capacitor used to power a high power laser has a capacitance of 0.5 F. The dielectric between the plates is ceramic ($\varepsilon_r = 1.5 \times 10^4$). They are 1.0 cm apart. Determine the area of overlap of the two plates.

6   How does the capacitance of a capacitor vary with the:
     a separation, d, of the capacitor's plates
     b area, A, of overlap of the two plates?

7   Figure 11.12 shows two identical parallel plate capacitors in series with a battery and a switch. The battery has negligible internal resistance.

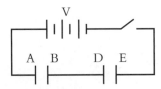

Figure 11.12

     a When the switch is closed:
        i   what happens to plate A?
        ii   what happens to plate B?
        iii where do the electrons from plate D go?
        iv   what happens to plate D?
        v   what happens to plate E?
     b If each plate has a charge of magnitude Q, what is the effective capacitance of the two capacitors in series?
     c What is the voltage across each of the capacitors?
     d What is the capacitance of one of the capacitors?
     e Suggest how the capacitance of two capacitors in series is related to the individual capacitance of one of the two capacitors.

8 What is the combined capacitance of a 4.0 μF and a 6.0 μF capacitor connected in series?

9 An 8 μF capacitor is in series with a 4 μF capacitor and a 6.0 V emf source with negligible internal resistance. Calculate the:
a combined capacitance of the two capacitors
b charge on each of the plates of the two capacitors
c voltage across each of the capacitors.

10 A 60 μF capacitor is in series with a 30 μF capacitor and a 12 V emf source. Determine the voltage across the 60 μF capacitor.

11 Figure 11.13 shows two identical 5 μF capacitors in parallel with a switch and a 6.0 V emf source with negligible internal resistance.

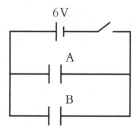

Figure 11.13

a What will the voltage across capacitor A be when the switch is closed?
b How much charge will build up on each of the plates of capacitor A?
c Since the same thing must be happening to capacitor B, what is the capacitance of the two capacitors in parallel?
d Write an equation for the combined capacitance of two capacitors, C_1 and C_2.

12 Figure 11.14 shows three capacitors in a circuit with a 12 V supply.

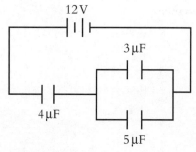

Figure 11.14

Determine the:
a voltage across the 3 μF capacitor
b charge on the plates of the 3 μF capacitor
c energy stored in the 3 μF capacitor.

13 A 220 µF capacitor is charged by a 6.0 V cell.
  a Calculate how much:
     i   charge has flowed
     ii energy has been lost from the cell
     iii energy has been stored by the capacitor.
  b How do you account for the difference between your answers to parts **a ii** and **a iii**?

14 Figure 11.15 shows how the current in an RC circuit varies with time when the
   circuit is connected to a 6.0 V emf source with negligible internal resistance.

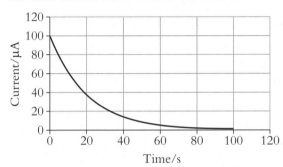

Figure 11.15

  a Use the graph to find the time constant, τ, of the RC circuit.
  b Show that the capacitance of the capacitor is 330 µF.
  c What feature of the graph can be used to determine the charge on the plates of
     the capacitor?

15 The equation for the current flowing in an RC circuit when a capacitor is charging is:

   $I = I_0 \, e^{-\frac{t}{RC}}$

  a What will the current be when t = RC?
  b When the current has fallen to less than 1% of I_0, the capacitor is considered fully
     charged. How much time must elapse for this to occur?
  c Sketch a graph of I against t.
  d Sketch a graph of how the charge, Q, on the capacitor plates varies with t.
  e State the equation for Q against t.

16 A 470 µF capacitor is connected to a 12 V emf supply until it is fully charged. It then
   discharges through a 22 kΩ resistor. Calculate the charge on the plates of the:
  a fully charged capacitor
  b capacitor after
     i   10.34 s
     ii 20.68 s
     iii 15.0 s.

? Exam-style questions

1 **Which of the following situations will *not* produce an induced emf?**
   A A coil of wire in which an alternating current is flowing.
   B A single wire in which an alternating current is flowing.
   C A coil of wire in a circuit with a battery that is switched on.
   D A coil of wire in a circuit with a constant current flowing.

2 **In an ac generator, a coil of N turns is rotated in a magnetic field of strength, B, at an angular frequency, ω, to produce a peak voltage, V. If the coil's turns are changed to $2N$, the magnetic field strength is changed to $2B$ and the angular frequency is changed to 2ω, what will the peak voltage be?**
   A $\dfrac{V}{4}$
   B V
   C $4V$
   D $8V$

3 **Which of the following combinations is correct for a step-down transformer (note: voltage ratio is $\dfrac{\text{primary voltage}}{\text{secondary voltage}}$ and current ratio is $\dfrac{\text{primary current}}{\text{secondary current}}$)?**
   A Voltage ratio = < 1; Current ratio = < 1
   B Voltage ratio = < 1; Current ratio = > 1
   C Voltage ratio = > 1; Current ratio = < 1
   D Voltage ratio = > 1; Current ratio = > 1

4 **How is the time constant, τ, of an RC circuit best described?**
   A The time it takes for the current in the circuit to halve.
   B The time it takes for the current in the circuit to fall to 37% of its initial value.
   C Half the time it takes for the current in the circuit to fall to zero.
   D The total time it takes for the current in a circuit to fall to zero.

5 **Which of the following units are equivalent to 1 farad?**
   A 1 joule per coulomb
   B 1 amp per volt
   C 1 amp-second per volt
   D 1 volt per coulomb

6   Figure 11.16 shows how the flux associated with a coil of wire of 200 turns varies with time.

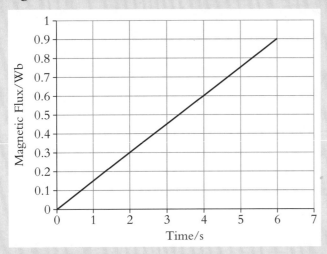

Figure 11.16

Use the graph to calculate the induced emf in the coil. **[3]**

7   Figure 11.17 shows a magnet falling through a coil of wire attached to an oscilloscope, and the resulting oscilloscope trace.

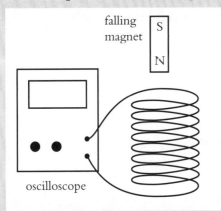 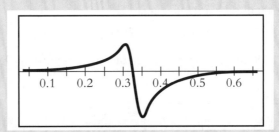

Figure 11.17

a   Explain why the trace shows an increasing voltage from 0 to 0.3 s. **[2]**

b   Explain why the trace shows a voltage that is negative from 0.35 to 0.6 s. **[1]**

c   Explain why the maximum negative voltage is greater than the maximum positive voltage. **[1]**

d   The coil is replaced with another coil of similar dimensions but twice the number of turns. The same magnet is dropped. What would you see on the oscilloscope trace? **[2]**

8   Figure 11.18 shows how the magnetic flux through a coil of 500 turns varies in time.

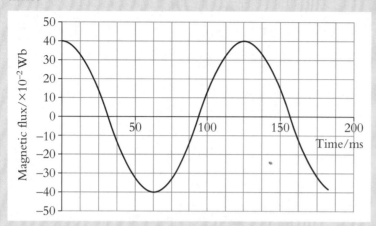

Figure 11.18

a State the maximum value of the magnetic flux linkage with the coil. **[1]**

b Show on the graph, by labelling with a M, a time when the induced emf is a maximum. **[1]**

c Show on the graph, by labelling with an O, a time when the induced emf is zero. **[1]**

d Use the graph to determine the maximum induced emf in the coil. **[3]**

9   **An induced emf is generated by rotating a coil in a magnetic field. State the effect on the induced emf of:**

a having a stronger magnetic field strength **[1]**

b having more turns on the coil **[1]**

c having a coil with a smaller area **[1]**

d rotating the coil at a larger angular frequency. **[1]**

10 **Figure 11.19 shows three capacitors in a circuit with a 6 V supply.**

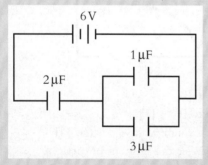

Figure 11.19

Determine the:

a voltage across the 2 μF capacitor

b charge on each of the plates of the 2 μF capacitor **[1]**

c energy stored by the 2 μF capacitor. **[2]**

11 Figure 11.20 shows how the magnitude of the charge on each of the plates of a capacitor varies with the voltage across the plates.

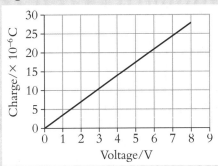

Figure 11.20

a Explain how this graph shows that $Q = CV$. **[2]**
b Use the graph to find the capacitance of the capacitor. **[2]**
c Use the graph to determine how much energy has been stored by the capacitor when connected to a 4 V supply. **[2]**

12 Figure 11.21 shows how the charge on a capacitor varies with time when it is discharged through a resistance of 100 kΩ.

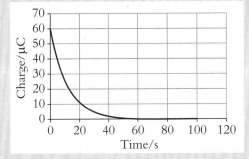

Figure 11.21

a Use the graph to determine the initial current flowing in the circuit. **[2]**
b Determine the voltage across the fully charged capacitor. **[1]**
c Calculate the capacitance of the capacitor. **[1]**
d Show that the time constant for the circuit is 12 s. **[2]**

13 Figure 11.22 shows how the voltage across a charged capacitor varies with time whilst the capacitor is discharging.

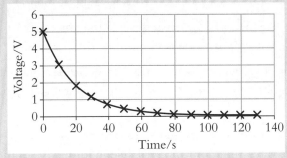

Figure 11.22

a Use data from the graph to show that the voltage varies exponentially with time. **[3]**
b Use the graph to show that the time constant, τ, of the circuit is 20 s. **[2]**

12 Quantum and nuclear physics

Chapter outline

In this chapter, you will:

- Describe the main features of the photoelectric effect experiment, understand that the photoelectric effect provides experimental evidence for the particle nature of light, and understand the concept of a photon and be able to solve problems involving the photoelectric effect both graphically and algebraically.
- Understand what a de Broglie wavelength is and be able to discuss the experimental evidence for matter waves.
- Describe an experiment to show the wave nature of electrons.
- Understand and be able to solve problems involving pair production and annihilation.
- Understand the quantisation of angular momentum and the Bohr model for a hydrogen atom and be able to outline the main features of a wave function to describe matter.
- Use the two forms of Heisenberg's uncertainty principle and be able to solve problems involving order of magnitude estimates.
- Describe qualitatively the concept of quantum tunnelling and the factors that affect the probability of this phenomenon.
- Describe a scattering experiment and the minimum in the scattered intensity in terms of the de Broglie wavelength of the diffracted particles and describe the deviation from Rutherford scattering in high energy interactions.
- Understand that nuclei also exist in discrete energy levels, and be able to describe experimental evidence for nuclear energy levels, solve problems involving radioactive decay, decay constants and half-lives for any time intervals.
- Describe methods for determining short and long half-lives of radioactive isotopes.

KEY TERMS

Work function, φ: The minimum amount of energy required by an electron to escape a metal surface.

Planck constant, h: A fundamental constant, equal to the energy of a quantum of electromagnetic radiation divided by its frequency, with a value of 6.63×10^{-34} J s

De Broglie wavelength: The wavelength, λ, that describes the wave-like behaviour of a particle; $\lambda = \dfrac{h}{p}$, where p is the momentum of the particle.

Schrödinger's wave function, Ψ: A wave function used to describe a particle, in which the square of its amplitude is proportional to the probability per unit volume of finding the particle.

The Copenhagen interpretation of Schrödinger's wave function: A way of considering that the complex wave function for a particle, with many solutions, becomes a simple single solution when the particle is observed. This is best thought of as: if you observe a particle to be behaving like a wave/particle then it is a wave/particle.

Heisenberg's uncertainty principle: The idea that it is not possible to know with perfect precision all aspects of a particle's characteristics. This takes two forms: $\Delta x \Delta p \geq \dfrac{h}{4\pi}$ and $\Delta E \Delta t \geq \dfrac{h}{4\pi}$

Pair production: The idea that in some circumstances a photon of sufficient energy can be transformed into a particle–anti-particle pair.

Annihilation: The idea that when a particle and its anti-particle interact they will be transformed into electromagnetic energy in the form of two photons. (Two photons are necessary to obey the law of conservation of momentum.)

Quantum tunnelling: A phenomenon in quantum mechanics that uses the idea of a particle's wave function having a non-zero amplitude everywhere to allow the particle to exist in a situation in which classically it has insufficient energy to exist. In effect, the particle seems to 'borrow' energy from its surroundings, make the transition from one situation to another and then 'give back' the energy.

Decay constant, λ: The probability that a given nucleus will decay within a time of one second. It is related to the half-life, $t_{\frac{1}{2}}$ by the equation $\lambda = \dfrac{\ln(2)}{t_{\frac{1}{2}}}$.

Exercise 12.1 – The interaction of matter with radiation

1   Calculate the energy of the following photons, giving your answers in joules and electronvolts.
    a   A radio wave photon of wavelength 2.5 m.
    b   An infrared photon of wavelength 6.0 μm.
    c   A visible photon of wavelength 623 nm.
    d   An X-ray photon of wavelength 1.5×10^{-10} m.

2   A 5 mW laser emits light of wavelength 630 nm. Calculate the:
    a   energy of a photon of light at this wavelength
    b   number of photons emitted by the laser in one second.

3   Albert Einstein was awarded the Nobel Prize for physics for his pioneering work on the photoelectric effect.
    a   Outline what Einstein showed using the photoelectric effect.
    b   Why was this work so pioneering?
    c   Suggest why the photoelectric effect is such an important topic in physics.

4   Figure 12.1 shows a negatively charged metal plate attached to a gold-leaf
    electroscope. The metal plate can be illuminated by different wavelengths of light
    from a variable light source above it.

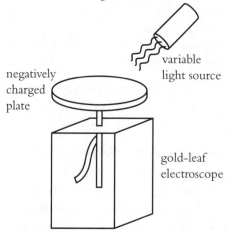

Figure 12.1

a   When the metal plate is illuminated with light of wavelength 650 nm, nothing
    happens to the angle of the gold leaf of the electroscope – even when illuminated
    for a long time.
    i   Explain this observation.
    ii How does this observation suggest that light is not behaving like a wave?
b   When the metal plate is illuminated with light of wavelength 450 nm, the angle of
    the gold leaf on the electroscope decreases immediately.
    i   Explain this observation.
    ii How does this observation suggest that light is behaving like a stream of
        particles?

5   A negatively charged zinc plate is attached to a coulombmeter. The zinc plate is
    illuminated with light of wavelength 440 nm. The coulombmeter shows a decrease in
    the amount of charge on the zinc plate.
    a   What would you expect the coulombmeter to show if the intensity of the
        illuminating light was increased?
    b   Explain your answer to part **a** in terms of light as a stream of discrete particles of
        energy.
    c   Explain what effect, if any, the increase in intensity of the illuminating light will
        have on the maximum amount of kinetic energy of the photoelectrons.

6   The work function for a particular metal surface is 3.2 eV.
    a   Calculate the threshold frequency for the metal surface.
    b   What is the longest wavelength of light that could produce photoelectrons from
        this metal surface?
    c   The metal surface is illuminated with UV light of wavelength 6.5×10^{-8} m.
        Calculate the maximum kinetic energy of a photoelectron.

7   Photoelectrons were emitted from the surface of potassium. They travelled
    at 4.5×10^5 m s^{-1}. The work function of the potassium surface was 1.5 eV.
    Determine the wavelength of the incident light on the potassium surface.
    (Mass of an electron = 9.1×10^{-31} kg.)

8 The work function of a copper surface is 4.2 eV.

   a Determine the threshold frequency for the copper surface.

   b Which part of the electromagnetic spectrum will contain radiation that is just about capable of producing photoelectrons from a copper surface?

   c Calculate the maximum speed at which a photoelectron can leave the copper surface if it is illuminated with radiation of frequency 2.2×10^{15} Hz.

9 Einstein's photoelectric effect equation is often written as: $\mathrm{KE_{max}} = hf - \varphi$

   a State what each of the terms in the equation represent.

   b Sketch a graph of $\mathrm{KE_{max}}$ (y-axis) against f (x-axis).

   c What information does the gradient of your graph provide?

   d Explain the significance of the intercept on the x-axis.

10 Figure 12.2 shows how the maximum kinetic energy of a photoelectron from a metal surface varies with the frequency of the illuminating radiation.

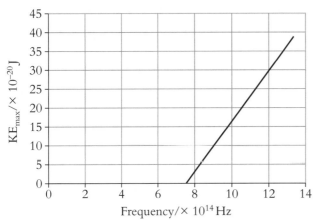

Figure 12.2

   a Use the graph to determine:

     i the work function for the metal surface

     ii a value for Planck's constant.

   b Sketch the relationship you would expect for the maximum kinetic energy of photoelectrons from a metal surface with a larger work function.

11 An electron is accelerated through a potential difference of V volts.

   a How much kinetic energy will the electron gain?

   b Show that the kinetic energy of the electron can be expressed as $\dfrac{p^2}{2m}$, where p is the momentum of the electron and m is the electron's mass.

   c Show that the momentum of the electron can be expressed as $\sqrt{2meV}$.

12 By the 1920s, Einstein's photoelectric effect was well established. It was accepted that light (which had once been recognised only as a wave) could behave like a stream of particles. Outline what de Broglie proposed in his PhD thesis of 1923.

13 Outline Davisson and Germer's experiment that supported de Broglie's idea that particles could exhibit wave-like properties.

14 a Calculate the effective wavelength of:
     i   an electron travelling at 2.0×10^7 m s^{-1} ($m_e = 9.1 \times 10^{-31}$ kg)
     ii a 160 g cricket ball travelling at 140 km h^{-1}
     iii a 70 kg human walking at 1.0 m s^{-1}.
    b i Which of the three examples in part **a** is most likely to behave like a wave?
      ii How would a human have to move to behave like a wave? How does this help
         explain why humans behave like particles, not waves?

15 a Calculate the effective wavelength of an electron that has been accelerated
       through a potential difference of:
     i   400 V
     ii 100 V
    b Would the electrons in part **a** show significant signs of diffraction by a crystal
       lattice with atoms spaced 3.0×10^{-10} m apart?

16 Figure 12.3 is a Feynman diagram.

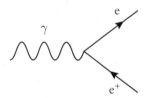

Figure 12.3

    a What quantum process is occurring in Figure 12.3?
    b Show that this process obeys the conservation laws of charge, baryon number,
       lepton number and strangeness.
    c i What must the minimum energy of the photon be?
      ii What will the 'temperature' of the photon be?

17 The mass of a proton is 938 MeVc^{-2}.
    a Calculate the minimum energy, in joules, of a gamma ray photon that will be able
       to produce a proton–anti-proton pair.
    b i Why is it most likely that a proton–anti-proton pair will only be produced by a
         gamma ray photon with significantly more energy than your answer to part **a**?
      ii What happens to the extra energy that the photon had if a proton–anti-proton
         pair is produced?

18 Figure 12.4 shows a Feynman diagram involving the interaction of a proton and an
    anti-proton.

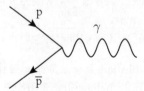

Figure 12.4

    a What is this process called?
    b Calculate the:
     i   energy of the photon
     ii wavelength of the photon.
    c In which part of the electromagnetic spectrum does this photon belong?

19 According to de Broglie, electrons in atoms should exhibit wave properties. And according to classical electrodynamics, charged particles that are accelerating must emit electromagnetic radiation. Electrons in orbits of atoms do not emit electromagnetic radiation unless they move from a higher energy level to a lower energy level.

    a If the electron exists as a wave, what kind of wave must it be for it not to be emitting any electromagnetic radiation?

    b If this electron wave takes up the length that the circumference of the orbit provides, write an expression for the wavelength of the wave as a function of the radius of the orbit.

    c For the $n = 1$ orbit, the wave exists in its fundamental state (as one complete wave). For the $n = 2$ orbit, the wave exists as two complete waves, and so on. Write an expression for the wavelength of the electron wave as a function of its orbital radius.

    d Using de Broglie's equation, $\lambda = \dfrac{h}{p}$, show that the angular momentum of the electron is quantised and given by the equation $mvr_n = \dfrac{nh}{2\pi}$, where r_n is the radius of the nth energy level.

20 This question is about how much energy an electron can have in a hydrogen atom.

    a By equating the centripetal force and the electrical force acting on an orbiting electron in a hydrogen atom, show that the kinetic energy of an electron in a hydrogen atom is given by $KE = \dfrac{ke^2}{2r}$.

    b Use Bohr's condition of the angular momentum of the electron, $mvr = \dfrac{nh}{2\pi}$, to show that the radius of the orbit of an electron in a hydrogen atom is quantised and given by $r = \dfrac{h^2 n^2}{4\pi^2 ke^2 m}$.

    c The total energy of the electron in the hydrogen atom is given by the sum of its kinetic energy and its electrical energy.

        i Show that $E_{\text{total}} = -\dfrac{ke^2}{2r}$.

        ii Hence show that E_{total} is quantised and given by $E_{\text{total}} = -\dfrac{2\pi^2 e^4 mk^2}{h^2 n^2}$.

        iii For $n = 1$, calculate the total energy of the electron in the hydrogen atom. Give your answer in electronvolts. (Use these values for the constants: $m = 9.109 \times 10^{-31}$ kg, $e = 1.602 \times 10^{-19}$ C, $k = 8.988 \times 10^9$ N m^2 C^{-2}, $h = 6.626 \times 10^{-34}$ J s.)

21 Erwin Schrödinger advanced the work of de Broglie by introducing the concept of a wave function, Ψ, to help describe how particles could exhibit wave properties.

a Explain the significance of Ψ^2.

b Figure 12.5 shows how the function Ψ^2 varies with distance from the nucleus, r, for the energy level $n = 1$.

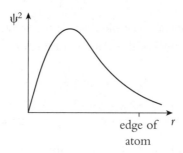

Figure 12.5

i With reference to Figure 12.5, suggest the most likely place to find the electron in a hydrogen atom.

ii How does Figure 12.5 show that it is possible, but not very likely, for the electron to exist outside the atom?

22 a Outline what Heisenberg said about how the uncertainty in the momentum of a particle was related to the uncertainty of its position in space.

b Figure 12.6 shows the Schrödinger wave function, Ψ, for a fast-moving free electron.

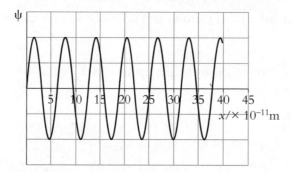

Figure 12.6

i Use Figure 12.6 to determine the wavelength of the free electron.

ii Use de Broglie's equation to determine the momentum, p, of the electron.

iii The value you should have calculated has no uncertainty; it is absolute. What does Heisenberg's uncertainty principle suggest is the uncertainty in its position in space?

iv What does Heisenberg's uncertainty suggest is the *actual* location of the free electron?

c Outline Heisenberg's uncertainty principle as applied to the uncertainty in the energy of a particle and the uncertainty in time for which it can exist.

d An electron in the ground state of a hydrogen atom might be able to exist outside the atom for a short time.

i Explain what evidence you have seen to support this statement.

ii Use Heisenberg's uncertainty principle to find how long the electron could exist outside the hydrogen atom.

iii Suggest and explain whether it would be possible to observe the electron existing outside the hydrogen atom.

23 Consider an electron in the ground state of a hydrogen atom.

   a How much energy does the electron need to gain for it to jump up to the next energy level?

   b If the electron were to gain this amount of energy, use Heisenberg's uncertainty principle to show that it can exist in the higher energy level for 3.2×10^{-17} s.

24 Consider a proton colliding with another proton in the core of the Sun to produce energy by thermonuclear fusion.

   a The temperature of the Sun's core is about 1.0×10^{7} K. Calculate the kinetic energy of a proton at this temperature.

   b For the proton to collide it must be about 3×10^{-15} m (3 fm) from the other proton. Calculate the electrical potential energy that the proton would have at this distance from the other proton.

   c By what factor is the kinetic energy of the proton smaller than the electrical potential energy it requires to approach the other proton to within 3 fm?

   d Does classical mechanics allow for the proton to fuse with the other proton?

   e The Sun produces energy – this is clear evidence that protons must be able to approach each other to within 3 fm. Consider the proton's Schrödinger wave function and suggest how the proton can exist beyond the energy barrier that the electrical potential energy provides.

   f What is this quantum mechanical process called?

   g Give two examples of this process (when applied to electrons) being used in everyday life.

25 Consider a particle and the possibility of quantum tunnelling past an energy barrier.

   a Suggest how the magnitude of the probability density function, Ψ^2, varies through the energy barrier with:

      i magnitude of the energy barrier, ΔE

      ii the width of the energy barrier, d

      iii the mass of the particle, m.

   b Sketch a graph to show how the probability of finding a particle varies with distance through an energy barrier.

Exercise 12.2 – Nuclear physics

1   **a**   Consider a cube of length, x, and mass, m. Write an expression for the cube's:

        i   volume

        ii   density.

   b   Consider a cube made from eight smaller cubes, each of length, x, and mass, m. Write an expression for the cube's:

        i   volume

        ii   length

        iii density.

   c   Consider a cube made from 27 smaller cubes, each of length, x, and mass, m. Write an expression for the cube's:

        i   volume

        ii   length

        iii density.

   d   Consider a cube made from A smaller cubes, each of length, x, and mass, m. Write an expression for the cube's:

        i   volume

        ii   length

        iii density.

   e   How does the:

        i   length of the cube vary with the number of smaller cubes from which it is made?

        ii   density of the cube vary with the number of smaller cubes from which it is made?

2   The radius of a proton or a neutron is 1.2×10^{-15} m (the *Fermi radius*).

   a   If the mass of a nucleon is 1.7×10^{-27} kg, calculate the:

        i   radius of a $^{12}_{6}\text{C}$ nucleus

        ii   density of a $^{12}_{6}\text{C}$ nucleus

        iii radius of a $^{235}_{92}\text{U}$ nucleus

        iv density of a $^{235}_{92}\text{U}$ nucleus.

   b   What do you observe about the density of these different atomic nuclei?

3   In Rutherford, Geiger and Marsden's famous experiment, alpha particles were fired at a thin piece of gold foil. The deflections of the alpha particles were carefully observed and recorded.

   a   What conclusions were made from the following observations?

        i   Most of the alpha particles passed straight through the piece of gold foil undeflected.

        ii   A small number of alpha particles were deflected through large angles.

        iii A very small number of alpha particles were deflected backwards.

   b   Rutherford used alpha particles of kinetic energy 7.7 MeV. The atomic number of gold is 79.

        i   Equate the alpha particle's kinetic energy with its electrical potential energy at its closest distance from the gold nucleus. Then, calculate the closest distance that an alpha particle could get to the gold nucleus. (Assume that, during the interaction, the gold nucleus does not move.)

        ii   Calculate the radius of the nucleus of the gold atoms.

        iii Is the closest approach distance a reasonable estimation of the radius of a gold nucleus?

4 Later observations of scattering, using alpha particles with higher kinetic energies, did not agree with Rutherford's experimental results.

  a Which of the four fundamental forces was responsible for the disagreement between the two sets of results?

  b Outline what was happening to the higher energy alpha particles to make the observations different.

5 In order to make more detailed observations of nuclei, it was necessary to scatter high energy electrons from nuclei, rather than alpha particles.

  a Suggest a reason why using electrons will not show the kind of deviations from expected scattering theory that the alpha particles had shown.

  b Calculate the radius of a nucleus of a gold atom.

  c A beam of electrons of de Broglie wavelength 3.1×10^{-15} m is directed at a gold nucleus. Calculate the angle at which a minimum will be formed in the electron diffraction pattern.

  d When electrons have a de Broglie wavelength that is similar in size to the size of a nucleus, their mass becomes larger than it usually is. One suggestion to overcome this was to use electrons of much lower kinetic energy. Suggest, and explain, whether this suggestion would produce usable diffraction patterns.

6 **a** Outline the observational evidence for nuclei to exist in discrete energy levels.

  b This equation shows the alpha decay of a bismuth nucleus into a thallium nucleus:

   $$^{212}_{83}\text{Bi} \rightarrow {}^{208}_{81}\text{Tl} + {}^{4}_{2}\alpha$$

   The masses of the Bi, Tl and α particles are, respectively, 211.946 u, 207.937 u and 4.0015 u.

   Calculate the maximum kinetic of the alpha particle.

  c Explain why the alpha particle is likely to have less kinetic energy than this.

7 Figure 12.7 shows some of the nuclear energy levels for neptunium-237.

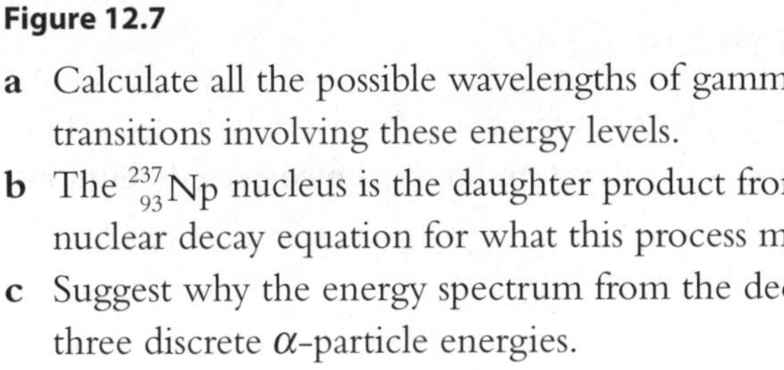

102 keV
above E_0

59 keV
above E_0

E_0
ground state

Figure 12.7

  a Calculate all the possible wavelengths of gamma rays that can be emitted from transitions involving these energy levels.

  b The $^{237}_{93}\text{Np}$ nucleus is the daughter product from an α-decay process. Write a nuclear decay equation for what this process must be.

  c Suggest why the energy spectrum from the decay of the parent nucleus consists of three discrete α-particle energies.

8 The nuclide $^{90}_{38}Sr$ is unstable and decays by β^- emission.

a Write a nuclear decay equation for the decay of $^{90}_{38}Sr$.

b Explain why the kinetic energy of the β^- particle can vary from zero up to a maximum value.

c How do conservation laws support the idea that there must be another particle emitted with the β^- particle?

9 The nuclide $^{64}_{29}Cu$ undergoes electron capture.

a Write a nuclear decay equation for the electron capture process involving $^{64}_{29}Cu$.

b How do conservation laws support the idea that there must be another particle emitted along with the daughter product?

10 A neutron is an unstable particle, which will undergo β^- decay whether the neutron is inside a nucleus or isolated from a nucleus. A proton is a stable particle that does not decay when it is isolated from a nucleus, but it is able to decay when it is inside a nucleus.

a Explain why the neutron decays whether it is inside a nucleus or not.

b Explain how a proton is able to decay only when it is inside a nucleus.

11 **a** Explain what is meant by the following terms.

i Half-life

ii Decay constant

iii Activity

b How is *decay constant* related to *half-life*?

c Calculate the decay constant of:

i $^{40}_{19}K$ (half-life = 1250 million years)

ii $^{13}_{7}N$ (half-life = 9.96 minutes)

iii $^{60}_{27}Co$ (half-life = 5.27 years).

12 The nuclide $^{24}_{11}Na$ is unstable and has a decay constant of $1.28 \times 10^{-5} \, s^{-1}$.

a Calculate the half-life of $^{24}_{11}Na$.

b As a fraction of its initial activity, what would the activity of a sample of $^{24}_{11}Na$ be after:

i 15 hours

ii 30 hours?

13 The isotope $^{137}_{55}Cs$ is used to treat malignant tumours. Its half-life is 28 years. Calculate the activity of 3.0 mg of freshly prepared $^{137}_{55}Cs$.

14 A sample of radioactive material is placed in front of a Geiger–Muller tube and its corrected count rate is 470 counts s^{-1}. After 20 minutes, the corrected count rate is 380 counts s^{-1}.

a Explain what is meant by *corrected count rate*.

b Determine the decay constant for the radioactive material.

c Determine the half-life of the radioactive material.

d Explain why this method of finding the half-life of a radioactive material is inappropriate for a radioactive substance that has a half-life of several million years.

15 Outline how to determine the half-life of a pure radioactive material for which there is no observable change in the count rate measured by a GM tube.

16 $^{14}_{6}C$ is an isotope of carbon that decays by β^- emission; all organic material contains small traces of $^{14}_{6}C$. The half-life of $^{14}_{6}C$ is 5730 years. Radiocarbon dating is a method that uses this data to determine the age of an object containing organic material. Scientists used radiocarbon dating to determine the amount of $^{14}_{6}C$ in a historic artefact. They found it was 92% of that in living tissue. How old is the artefact?

? Exam-style questions

1 **Which of the following is the best estimate of the order of magnitude of a typical work function of a metal surface?**
A 10^{-21} J
B 10^{-19} J
C 10^{-17} J
D 10^{-13} J

2 **Which of the following statements about the stopping voltage is correct?**
A The stopping voltage is independent of the intensity of the illuminating radiation.
B The stopping voltage is inversely proportional to the intensity of the illuminating radiation.
C The stopping voltage is proportional to the intensity of the illuminating radiation.
D The stopping voltage is proportional to the square of the illuminating radiation.

3 **Aidan has a mass of 80 kg and walks along at a speed of 1.5 m s^{-1}. Jennifer has a mass of 60 kg and jogs at a speed of 2.0 m s^{-1}. What is the ratio of their de Broglie wavelengths, $\dfrac{\lambda_{\text{Aidan}}}{\lambda_{\text{Jennifer}}}$?**
A 0.75
B 1.00
C 1.25
D 1.33

4 **Which of the following statements is not one of the three assumptions of the Bohr model of the atom?**
A Electrons exist in atoms in discrete energy levels.
B Electrons exist in atoms as particles that orbit around the nucleus.
C Electrons may move from one energy level to another by emitting or absorbing electromagnetic radiation.
D The angular momentum of electrons in atoms is quantised.

5 **Complete this sentence: The density of a nucleus is …**
A proportional to A, the number of nucleons present.
B proportional to A^3, the cube of the number of nucleons present.
C proportional to $A^{1/3}$, the cube-root of the number of nucleons present.
D independent of the number of nucleons present.

6 **a** Explain what is meant by *work function for a metal*.

b Explain what is meant by *threshold frequency for a metal surface*.

c A metal surface is illuminated with light of wavelength 450 nm. The work function of the metal is 1.5 eV. Determine the maximum kinetic energy of the electrons emitted from the metal surface.

d If the illuminating power in part **c** is 3W and one electron is emitted from the metal surface for every eight incident photons, calculate the current produced by the incident radiation.

7 **Figure 12.8 shows a pair of zinc electrodes attached to a variable power supply and a sensitive ammeter. The electrodes each have a work function of 4.25 eV. One of the electrodes is illuminated with UV light of wavelength 260 nm. The ammeter shows a current flowing in the circuit.**

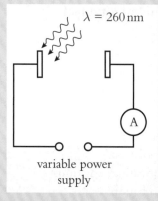

Figure 12.8

a Calculate the maximum kinetic energy of the photoelectrons from the illuminated electrode. **[2]**

b The variable power supply is adjusted and the current falls to zero. Suggest which terminal on the power supply is negative. **[1]**

c Determine the minimum terminal voltage required to prevent a current from flowing. **[1]**

8 **Figure 12.9 below shows accelerated electrons passing through a thin piece of graphite crystal inside an evacuated tube.**

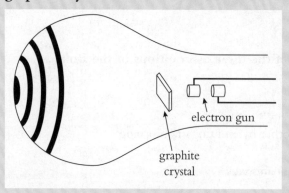

Figure 12.9

a Explain why the tube must be evacuated. **[1]**

b Explain how the pattern on the fluorescent screen of the tube provides evidence of the wave nature of electrons. **[2]**

c **i** The electrons from the electron gun have been accelerated through a potential difference of V. Use $KE = \dfrac{p^2}{2m}$ to write an expression for the momentum, p, of the electrons as a function of V. **[1]**

    ii Derive an expression for the de Broglie wavelength of the electrons. **[1]**

d The distance between the graphite crystal and the fluorescent screen is 20.0 cm. The electrons have been accelerated through a potential difference of 1.0 kV. If the radius of the third observed ring on the fluorescent screen is 3.5 cm, calculate the spacing of the carbon atoms in the graphite crystal. **[3]**

9 **Answer these questions by applying Heisenberg's uncertainty principle to a 70 kg athlete jumping over a 3 m high wall.**

  a Calculate how much gravitational potential energy the athlete must gain (the athlete's centre of mass is 1 m above the ground). **[1]**

  b Calculate the amount of time for which the athlete could gain this energy. **[2]**

  c Suggest why you cannot use a quantum mechanical argument to explain why the athlete can jump over the wall. **[2]**

10 **A sample of $^{241}_{95}$Am (an α-emitter) for use in school physics departments has an activity of 5 µCi. (1 Ci = 3.7×10^{10} Bq.) The half-life of $^{241}_{95}$Am is 433 years.**

  a Calculate the decay constant for $^{241}_{95}$Am. **[1]**

  b Determine the:

    i number of $^{241}_{95}$Am nuclei in the originally prepared sample **[2]**

    ii mass of $^{241}_{95}$Am in the originally prepared sample. **[2]**

  c Explain why there is not likely to be a Trading Standards issue for the samples of $^{241}_{95}$Am that are delivered to schools within a year of their preparation. **[2]**

11 **The isotope $^{99}_{43}$Tc is a gamma emitter with a half-life of 6.0 hours. A sample of 11 µg of $^{99}_{43}$Tc is placed 2 cm in front of a Geiger Muller tube, whose front window has an area of 1 cm^2.**

  a Calculate the decay constant for $^{99}_{43}$Tc. **[1]**

  b Determine the number of atoms of $^{99}_{43}$Tc in the sample. **[2]**

  c Hence determine the activity of the sample. **[2]**

Option A: Relativity

Chapter outline

In this chapter, you will:

- Understand the concept of a reference frame and use the Galilean transformation equations in two reference frames to determine whether the force on a moving charge, or current, is electric or magnetic in a given reference frame.
- Determine qualitatively the nature of a field as observed in different reference frames.
- Know the two postulates of special relativity, understand the concept of clock synchronisation and be able to use the Lorentz transformation equations to show how measurements of space and time can be converted in two different reference frames.
- Solve problems involving the addition of velocities, derive the time dilation and length contraction equations using the Lorentz transformation equations.
- Solve problems using the muon decay experiment as evidence of time dilation and length contraction.
- Using a spacetime (Minkowski) diagram, be able to represent an event as a point, represent the positions of a moving particle by a curve (the worldline), represent more than one inertial reference frame, and determine the angle between a worldline for a given speed and the time axis.
- Solve problems involving simultaneity and kinematics, and represent time dilation and length contraction.
- Recall, describe and resolve the twin paradox.
- **HL** Distinguish between total energy and rest energy, describe the laws of conservation of momentum and conservation of energy in special relativity and determine the potential difference necessary to accelerate a particle to a given speed or energy.
- **HL** Solve problems involving relativistic energy and momentum in particle interactions and decay events.
- **HL** Understand the concept of the equivalence principle and use the equivalence principle to explain light bending near a massive object and to explain gravitational time dilation.
- **HL** Understand the nature of gravitational red shift, describe the Pound–Rebka–Snider experiment and calculate gravitational frequency shifts.
- **HL** Understand the concept of a Schwarzschild black hole and be able to calculate its radius, be able to use the equation for gravitational time dilation near the event horizon of a black hole and apply the ideas of general relativity to the universe as a whole.

Galilean transformations: A set of equations that link together two frames of reference by their relative velocities; $x = x' + vt$, $x' = x - vt$, $u' = u - v$

Lorentz transformation: A factor that reconciles Maxwell's laws of electromagnetism for all inertial frames of reference; $\gamma = \dfrac{1}{\sqrt{1 - \dfrac{v^2}{c^2}}}$ such that $x' = \gamma(x - vt)$ and $t' = \gamma\left(t - \dfrac{v}{c^2}x\right)$.

Inverse Lorentz transformation: $x = \gamma(x' + vt')$ and $t = g\left(t' + \dfrac{v}{c^2}x'\right)$.

Spacetime interval, Δs: $\Delta s^2 = (c\Delta t)^2 - \Delta x^2$

HL **Relativistic momentum:** A way of ensuring that the conservation of momentum is obeyed by use of the Lorentz transformation; $p = \gamma m_0 v$.

HL **Energy–momentum equation:** $E^2 = (pc)^2 + (m_0 c^2)^2$.

HL **Schwarzschild radius and event horizon:** $R_S = \dfrac{2GM}{c^2}$ gives the radius of the event horizon – the radial distance at which the escape speed equals the speed of light.

Exercise A.1 – The beginnings of relativity

1   **a** State Newton's first law of motion.
   b Explain what is meant by *a frame of reference*.
   c Explain what is meant by *an inertial frame of reference*.

2   Pete and Jonathan are sitting on a bus travelling forwards at 15 m s^{-1}. Pete is 3 m in front of Jonathan. Pete throws a chocolate bar to Jonathan at a speed of 6 m s^{-1}. Ellie and Oscar saw Pete throw the chocolate bar: Ellie was sitting on the bus, and Oscar was standing on the road watching the bus pass by.
   a At what speed does Ellie see the chocolate bar travelling?
   b Does the bus's speed affect Ellie's observation of the chocolate bar's speed? Explain your answer.
   c At what speed does Oscar see the chocolate travelling?
   d Does the bus's speed affect Oscar's observation of the chocolate bar's speed? Explain your answer.
   e In Ellie's frame of reference, how far did the chocolate bar travel?
   f Show that, in Ellie's frame of reference, the time taken for the chocolate bar to complete its journey from Pete to Jonathan is 0.5 s.
   g Oscar also measures the time of the chocolate bar's journey as 0.5 s. How far did Oscar see the chocolate bar travel?
   h Have Ellie and Oscar used the same physics laws to find the distance, speed and time for the chocolate bar?
   i How was Newton able to explain why the laws of physics are the same for different frames of reference, even if two observers see the same event differently?
   j Write Einstein's first postulate of special relativity.

3 Use the Galilean transformations to solve the following examples.

 a A student standing by a two-lane road sees a truck travelling at 12 m s^{-1}. A car is travelling at 18 m s^{-1} in the same direction. Determine the velocity of the:

   i car as observed by the truck driver

   ii truck as observed by the car driver.

 b A nitrogen molecule moving vertically upwards at 500 m s^{-1} passes an oxygen molecule travelling vertically downwards at 438 m s^{-1}. Determine the velocity of the:

   i nitrogen molecule as observed by the oxygen molecule

   ii oxygen molecule as observed by the nitrogen molecule.

4 a Figure A.1 shows two electrons, e_1 and e_2, at rest relative to each other, and a stationary observer.

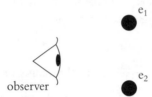

Figure A.1

   i What kind of force would an observer see between the two electrons?

   ii In which direction is this force on the electron e_1?

 b Figure A.2 shows two electrons, e_1 and e_2, and an observer all moving along at the same speed, v.

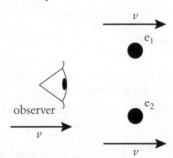

Figure A.2

   i Does the observer see the same kind of force between the two electrons as in part **a**?

   ii Is the force still in the same direction as it was in part **a**?

 c Explain your answers to part **b**.

 d Figure A.3 shows an electron, e_1, a small distance from a wire in which there is a current, I, flowing. e_1, the wire and the observer are all stationary.

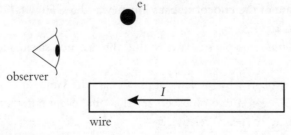

Figure A.3

i Explain why the wire is electrically neutral.
ii Explain why there is no electrical force on the electron, e_1.
iii What does the current in the wire create around the wire?
iv Explain why there is no magnetic force on the electron e_1

e Figure A.4 shows an electron, e_1, moving along with speed, v, parallel to the current-carrying wire. The observer and the wire are stationary.

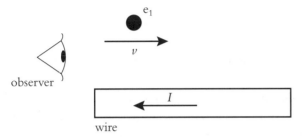

Figure A.4

i What kind of force does the observer see between the electron, e_1, and the wire?
ii Explain how this force is created.
iii In which direction does this force act on the electron e_1?

f Figure A.5 shows an observer, an electron, e_1, and electrons in a wire all moving with a speed, v.

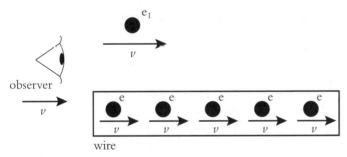

Figure A.5

i The current (moving electrons) in the wire will cause a magnetic field to occur around it. Explain why the observer does not see a magnetic force acting on e_1.
ii Einstein's first postulate of special relativity is that the laws of physics must be the same in all inertial frames of reference. So, if there is no magnetic force on the electron, e_1, then the force on e_1 must be electrical. What kind of charge must the wire have acquired for the force on e_1 to be electrical? (Remember which direction this force has to be in.)
iii Suggest how the wire can have acquired this extra charge.

5 Two protons, separated by a distance, d, are moving with the same velocity, v.

a In the frame of reference of the two protons, S, an observer sees both protons stationary relative to himself. The observer sees that there is a force between the two protons.

i What kind of force does the observer see between the two protons?
ii Write an expression for the magnitude of this force.
iii In which direction is this force?

b In the frame of reference of a stationary observer, S', an observer sees both protons moving.

    i Does the observer see an electrical force between the two protons?

    ii Write an expression for the magnitude of this force.

    iii In which direction is this force?

    iv Is it reasonable for the observer to think of the two protons as currents? Explain your answer.

    v There will be a magnetic force between these two 'currents'. In which direction will this magnetic force be?

c Do the observers in the frames of reference, S and S', seem to be observing the same thing? Explain your answer.

d According to Einstein's first postulate, the laws of physics must be the same for any observer in any frame of reference. This means that each observer, in S and S', must observe the event similarly. Suggest how it is possible for both observers to see the same thing.

6   Figure A.6 shows two long, parallel plates connected to a battery. When the battery is switched on, its effect propagates along the parallel plates at a speed v.

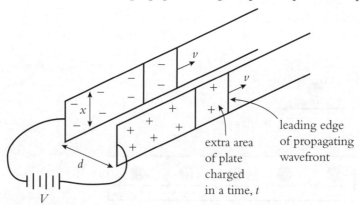

Figure A.6

Behind the leading edge of the propagating wavefront the plates are charged; the left-hand plate negatively and the right-hand plate positively.

a Explain why the right-hand plate becomes positively charged and the left-hand plate becomes negatively charged.

b In a time, t, how far will the leading edge of the propagating wavefront travel?

c If the height of the parallel plates is x, what new area of each plate becomes charged in a time, t?

d Give an expression for the charge density, σ, on the plates.

e The two parallel plates are a capacitor, so the electric field between the two plates is given by $E = \dfrac{\sigma}{\varepsilon_0}$. Derive an expression for E in terms of I, x and v.

f The two plates, each carrying a current, must also produce a magnetic field. If we consider the plates to be like a solenoid, then the magnetic field strength, B, is given by $B = \mu_0 \dfrac{I}{x}$. Derive an expression for B in terms of E.

g In a time, t, what is the extra area through which the magnetic field, B, acts?

h What is the rate of change of magnetic flux?

i   According to Faraday, the rate of change of magnetic flux equals the emf generated. This emf is the potential difference supplied by the battery, V. The electric field strength, E, is $E = \dfrac{V}{d}$.

Use your answer to part **h** derive an expression for E in terms of B.

j   Use your answers to parts **h** and **i** to derive an expression for v, which is independent of B and E.

k $\varepsilon_0 = 8.85 \times 10^{-12}$ C^2 N^{-1} m^{-2} and $\mu_0 = 4\pi \times 10^{-7}$ N A^{-2}. Use these values to find the speed, v, at which the electric and magnetic fields propagate along the space between the parallel plates. This is the speed of light, c.

7   a   With reference to your answer from question **6j**, suggest why electromagnetic waves are able to propagate through a vacuum.

b   Is the speed at which electromagnetic waves can move affected by the medium between the two parallel plates? Explain your answer.

c   Does the speed at which light travels depend on the way in which the pair of parallel plates are moving?

d   Does the speed at which light travels depend on the speed at which the medium between the two plates is moving?

e   How did Maxwell's speed of light contradict the Galilean transformation ideas?

f   The Galilean transformations had been complementary with Newtonian mechanics. What did Lorentz – and, later, Einstein – conclude was necessary for Maxwell's speed of light to be consistent with the established Newton's laws of motion?

Exercise A.2 – Lorentz transformations

1   The Michelson–Morley experiment is important for the history of physics.

a   Outline the purpose of the Michelson–Morley experiment.

b   What did the results from the experiment suggest about the:

i   existence of the aether

ii   dependence of the speed of light on the velocity of the Earth?

c   Which postulate of relativity did the Michelson–Morley experiment verify?

2   An observer in an inertial frame of reference, S, observes an event occur at (x, t). An observer in a reference frame, S', moving with a speed, v, relative to S, observes the same event occur at (x', t')

a   Use the Lorentz transformations to show how:

i x' is related to v, x and t

ii x is related to v, x' and t'

iii t' is related to v, t and x

iv t is related to v, t' and x'.

b   What assumption is made in expressing these equations?

3 A teacher lines up ten students, each with an identical stopwatch. There is 10 m between each student. The teacher stands 10 m away from the first student in the line. The students start their stopwatches when the teacher waves her hand in the air. An eleventh student runs along the line and the ten students stop their stopwatch when he is level with them.

a Explain why the teacher is happy to consider that all of the students start their stopwatches at the same time.

b The student closest to the teacher will, in fact, start the stopwatch a little earlier than the student furthest away. Determine the time interval between the students 10 m and 100 m away starting their stopwatches.

c The teacher wants the stopwatches to be synchronised. If a student is a distance, x, from the teacher, what value must their stopwatch read when they see the teacher waving her hand?

4 An observer in an inertial frame of reference, S, wants to measure the length of an object. They would find the position of one end of the object, x_1, at a time t_1, and the position of the other end of the object, x_2, at a time t_2, and then say that the length of the object, Δx, is $x_2 - x_1$.

Another observer in frame S', moving at a speed, v, relative to S, wants to measure the length of the same object.

a Using the Lorentz transformation, write expressions for x_1' and x_2'.

b If $\Delta x' = x_2' - x_1'$, show that $\Delta x' = \gamma\left(\Delta x - v\Delta t\right)$

5 An observer in frame S wants to measure how long something takes to occur. They will measure the start time of an event, t_1, at a place x_1, measure the end time of the event, t_2, at a place x_2 and then say that the event took a time of $\Delta t = t_2 - t_1$.

Another observer in frame S', moving at a speed, v, relative to S, wants to measure how much time the event has taken.

a Using the Lorentz transformation, write expressions for t_1' and t_2'

b If $\Delta t' = t_2' - t_1'$, show that $\Delta t' = \gamma\left(\Delta t - \dfrac{v}{c^2}\Delta x\right)$

6 a Use a spreadsheet package (such as Microsoft Excel®) to draw the graph of γ against v. Use values of v from 0 to just less than c.

b At what value of v does γ begin to increase significantly above $\gamma = 1.0$?

c What is the value of γ when v is:

i $0.01c$?

ii $0.1c$?

iii $0.5c$?

iv $0.9c$?

d What is the value of v when γ is:

i 1.5?

ii 2.0?

iii 5.0?

7 An observer on Earth sees a rocket travelling away from Earth at a speed of $0.7c$. The rocket fires a missile forwards at a speed of $0.3c$ relative to it.

   a Calculate the speed that the observer on the Earth measures for the missile.

   b Suppose that, instead of firing a missile, the rocket fired a laser. By calculating the speed that the observer on the Earth measures for the leading edge of the laser beam from the rocket, show that the relativistic addition of velocities is consistent with the second postulate of relativity.

8 A space craft launches two pods in opposite directions. Pod A leaves the space craft at a speed of $0.6c$ and pod B leaves the space craft at a speed of $0.7c$. What speed does pod A measure for pod B?

9 A relativistic red car is observed by an observer on the road to be travelling at $0.5c$. The driver in the car observes a relativistic blue car passing him at a speed of $0.5c$. Determine the speed that the observer on the road measures for the blue car.

10 **a** Explain what is meant by *invariant*.

   b Define the spacetime interval, Δs.

   c By using the Lorentz transformations show that the spacetime interval is invariant.

11 **a** Which quantities are invariant in all inertial frames of reference?

   b Define the following terms.

     i Rest mass.

     ii Proper length.

     iii Proper time.

12 Figure A.7 shows a light source on the floor of a closed container of height H. The container is initially at rest with respect to the ground. An observer inside the container uses a clock to measure the time it takes for light to travel from the source to the top of the container.

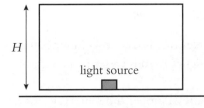

Figure A.7

   a **i** Write an expression for the time it takes for light to travel from the source to the top of the container to give the value that the observer inside the container measures. Call this t.

     ii If another observer, outside the container, also measures the time it takes for the light to reach the top of the container, will this observer measure the same time? Explain your answer.

   b Assume that the container is set in motion so that it moves sideways at a constant speed of v relative to the ground, as shown in Figure A.8.

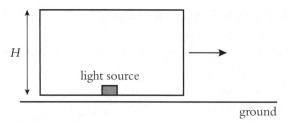

Figure A.8

 i For the observer inside the container, is the time it takes for the light to reach the top of the container the same as when the container was at rest? Explain your answer.

 ii For the observer outside the container, the light beam now has to travel a horizontal distance as well as a vertical distance to reach the top of the container. If this observer measures the time for the light beam to reach to the top of the container as t', write an expression for the total distance that the light beam has travelled.

 iii This total distance travelled is measured by the observer outside the container as taking a time t'. Show that $t'^2 = \dfrac{t^2}{1 - \dfrac{v^2}{c^2}}$ and that $t' = \gamma t$.

 c Explain why this phenomenon is called *time dilation*.

13 In the frame of reference, S, the two ends of a table are located at the coordinates x_1 and x_2 such that the proper length of the table, $L = x_2 - x_1$. An observer in the frame of reference, S', moving with a speed, v, relative to S measures, at the same time, the coordinates of the ends of the table to be at x'_1 and x'_2 such that the length of the table measured in S' is $L' = x'_2 - x'_1$.

 a Using the Lorentz transformations, show that $L = \gamma\left(x'_2 - x'_1\right)$.

 b Hence show that $L' = \dfrac{L}{\gamma}$

 c Suggest why this phenomenon is called *length contraction*.

14 A student standing on the Earth's surface observes that it takes two minutes for a nearby kettle to boil. Overhead, one of the student's friends passes by in a space rocket travelling at a speed of $0.8c$.

 a Explain why the student on the Earth measures a proper time interval.

 b Calculate the value of γ for the space rocket.

 c Determine how much time the student's friend in the space rocket measures for the kettle to boil.

15 An observer on the ground measures a building to be 100 m long. Calculate the length of the building measured by another observer sitting in a car travelling at $0.85c$ relative to the ground.

16 **a** An observer in a car passes a stationary observer at a speed of $0.75c$. Just at the moment the car passes the stationary observer, the stationary observer measures the time interval between two signal lights, in the same place, being switched on to be 5.00×10^{-3} s. Calculate the time interval measured by the observer in the fast car between the switching on of the two lights.

b On another occasion, the car is passing the stationary observer at a speed of $0.75c$. The stationary observer now sees that two different lights switch on at exactly the same time, as shown in Figure A.9.

Figure A.9

Explain why the observer in the car does not see both lights being switched on at the same time.

17 Anand is on board a space rocket travelling towards Proxima Centauri when he passes Louis observing from the Earth. Louis observes that Anand's space rocket is travelling at $0.9c$ with respect to the Earth. Proxima Centauri is 4.0 light-years from the Earth.

a Calculate the time it takes for Anand's space rocket to reach Proxima Centauri as measured by Louis on the Earth. (You may assume that the Earth remains stationary during this time.)

b Calculate the time that Anand measures for him to reach Proxima Centauri.

c Which of your answers to **a** and **b** is a proper time?

Exercise A.3 – Spacetime diagrams

1 Figure A.10 shows three examples in a spacetime diagram for particles, p, q and w.

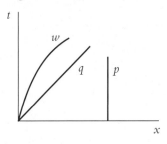

Figure A.10

a Describe what is happening to p.

b Describe what is happening to q.

c Describe what is happening to w.

2   Figure A.11 shows an example of a spacetime diagram in which a particle, r, and a photon, s, have their worldlines.

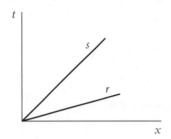

Figure A.11

a   State what the gradient of the worldline for s shows.
b   Explain why the worldline for r is not possible.

3   Figure A.12 shows a Minkowski diagram on which a single event, M, has been plotted. Note that the y-axis on this (and subsequent) diagrams is labelled ct, so has units of metres.

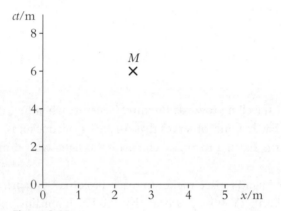

Figure A.12

Use the diagram to find:
a   where the event occurred
b   at what time the event occurred.

4   Figure A.13 shows a Minkowski diagram on which two wordlines, A and B, are shown.

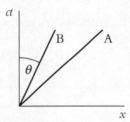

Figure A.13

a   Worldline A represents a photon. Show that the gradient of this worldline must be 1.
b   Worldline B represents a particle travelling at a constant speed, v. Show that the angle that the worldline B makes with the ct axis is given by the expression:

$$\theta = \tan^{-1}\left(\frac{v}{c}\right).$$

c With reference to the angle, θ, that a worldline makes with the y-axis, outline why it is a good idea to plot ct on the y-axis of the Minkowski diagram.

d What is the maximum angle, θ_{max}, that a worldline can have? Explain your answer.

5 Draw a Minkowski diagram to include a worldline for:

a a photon moving in the positive x direction; label this P^+

b a photon moving in the negative x direction; label this P^-

c an object moving in the positive x direction with a speed of $v = 0.3c$ (and show the angle, θ^+, that this worldline makes with the ct axis); label this Q^+

d an object moving in the negative x direction with a speed of $0.8c$ (and show the angle, θ^-, that this worldline makes with the ct axis); label this Q^-.

6 Figure A.14 shows a Minkowski diagram with two sets of axes for two inertial reference frames, S and S', where S' moves with a constant speed, v, relative to S. A single event, M, is shown.

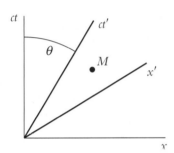

Figure A.14

a State an expression for the angle, θ, between the ct axis and the ct' axis.

b Copy Figure A.14 and show how to find the co-ordinates of:

  i M in S

  ii M in S'.

c State an expression for how:

  i x' is related to x

  ii ct' is related to ct.

7 Figure A.15 shows a Minkowski diagram with two sets of axes for the reference frames S and S'. Five events are shown, labelled A, B, C, D and E.

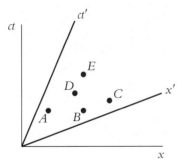

Figure A.15

a **i** In S, which two events occur simultaneously?

  ii Outline why it is obvious that these two events do not occur simultaneously in S'.

b i In S, which two events occur at the same place?

  ii Outline why it is obvious that these two events do not occur in the same place in S′.

c i In S′, which two events occur simultaneously?

  ii Outline why it is obvious that these two events do not occur simultaneously in S.

d i In S′, which two events occur in the same place?

  ii Outline why it is obvious that these two events do not occur in the same place in S.

e Between which two events, and in which reference frames, is it possible to measure a proper:

  i time?

  ii length?

8   Figure A.16 shows a Minkowski diagram in which a car, of proper length 5 m in S, is stationary in S. S′ moves with a constant speed, v, with respect to S.

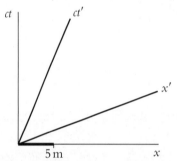

Figure A.16

a Copy Figure A.16 and show what its length will be when measured in S′.

b Is the length of the car in S′ longer, the same or shorter than its length in S?

c What can you say about the scale of the axes in S and S′?

9   Figure A.17 shows a Minkowski diagram showing two events, E_1 and E_2, which occur at the same place $(x = 0)$ in S. A passing observer, travelling at a constant speed, v, relative to S also observes the two events in S′.

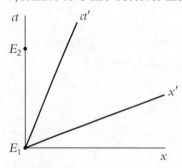

Figure A.17

a Copy Figure A.17 and show the time that the observer in S′ measures between E_1 and E_2.

b Is the time interval in S′ longer, the same or shorter than it is in S?

10 **a** Sketch a spacetime diagram and place an event, *X*, somewhere centrally on the diagram.
    b Add to your diagram the worldline for a photon emitted:
    i   forwards from *X*
    ii backwards from *X*.
    c Hence describe the region of the spacetime diagram in which photons from the event, *X*, can be observed.
    d What is the significance of this region?

11 Figure A.18 shows a spacetime diagram in which two events, *Y* and *Z*, occur.

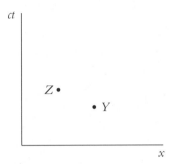

Figure A.18

    a By drawing suitable worldlines from event *Y*, show whether it is possible that event *Z* was caused by event *Y*.
    b Explain your reasoning.

12 **a** Outline what is meant by *the twin paradox*.
    b Which of the two twins actually ages the most?
    c Explain why the observations of the ages of the twins in the two frames of reference are not symmetrical.

13 Two identical twins, Minky and Som, conduct their own twin paradox. Minky stays at home on Earth, whilst Som travels to a nearby star, Fazer, which is 10 light-years away, at a speed of $0.9c$. When Som reaches Fazer, she turns around and returns to the Earth, once again at a speed of $0.9c$.
    a Calculate how much time Minky measures for Som to reach Fazer.
    b Calculate how much Som has aged in her reference frame of the moving space ship.
    c In Som's reference frame, she sees that Minky has been on a journey. How much has Minky aged according to Som when Som reaches Fazer?
    d Why is it necessary for Som to begin with a new reference frame, S'', when she turns around at Fazer to head back to the Earth?
    e Draw a Minkowski diagram to illustrate Som's journey as observed by Minky in S and by Som in S' and S''.
    f What happens to Som's measurement of the Earth clocks when she turns around at Fazer?
    g When Som returns to Minky, how much older has Minky become than Som?

HL Exercise A.4 – Relativistic mechanics

1   a   Define the term *rest energy*, E_0.

     b   How is the rest energy of a particle related to its total energy, E?

     c   Show that the rest energy of an electron is 0.51 MeV.

     d   Calculate the total energy, E, of an electron travelling at a speed of $0.9c$.

2   Calculate the speeds of the following particles.

     a   Particle p that has total energy that is three times its rest energy.

     b   Particle q that has total energy that is five times its rest energy.

     c   Particle r that has total energy that is 10 times its rest energy.

3   Protons in the Large Hadron Collider (LHC) at CERN can be accelerated to a total energy of 7 TeV. If the rest energy of a proton is 938 MeV, calculate the speed at which protons in the LHC can travel. (Use 10 significant figures.)

4   Giving your answers in MeV, calculate the kinetic energy, KE, of:

     a   an electron that has a gamma factor of 2.5

     b   a proton that has a gamma factor of 3.0

     c   particle c, of rest mass 1.5 g, that has a gamma factor of 5.0.

5   An electron is travelling at a speed of $0.99c$.

     a   Calculate the relativistic kinetic energy, in MeV, of the electron.

     b   Calculate the ratio of the relativistic kinetic energy to the Newtonian kinetic energy, $\dfrac{\text{KE}_{\text{rel}}}{\text{KE}_{\text{Newt}}}$ for this electron.

6   a   Calculate the energy required to accelerate an electron from rest to a speed of:

       i $0.9c$

       ii $0.95c$

       iii $0.99c$.

     b   Sketch a graph to show how the amount of energy required to accelerate an electron varies with its final speed.

     c   How does your sketch help to explain why it is impossible for a particle with a mass to travel at the speed of light?

7   a   Distinguish between the Newtonian momentum and the relativistic momentum of a particle of rest mass, m_0, travelling at a speed of v.

     b   State how the total energy, E, of a relativistic moving particle is related to its rest energy, E_0.

     c   Show that $E^2 - p^2c^2 = \gamma^2 m_0^2 c^2 \left(c^2 - v^2\right)$.

     d   Show that $E^2 - p^2c^2 = m_0^2 c^4$.

     e   State the relationship between the total energy, E, the momentum of the particle, p, and the rest mass, m_0.

8   a   Calculate the total energy, E, of an electron travelling at a speed of $0.85c$.

     b   Calculate the kinetic energy of the electron.

     c   Calculate the momentum of the electron.

9 An electron is accelerated from rest through a potential difference of 400 kV.

  a State how much kinetic energy the electron will have gained.

  b Show that a classical, Newtonian, calculation produces an unreasonable value for its speed.

  c What will the total energy of the electron be?

  d Calculate the momentum of the electron.

  e Calculate the actual speed of the electron.

10 A proton of rest mass, m_0, and charge, e, is accelerated from rest through a potential difference of V volts.

  a Show that: $\gamma = 1 + \dfrac{eV}{E_0}$.

  b **i** Calculate the total energy, E, of a proton that has been accelerated through a potential difference of 400 MV.

  ii Calculate the momentum of the proton.

  iii Hence calculate the speed of the proton.

11 **a** A proton is accelerated from rest through a potential difference, V, so that its final speed is $0.9c$. Calculate the value of V.

  b Compare the voltage required in part **a** with the voltage required to accelerate an electron to the same final speed.

HL Exercise A.5 – General relativity

1 Outline what is meant by *principle of equivalence*.

2 Consider an observer, O, drinking a cup of tea inside a closed container that is not within any kind of gravitational field. The observer is not able to extract any information of any kind from outside the container. You may ignore the mass of the observer.

  a Firstly, consider that the container is at rest with respect to the rest of the universe around it.

  i If the observer, O, releases his cup of tea, suggest what O would expect the cup of tea to do.

  ii How would O explain the behaviour of the cup of tea?

  b Consider that the container is moving at a constant velocity through space, again outside the effect of any gravitational field.

  i If O drops his cup of tea again, what would O expect the cup of tea to do?

  ii Would O be able to know if he is in a container moving through space at a constant velocity?

  iii How would O explain the behaviour of the cup of tea?

  c Consider that the container is accelerating upwards with respect to the universe around it.

  i If O drops his cup of tea again, what would O expect the cup of tea to do?

  ii Would O be able to tell the difference between his container accelerating and the container being within a gravitational field?

  iii Hence suggest two ways in which O could explain what happens to his dropped cup of tea.

  d How does O's observations of the dropped cup of tea confirm Einstein's equivalence principle?

3   Consider an observer standing on one side of a closed container. The observer is holding a toy laser, which he points horizontally towards the opposite wall of the container.

    a   The container is in deep space, well away from any large masses, and is not moving with respect to the rest of the universe.

        i   Where will the observer expect to see the light from the toy laser when it hits the opposite wall of the container?

        ii   How will the observer describe the path taken by the light from the laser?

    b   Now suppose that the container is moving upwards with a constant velocity through space, once again well away from the gravitational effects of any large masses.

        i   Where will the observer expect to see the light from the laser hit the opposite wall?

        ii   Is it possible for the observer to know the difference between the container being stationary in space and the container moving with a constant velocity through space?

    c   Consider what happens when the container accelerates upwards with a constant acceleration.

        i   Where will the observer expect to see the light from the laser hit the opposite wall?

        ii   How will the observer describe the path of the light from the laser?

        iii   Explain your reasoning.

        iv   Is it possible for the observer inside the closed container to know the difference between the container accelerating with a constant acceleration and the container being situated in a gravitational field caused by a large mass?

        v   What does this suggest happens to the path of a beam of light if it passes near a large mass?

4   Duangjian is an observer sitting at the front of a space rocket that is accelerating through deep space, with an acceleration of a. Duangian measures the proper length of the space rocket to be l.

    a   Explain why Duangjian's measurement of the length of the rocket is a proper length.

    b   At time $t = 0$, a light bulb at the rear of the space rocket illuminates. Write an expression for the time, Δt, that Duangjian measures for the light to reach her from the light bulb.

    c   During this time, the speed of the space rocket will have increased. Write an expression for the increase in speed, Δv, of the space rocket.

    d   Show that $\Delta v = \dfrac{al}{c}$.

    e   During the time, Δt, that the light is travelling from the light bulb to Duangjian, Duangjian will have travelled forwards, causing a Doppler red shift of the observed light. Show that the change in frequency of the light observed by Duangjian is given by $\Delta f = f \dfrac{al}{c^2}$.

    f   According to the equivalence principle, is it possible for Duangjian to know the difference between her being inside an accelerating space rocket and her being in a space rocket that is sitting stationary in a gravitational field?

    g   What does this suggest will happen to a photon that is emitted upwards from the Earth's surface?

5 The Burj Khalifa building in Dubai has an observation centre 555 m above the ground.

   a Calculate the change in frequency of a photon of wavelength 500 nm emitted from the ground and observed at the observation centre of the Burj Khalifa.

   b Has the photon become more or less energetic?

   c Two identical clocks are located at the base of the Burj Khalifa and on the wall of the observation centre. Over the course of a day, by how much do the two clocks differ?

   d Suggest, therefore, how a gravitational field affects the passage of time.

   e Outline why it is necessary for GPS satellites to take into account the effect of gravitational time dilation.

6 Outline Pound, Rebka and Snider's famous 1959 experiment. Explain why their results provided empirical verification of the general theory of relativity.

7 In the Pound, Rebka and Snider experiment, the source and detector were separated by a vertical distance of 22.6 m.

   a Calculate the fractional difference in frequency that would occur for the gamma rays they used.

   b Explain why it is necessary to be able to measure very small changes in frequency.

8 Suppose you drew a straight line, as in Figure A.19.

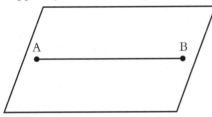

Figure A.19

   a Is it fair to say that the shortest distance between A and B is the length of the line you have drawn?

   b Now suppose you curl your piece of paper, as in Figure A.20. Is your line still straight, or is it curved?

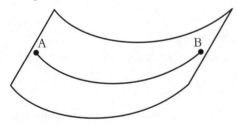

Figure A.20

   c Whether a line is deemed to be straight or curved depends on the surface on which it is drawn. How did Einstein use this idea to explain the bending of light near a large mass?

   d Outline what is meant by *gravitational lensing*.

9 In 1919, Sir Arthur Eddington carried out an experiment involving the Earth, the Moon, the Sun and a distant star.

    a What was the purpose of Eddington's experiment?

    b Suggest why Eddington carried his experiment out during a total solar eclipse.

    c Sketch a diagram to show Eddington's observations of the:

        i path of light from the star to the Earth

        ii apparent position of the star.

    d How did Einstein explain the path of the light from the star to the Earth?

10 **a** Explain what is meant by a *black hole*.

    b Explain what is meant by *event horizon*.

    c Explain what is meant by *Schwarzschild radius*.

    d Calculate the Schwarzschild radius for the:

        i Earth ($M_E = 6 \times 10^{24}$ kg)

        ii Sun ($M_S = 2 \times 10^{30}$ kg).

11 According to the Oppenheimer-Volkoff limit, a star must have a mass of at least three solar masses to become a black hole. The mass of our Sun is 2×10^{30} kg.

    a Calculate the minimum Schwarzschild radius of a black hole.

    b How would you expect this radius to change with time? Explain your reasoning.

12 Consider a black hole of mass 30 M_S.

    a Calculate the Schwarzschild radius.

    b An observer in a space ship is passing the black hole at a distance of 100 R_S. They send out two signals, separated by one second, to a distant space station. Calculate the separation of the two signals as observed at the space station.

    c Suppose that the observer in the space ship moves to 10 R_S from the black hole. As before, they send two signals separated by one second. Calculate the separation of the two signals as observed at the distant space station.

    d If the observer continues to travel towards the Schwarzschild radius, outline what the observer at the space station will notice about the separation of the two signals.

    e In performing the calculations for this question, what assumption is made about the black hole?

13 **a** Explain why Einstein introduced the cosmological constant into his solution for his equations showing the 'size' of the universe.

    b How did Einstein's prediction of the size of the universe contradict Hubble's later findings?

    c Explain what is meant by *the critical density of the universe*.

    d Outline how recent measurements of the mass and energy in the universe have led astrophysicists to believe that the universe is expanding at an accelerating rate.

Exam-style questions

1   **This question is about the Michelson–Morley experiment.**

  a Sketch a diagram of the apparatus used by Michelson and Morley. Add rays of light to show how an interference pattern is formed for the observer. **[4]**

  b In part of the experiment, the whole set of apparatus was rotated through 90°. Why did Michelson and Morley do this? **[1]**

  c Explain the purpose of the moveable mirror. **[1]**

  d What did Michelson and Morley notice from their results? **[1]**

  e Explain how their results helped to confirm what Einstein and Maxwell had predicted for the speed of light. **[2]**

2   **An observer in the inertial reference frame S notices that the relativity express train is passing along the train tacks at a speed of $0.75c$. At a time of $t = 3.0$ s, the observer in S notices that a friend drops his mobile phone at a position of $x = 500$ m. Another observer sitting inside the relativity express also observes the dropped mobile phone.**

  a Calculate the value of the gamma factor, γ. **[2]**

  b Assuming that both observers have clocks that read zero when the origins of their reference frames coincide, determine the:

    i position, x', where the observer in S' sees the dropped phone

    ii time at which the observer in the S' sees the dropped phone. **[2]**

3   **A fast train is travelling at a speed of $0.6c$ relative to the ground. An observer inside the train measures the train to be 400 m long. The observer in the train switches on a torch so that the light beam travels towards the front of the train.**

  a Determine how much time the light takes to reach the front of the train as observed by the observer on the train? **[1]**

  b Calculate the value of γ for the train. **[2]**

  c Use the Lorentz transformations to calculate how long the train is as observed by the observer on the ground. **[2]**

  d Calculate how much time an observer on the ground measures for the light from the torch to reach the front of the train. **[2]**

4   John is sitting in the middle of a carriage on the relativity express, travelling at
a constant speed of 0.8c with respect to Mary, who is standing by the side of the
railway track (see Figure A.21).

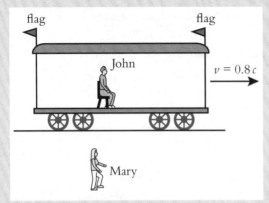

Figure A.21

Just at the moment that John and Mary are alongside each other, the two flags
at each end of the carriage fall off the train. Mary says that the two flags fell
simultaneously (at exactly the same time).

a   State whether John also thinks that the two flags fell simultaneously. **[1]**

b   Explain your reasoning for part **a**. **[2]**

c   John measures the length of the train carriage to be 25 m.

   i   Explain why John's measurement of the length of the carriage is a proper length.

   ii Calculate the value of the length of the carriage as measured by Mary. **[3]**

5   A muon is a sub-atomic particle (a member of the lepton family) that is unstable.
It has a half-life of $t_{\frac{1}{2}} = 3.1\,\mu s$ when measured in a frame of reference where the
muon is at rest.

Muons are produced in large numbers in the Earth's upper atmosphere, at an
altitude of about 15 km, by cosmic rays colliding with atoms to produce pions.
These pions then decay into muons (and muon neutrinos). When produced, muons
travel at a speed of 0.97c towards the Earth's surface, where they are detected.

a   According to an observer on the Earth, what is the muon's half-life? **[1]**

b   According to an observer on the Earth, how far do muons travel through the atmosphere in
one half-life? **[1]**

c   Show that, in the muon's frame of reference, the muon's proper half-life and the distance
it travels in this time are consistent with it moving at a speed of 0.97c relative to the
Earth. **[2]**

d   How many half-lives must pass before the muons reach the Earth's surface? **[2]**

e   Outline why so many muons are observed at the Earth's surface. **[2]**

6   Figure A.22 shows a Minkowski diagram in which there are three events, A, B and C.
    A stationary observer at the origin in S and another observer, in the frame S′, who
    is passing by in a space rocket travelling at a constant speed relative to S, both
    observe the three events.

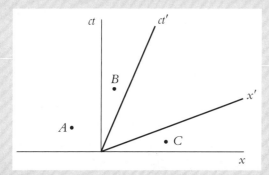

Figure A.22

a According to the observer in S, which event is observed:
   i   first?
   ii last? **[2]**
b According to the observer in S′, which event is observed:
   i   first?
   ii last? **[2]**

7   **HL** A photon produces an electron–positron pair. The electron moves away at a
    speed of 0.9c.
a Suggest why the positron does not move away in the opposite direction to the electron. **[2]**
b Calculate the kinetic energy of the electron. **[2]**
c Calculate the momentum of the electron. **[2]**

Option B: Engineering physics

Chapter outline

In this chapter, you will:

- Understand the concepts of torque and moments of inertia, calculate torque for single forces and couples and use moments of inertia to solve problems involving torque and angular acceleration.
- Solve problems involving objects in rotational and translational equilibrium.
- Solve problems using rotational quantities analogous to linear quantities, sketch and interpret graphs of rotational motion and use the conservation of angular momentum to solve problems involving rolling without slipping.
- Describe the first law of thermodynamics as a statement of the conservation of energy, use the correct sign convention for the quantities Q, ΔU and ΔW in the first law.
- Solve problems using the first law, and describe the second law of thermodynamics in its Clausius form, its Kelvin form and as a consequence of entropy.
- Describe and solve problems involving processes in terms of entropy changes.
- Understand the nature of a thermodynamic cycle and be able to sketch and interpret cycles on a p–V graph.
- Understand and be able to identify isovolumetric, isobaric, isothermal and adiabatic processes on a p–V diagram and solve problems involving adiabatic processes for monatomic gases using the equation: $p\,V^{\frac{5}{3}}$ = constant.
- Recognise the main features of a Carnot cycle and solve problems involving thermal efficiency.
- **HL** Understand the nature of density and pressure in a fluid and determine buoyancy forces in a fluid using Archimedes' principle, know Pascal's principle and be able to use it to solve problems involving pressure and density.
- **HL** Understand the concept of hydrostatic equilibrium, describe what an ideal fluid is and understand the concept of streamlines in fluid flow and use the concept of continuity to solve problems involving the flow of a fluid.
- **HL** Use the Bernoulli equation in conjunction with continuity.
- **HL** Describe the frictional drag force exerted on small spherical objects in a laminar fluid flow.
- **HL** Solve problems involving Stokes' law and determine the Reynolds number in simple situations.
- **HL** Understand the concept of a natural, or resonant, frequency and understand the meaning of a Q factor, be able to use it in describing qualitatively and quantitatively examples of under damped, over damped and critically damped oscillations.
- **HL** Solve problems using the Q factor.
- **HL** Understand the phase relationship between a periodic driving force and the resulting forced oscillations, sketch and interpret graphs involving the amplitude of vibration plotted against forcing frequency for an object close to its resonant frequency and describe the useful and destructive effects of resonance.

KEY TERMS

Angular acceleration, α: The rate of change of angular speed; $\alpha = \dfrac{\Delta \omega}{\Delta t}$

Torque, Γ: The turning moment produced by a force acting at a distance from a centre of rotation, $\Gamma = F\,r\sin\theta$, where F is the force, r the distance from the centre of rotation to the point at which the force acts and θ is the angle between the force and the line joining where the force acts and the centre of rotation.

Angular momentum, L: The rotational equivalent to linear momentum; $L = I\omega$

Angular kinetic energy, KE_{rot}: $KE_{rot} = \dfrac{1}{2} I\omega^2$

The first law of thermodynamics: $Q = \Delta U + W$

Adiabatic change: $p_1 V_1^{\frac{5}{3}} = p_2 V_2^{\frac{5}{3}}$ and $T_1 V_1^{\frac{2}{3}} = T_2 V_2^{\frac{2}{3}}$ suggesting that an adiabatic change is a steeper curve on the p–V diagram than that of an isothermal change.

Efficiency of a heat engine operating in a Carnot cycle, η: $\eta = 1 - \dfrac{T_{cold}}{T_{hot}}$

Entropy change, ΔS: $\Delta S = \dfrac{\Delta Q}{T}$

HL **Bernouilli equation:** $\dfrac{1}{2}\rho v^2 + \rho gz + p = \text{constant}$

HL **Stokes' law:** Viscous drag force on a sphere, $F = 6\pi\eta r v$, where η is the coefficient of viscosity, r the radius of the sphere and v the velocity of the sphere through the fluid.

HL **Reynolds number, R:** $R - \dfrac{vr\rho}{\eta}$, when $R < 1000$, laminar flow occurs; when $R > 2000$, the flow is turbulent.

HL **Q-factor:** $Q = 2\pi\dfrac{\text{energy stored in a system}}{\text{energy lost per cycle}} = 2\pi f_0 \dfrac{E_{stored}}{\text{power loss}}$

Exercise B.1 – Rigid bodies and rotational dynamics

1   **a** Calculate the angular speed, ω, of the:
   i   second hand of a clock
   ii minute hand of a clock
   iii hour hand of a clock.
   b The hour hand of a clock is 1.5 cm long, its minute hand is 2.0 cm long and its second hand is 2.5 cm long. Calculate the linear speed of the tip of the:
   i   second hand
   ii minute hand
   iii hour hand.

2   **a** Define the term *angular acceleration*.
   b A cylinder making 300 rotations in one minute slows down. After 5 seconds, it makes 120 rotations per minute. Calculate the cylinder's:
   i   initial angular speed
   ii final angular speed
   iii angular acceleration.

3 A disc rotating with an angular speed of $\omega = 40$ radians s^{-1} is subject to an angular acceleration of 5 radians s^{-2} for 6 seconds.

    a Sketch a graph to show how the angular speed of the disc varies with time.

    b Determine the:

       i final angular speed of the disc

       ii total number of rotations that the disc makes during the six second period.

4 The Sun has an equatorial radius of 6.96×10^5 km. It rotates with a period, at the equator, of 24.47 days. The Earth's equatorial radius is 6.37×10^3 km.

    Calculate the ratio of the Sun's:

    a angular speed at the equator to the Earth's angular speed at the equator, $\dfrac{\omega_S}{\omega_E}$

    b linear speed at its equator to the Earth's linear speed at its equator, $\dfrac{v_S}{v_E}$.

5 Calculate the:

    a angular acceleration of a rotating object that takes 4.0 seconds change its angular speed from 20.0 radians s^{-1} to 15 radians s^{-1}

    b time it takes for an initially non-rotating object to reach an angular speed of 600 radians s^{-1} if its angular acceleration is 15 radians s^{-2}

    c total angle turned through if an object initially rotating with an angular speed of 15 radians s^{-1} is subject to a constant angular acceleration of 2.0 radians s^{-2} until it reaches a final angular speed of 40 radians s^{-1}.

6 A car travelling at 10.0 m s^{-1} decelerates to rest at a constant rate over a distance of 50.0 m. The wheels, with their tyres, have a radius of 40.0 cm. Calculate the:

    a initial angular speed of the wheels

    b number of rotations that the wheels make whilst the car is slowing down

    c angular acceleration of the wheels

    d time it took the car to stop.

7 **a** Define the term *torque*.

    b State the units for torque.

    c Calculate the torque produced by a:

       i perpendicular force of 250 N acting at a distance of 60 cm from an axis of rotation

      ii force of 400 N acting 3.0 m from an axis of rotation at an angle of 30° to the line joining the axis of rotation and the point where the force is applied.

8 **a** Explain what is meant by a *couple*.

    b Explain why an object subjected to a couple will be in translational equilibrium, but not in rotational equilibrium.

    c What will happen to the angular speed of a rotating object if it is subject to a constant couple?

9 The lid of a jar of preserve has a radius of 3.5 cm. To unscrew the lid requires a couple of 15 N m.

    a If the lid is to be opened by hand, calculate the minimum force that must be applied to each side of the lid if it is to turn.

    b A kitchen gadget, with 15 cm long handles, can clamp onto the lid. Calculate the minimum force that must be applied to the gadget's handles to unscrew the lid.

    c Suggest why consumers are happy to buy such a gadget, rather than just use their hands.

10 **a** Define the term *moment of inertia, I*.

    b Describe why I is often thought of as analogous to the mass of an object.

    c State the equivalence of Newton's second law of linear motion for rotational motion.

11 Determine the moment of inertia, I of:

    a the point mass of 0.20 kg rotating about a centre of rotation of radius 0.40 m

    b two point masses, each of 0.20 kg, each rotating in the same way around an axis of rotation of radius 0.40 m.

    c two point masses, each of mass 0.20 kg, each rotating in the same way about an axis of rotation of radius 0.80 m.

    d What do you notice about how the

      i mass of a point mass affects its moment of inertia

      ii distance from the axis of rotation affects the moment of inertia?

12 Figure B.1 shows two point masses on a light rod.

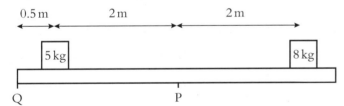

Figure B.1

    a Calculate the moment of inertia of the system if the axis of rotation is at point:

      i P

      ii Q.

    b The 5 kg mass is removed. Calculate the moment of inertia of the system if the axis of rotation is at Q.

    c What do you conclude from your answers to **aii** and **b**?

13 A circus performer rotates a 300 g flat plate on a thin rod by applying a force of 20 N tangentially to its rim. The plate's radius is 20.0 cm.

    a The moment of inertia of the plate is given by $I = \frac{1}{2}MR^2$. Calculate the angular acceleration of the plate.

    b As the plate rotates, the circus performer drops a 120 g lump of mashed potato onto it, 12 cm from the axis of rotation. The potato sticks to the plate. He continues to apply the same force. Calculate the new angular acceleration.

14   Figure B.2 shows a thin circular disc of mass 5.0 kg and radius 25 cm. A rope is
     wrapped around it. The end of the rope is pulled with a constant force of 20 N,
     making the disc spin, from rest, around a frictionless axis of rotation passing through
     the centre of the disc.

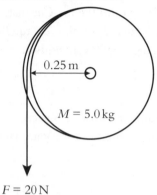

$F = 20\,\text{N}$

Figure B.2

   a Calculate the torque acting on the disc.
   b Calculate the angular acceleration of the disc.
   c Calculate how many rotations the disc will make in 5 seconds.

15   A cylinder of mass 6.0 kg and radius 0.3 m can rotate around an axis of rotation that
     passes through its centre of mass. If a constant force of 4.0 N is applied tangentially to
     the edge of the cylinder, calculate the angular speed of the cylinder after 8.0 seconds.

16   Figure B.3 shows a pulley wheel of mass, M, and radius, R, with a mass, m, attached
     by a light string. The moment of inertia of the pulley wheel about its centre of
     rotation is $I = \frac{1}{2}MR^2$. The mass, m, is allowed to fall freely.

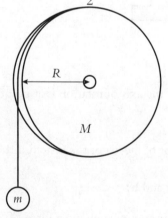

Figure B.3

   a State an expression for the torque acting on the pulley.
   b Does it matter how long the string holding the mass is?
   c Consider the string to be 0 cm long (i.e. the mass is positioned on the edge of
         the pulley). Write an expression for the total moment of inertia about the axis of
         rotation of the pulley wheel.

d Show that the angular acceleration of the pulley wheel, α, is given by the expression: $\alpha = \dfrac{mg}{R\left(\frac{1}{2}M + m\right)}$

e Show that the linear acceleration of the mass, m, is given by the expression,

$$a = \dfrac{mg}{\dfrac{M}{2} + m}$$

17 Figure B.4 shows a coin of radius, R, rolling along a horizontal surface at a linear speed, v. The coin does not slip.

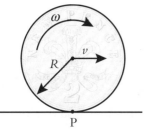

Figure B.4

a What is the linear speed caused by the rotation of the coin at point Q?
b State an expression for the total linear speed of point Q.
c State an expression for the linear speed of point P.
d Since the coin does not slip, what is the actual value of the instantaneous linear speed at P?
e Show that the instantaneous linear speed of point Q is $2v$.

18 A cylinder of radius R and mass M is rolling along a horizontal surface without slipping, as shown in Figure B.5.

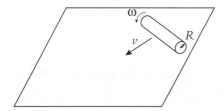

Figure B.5

a If the linear speed, v, of the cylinder along the surface is 20.0 cm s^{-1} and the radius of the cylinder is 1.5 cm, calculate how many rotations the cylinder makes in one second.
b Calculate the angular speed of the cylinder, ω.
c Show that, at any time, the fastest actual speed attained by any part of the cylinder is 40.0 cm s^{-1}.

19 a i State the equation for the kinetic energy of a body of mass, M, moving along with a linear speed, v.
   ii State the equation for the rotational kinetic energy of a body of mass, M, rotating at an angular speed, ω.
b Calculate the total kinetic energy of a cricket ball of radius 3.5 cm and mass 163 g rolling along a horizontal surface without slipping at a linear speed of 4.0 m s^{-1}.
(The moment of inertia of a sphere of mass, M, and radius, R, is $\frac{2}{5}MR^2$.)

20 A sphere of mass, M, and radius of 5.0 cm rolls, without slipping, down a sloping surface of length 1.5 m in a time of 6.0 s. (The moment of inertia of a sphere of mass, M, and radius, R, is $\frac{2}{5}MR^2$.)

    a Use the equations of linear kinematics to determine the speed of the sphere when it reaches the end of the sloping surface.

    b Calculate the angular speed of the sphere at the end of the sloping surface.

    c i Show that $gh = \frac{7}{10}v^2$, where h is the height of the top of the sloping surface above its bottom.

      ii Calculate h.

21 Consider two solid cylinders, A and B. A has a radius of 0.20 m and a mass of 1.25 kg, and B has a radius of 0.80 m and a mass of 20.0 kg. Both cylinders are released at the same time, from rest, to roll down a sloping surface, without slipping, so that they both end up 0.20 m below where they began.

    a Show that both cylinders will reach the bottom of the sloping surface travelling at the same speed.

    b Calculate the final speed of the cylinders at the bottom of the sloping surface.

    c Which famous experiment does this bring to mind?

    d How might you explain this to a young physics student?

22 Complete Table B.1 to show how some of the linear motion equations are related to rotational motion. The first equation has been done for you.

Linear motion	Rotational motion
$F = m\,a$	$\Gamma = I\,\alpha$
work done = force × perpendicular distance	work done =
power = force × velocity	power =

Table B.1

23 a A sphere of mass 2.5 kg and radius 6.0 cm is spinning about its axis at 300 rotations per minute. Calculate the sphere's angular:

      i speed

      ii momentum.

    b State the principle of conservation of angular momentum.

    c Suppose that, while spinning, a point mass of 4.0 kg fell onto the sphere and attached itself to the sphere's surface. Calculate the new rotation rate of the sphere with the mass attached.

Exercise B.2 – Thermodynamics

1   a What is the *internal energy* of a gas?

    b Calculate the internal energy of 3.0 moles of an ideal gas at a temperature of 300 K.

    c State what will happen to the internal energy of the gas in part **b** if the temperature of the gas is halved.

2. State what is meant by the following terms.
   a. An open system.
   b. A closed system.
   c. An isolated system.

3. Table B.2 lists four thermodynamic processes. State which quantity each process refers to and what happens to it.

Thermodynamic process	Details of relevant quantity
Isothermal	
Isovolumetric	
Isobaric	
Adiabatic	

Table B.2

4. 25 cm^3 of ideal gas at a pressure of 2.5×10^5 Pa and a temperature of 300 K has its thermodynamic state changed so that its pressure becomes 1.0×10^5 Pa.
   a. If the process is conducted isothermally, calculate the final volume of the gas.
   b. If the same process is conducted adiabatically, calculate the gas's final:
      i. volume
      ii. temperature.

5. A fixed amount of ideal gas at a pressure of 2.0×10^6 Pa is compressed by an isobaric process from a volume of 0.25 m^3 to a volume of 0.15 m^3.
   a. The internal energy, U, of the gas is given by the expression $U = \frac{3}{2} NkT$. Show that the change in internal energy of the gas can be expressed by $\Delta U = \frac{3}{2} p\Delta V$
   b. Calculate the change in internal energy of the gas.
   c. Calculate the work done, W, on the gas.
   d. Calculate the heat exchanged between the gas and its surroundings.

6. In practice, not all gases are ideal gases.
   a. How can we try to replicate an adiabatic process in real life?
   b. How can we try to replicate an isothermal process in real life?
   c. Explain why the gas that comes out of an aerosol can is always cold.

7. A sample of ideal gas expands isothermally doing 2.5 kJ of work on its surroundings. Determine the:
   a. change in its internal energy
   b. heat exchanged from its surroundings.

8. A sample of ideal gas is compressed by 4.5 kJ of work.
   a. If the process is isothermal, how much heat is exchanged between the gas and its surroundings, and in which direction?
   b. If the process is adiabatic, what happens to the temperature of the gas?

9 Figure B.6 shows a $p-V$ diagram on which two thermodynamic processes, A and B, are shown for a fixed amount of 2.0 moles of gas. The temperature at X and Y is 300 K.

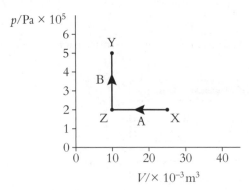

Figure B.6

  a i What type of thermodynamic process is process A?

    ii What type of thermodynamic process is process B?

  b i Calculate the amount of work done on the gas by process A.

    ii Is the gas at Z at a higher or a lower temperature than it is at X? Explain your reasoning.

    iii What can you say about the amount of heat, Q, exchanged between the gas and its surroundings during process A?

  c i Does process B involve any work being done on or by the gas? Explain your answer.

    ii Since the internal energy, U, of the gas at X and Y is the same (they are at the same temperature) what must be happening during process B?

10 Figure B.7 shows two more thermodynamic processes, C and D, also acting on a fixed amount of 2.0 moles of ideal gas. The temperature of the gas at X and Y is 300 K.

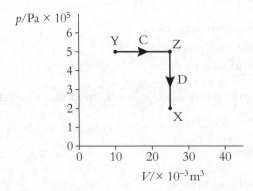

Figure B.7

  a i Calculate the amount of work done by the gas during process C.

    ii Is the gas at point Z at a higher or a lower temperature than at point Y?

    iii What must be happening to the gas during process C?

  b i Does the gas do any work on its surroundings during the process D? Explain your reasoning.

    ii What must be happening to the gas during process D?

11 Figure B.8 shows a thermodynamic cycle consisting of four thermodynamic processes, A, B, C and D, moving a fixed quantity of gas through four thermodynamic states, W, X, Y and Z.

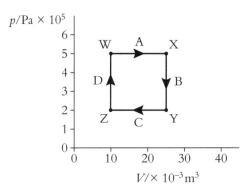

Figure B.8

a   For process A, calculate the work done by the gas on its surroundings.
b   Do processes B and D involve any work being done on or by the gas?
c   For process C, calculate the work done on the gas.
d   Calculate the net work done by the gas if the gas begins in state W and finishes in state W having undergone processes A, B, C and D.
e   How is this net work done by the gas represented on Figure B.8?
f   In terms of conservation of energy, how is it possible for the gas to move around the thermodynamic cycle producing a net amount of work done on its surroundings?

12 Figure B.9 shows another kind of thermodynamic cycle on a p–V diagram. In this cycle, there are two adiabatic processes, A and C, and two isovolumetric processes, B and D.

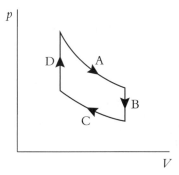

Figure B.9

a   This cycle describes what happens in an internal combustion engine, such as in a family car. What is the name of this kind of cycle?
b   How can you use the p–V diagram to find the net work done?
c   In which process does the gas:
   i   absorb heat from the surroundings?
   ii   release heat to the surroundings?
d   In which of the two processes in part **c** is most heat exchanged?
e   Draw a diagram of a simple heat engine that explains how work can be derived from heat.
f   How does your diagram show that the production of work from heat cannot be 100% efficient?

13 Figure B.10 shows a theoretical thermodynamic cycle that is deemed to be the most efficient thermodynamic cycle possible.

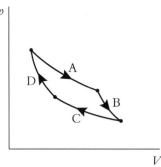

Figure B.10

a What is the name given to this kind of thermodynamic cycle?
b Identify the thermodynamic processes represented on the diagram by A, B, C and D.
c Along which process is the temperature of the gas highest?
d In which process is heat:
   i absorbed from the surroundings into the gas?
   ii lost to the surroundings from the gas?
e In which of the two processes in part **c** is most heat exchanged?

f Draw a diagram of a heat engine. Use it to show that efficiency of the heat engine can be given as $\eta = 1 - \dfrac{Q_c}{Q_H}$, where Q_c is the heat exchanged when the temperature of the gas is coldest and Q_H is the heat exchanged when the temperature of the gas is hottest.

14 In a pressurised water reactor (a kind of nuclear power station), pressurised water at a temperature of 327 °C is used to generate work. The cooled water reaches a temperature of 27 °C.
   a Calculate the maximum theoretical efficiency of such a power station.
   b In practice, this level of efficiency is not realised. Suggest why it is not possible to replicate this level of efficiency in a real nuclear power station.
   c **i** How could the theoretical efficiency be increased?
      ii Suggest why your answer is not possible in practice.

15 Figure B.11 shows a heat pump.

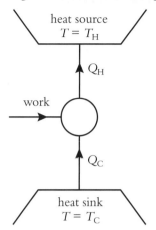

Figure B.11

a Describe in more detail what Figure B.11 shows.
b Suggest a real-life example of this.

16 The second law of thermodynamics states that it is not possible to make a heat engine that converts all of the heat exchanged into useful work. This law can be expressed in other forms.

a **i** Which interpretation of the second law has been described in the introduction to this question?
   ii Describe how this interpretation of the law is shown by the engine in a family motor car.
b **i** State the Clausius interpretation of the second law.
   ii Give an example of the Clausius interpretation of the second law from your own home.

17 Another way of interpreting the second law of thermodynamics is to say that, in any process, the net change in entropy is always positive.

a Define the term *change in entropy*.
b An ice cube sitting on a metal plate will melt quite quickly.
   i Explain why the ice cube will melt quickly.
   ii Explain how the net change in entropy is positive despite energy being removed from the surroundings of the ice cube.
   iii If the ice cube has a mass of 10 g, calculate the change in entropy of the ice cube. (The specific latent heat of fusion of water is 334 kJ kg^{-1}.)

18 **a** Describe how the net entropy is increasing when:
   i a cup of tea is left to cool
   ii a crystal of sodium chloride grows from a pool of sea water
   iii an athlete sweats to keep cool.
b Calculate the net entropy change when 2 kJ of heat are exchanged from a heat source at a temperature of 700 K to a heat sink at a temperature of 300 K.

HL Exercise B.3 – Fluids and fluid dynamics

1   Consider a cylinder of height, h, and cross-sectional area, A, filled with liquid of density, ρ. A point, P, is inside the cylinder at the bottom of the liquid.
   a Give an expression for the weight of the water above point P.
   b Show that the extra pressure, p_{liquid} , exerted at point P is given by $p_{liquid} = h\rho g$
   c If the atmospheric pressure above the cylinder is 1.0×10^5 Pa and $h = 30.0$ cm, calculate the pressure at the bottom of the cylinder.

2   **a** The density of mercury is 1.36×10^4 kg m^{-3}. Calculate the height of a column of mercury required to produce an excess pressure at its base equal to 1 atmosphere.
   b If water was used instead of mercury in part **a**, what height would the column of water need to be to produce the same excess pressure?

3   Figure B.12 shows the principle of hydraulics. A mass of 1.5×10^3 kg is to be raised by applying a force, F, on the left-hand piston. The cross-sectional area of the right-hand side of the hydraulic system is four times that of the left-hand side.

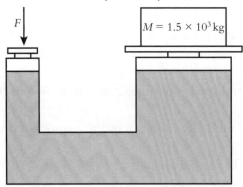

Figure B.12

   a State Pascal's principle.
   b Determine the size of the force, F, required to lift the mass.
   c If the mass is be raised 1.0 m, determine the distance through which the force, F, must be applied on the left-hand side.

4   **a** State Archimedes' principle.
   b Consider a cylinder, of cross-sectional area, A, and height, h, immersed in liquid of density, ρ. The top of the cylinder is level with the surface of the liquid. The bottom of the cylinder is a distance, h, below the surface.
     i Give an expression for the pressure in the liquid just underneath the cylinder at point P.
     ii Give an expression for the upwards force on the underside of the cylinder due to the pressure in the liquid at a depth, h.
     iii State an expression for the downwards force on the cylinder due to the atmospheric pressure, p_0.
     iv Derive an expression for the buoyancy force; that is, the net upwards force on the cylinder due to the liquid.
     v By finding an expression for the weight of the liquid displaced by the cylinder, show Archimedes' principle to be true.
     vi If the cylinder just floats, what must its density be?

5 A block of wood of density 1.1×10^3 kg m^{-3} has a mass of 100 kg. It is completely immersed in water.

    a Determine the net force on the block of wood.

    b Does the block of wood float or sink?

6 **a** A large, solid steel block of mass 68 000 tonnes is dropped into the sea. The density of steel is 7.8×10^3 kg m^{-3}.

      i Calculate the buoyancy force acting on the block of steel.

      ii Would the block of steel sink or float?

    b A large boat – called a TI-class supertanker – has a mass of 68 000 tonnes when empty. It displaces a volume of water given by 68 m × 380 m × 25 m.

      i Calculate the buoyancy force on this boat.

      ii Calculate the weight of the oil cargo it can carry without sinking.

7 **a** State the three assumptions necessary for an ideal fluid.

    b Define the volume flow rate of an ideal fluid.

    c Calculate the volume flow rate for an ideal fluid flowing through a pipe of cross-sectional area 20.0 cm^2 at a speed of 1.5 m s^{-1}.

    d If the pipe in part **c** became gradually narrower so that its radius became halved, what would be the:

      i volume flow rate

      ii speed of the fluid?

8 Figure B.13 shows an ideal fluid flowing in a tube of varying cross-sectional area.

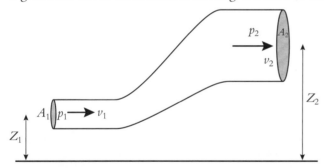

Figure B.13

The left-hand side of the tube has a cross-sectional area, A_1, and a pressure in the fluid of p_1. The right-hand side of the tube has a cross-sectional area, A_2 and a pressure in the fluid of p_2. The speed of the fluid through $A_1 = v_1$. The speed of the fluid through $A_2 = v_2$.

    a **i** What force is pushing the fluid along the left-hand side of the tube?

      ii In a time, Δt, how far does the fluid move along the left-hand side of the tube?

      iii Show that the work done on the fluid in the left-hand side of the tube in a time Δt is $W_1 = p_1 A_1 \, v_1 \Delta t$.

    b **i** What force is pushing the fluid along the right-hand side of the tube?

      ii In a time, Δt, how far does the fluid move along the right-hand side of the tube?

      iii Show that the work done on the fluid in the right-hand side of the tube in a time Δt is $W_2 = p_2 A_2 \, v_2 \Delta t$.

    c According to the continuity principle, the volume of fluid moving in a time Δt must be the same throughout the tube. Show that the net work done on the fluid in moving from the left-hand side to the right-hand side is $W_{net} = V (p_1 - p_2)$.

d To get the fluid from the left- to right-hand side, work must also be done against gravity to raise the fluid to a greater height.

    i Through what height does the fluid travel when moving from the left- to right-hand side?

    ii If the fluid has a density, ρ, how much work must be done against gravity to move a volume, V, through this height?

e If the fluid has a density, ρ, for the volume, V, state an expression for the change in kinetic energy in moving from the left- to right-hand side.

f Conservation of energy states that the total work done on the volume of fluid, V, is given by:

$$W_{total} = \Delta KE + \Delta GPE$$

    i Use your answers to parts **c**, **d** and **e** to expand this equation.

    ii Show the Bernoulli equation: $p_1 + \dfrac{1}{2}\rho v_1^2 + \rho g z_1 = p_2 + \dfrac{1}{2}\rho v_2^2 + \rho g z_2$

9 Figure B.14 shows some water flowing through a tube of constant width.

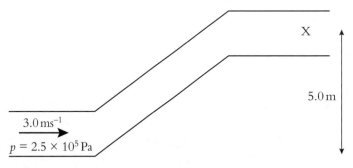

Figure B.14

Calculate the pressure at point X.

10 Figure B.15 shows some water flowing through a tube with variable width.

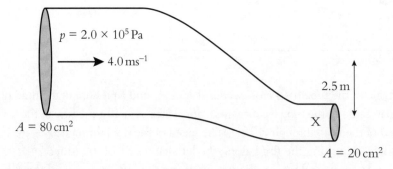

Figure B.15

  a Use the continuity equation to calculate the speed of the fluid at point X.

  b Use the Bernoulli equation to calculate the pressure at the point X.

11 Consider a tall cylinder full of water. It has a small hole in its side that is plugged with a rubber bung. The atmospheric pressure is 1.0×10^5 Pa.

  a Calculate the pressure at a point X inside the cylinder, 3.0 m below the surface of the water, just next to the bung.

  b The bung is now removed. Calculate the speed at which water leaves the hole.

12 Figure B.16 shows a cricket ball in its path from the bowler towards the batsman. One side of the ball is shiny and smooth. The other side of the ball is dull and rough.

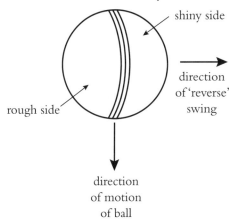

Figure B.16

Use Bernoulli's equation to explain why a talented bowler can make the cricket ball 'reverse' swing sideways in the direction shown in Figure B.16.

13 **a** Outline how Bernoulli's equation shows the lift force on an aeroplane's wing.
   b Outline how the Pitot tube extending from the nose of an aeroplane is able to measure the speed of the plane through the air.

14 Figure B.17 shows three examples of the streamlines in a fluid flowing in a tube.

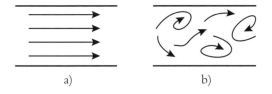 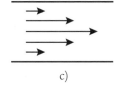

a)   b)   c)

Figure B.17

a For each example, identify whether the flow is non-viscous laminar, viscous laminar or turbulent.
b A sphere of radius, r, is moving through a viscous liquid of viscosity, η, at a speed, v:
   i State the size of the viscous drag force experienced by the sphere.
   ii By equating the weight of the sphere with its buoyancy force and its viscous drag force, show that the terminal velocity of the sphere is given by the expression:

$$V_{terminal} = \frac{2r^2 g\left(\rho_s - \rho_f\right)}{9\eta}$$

where ρ_s is the density of the sphere and ρ_f is the density of the fluid through which it is falling.
c A steel ball bearing of radius 1.0 cm is falling through water with viscosity 8.9×10^{-4} Pa s. ($r_{steel} = 7.8 \times 10^3$ kg m^{-3})
   i Calculate the ball's terminal velocity.
   ii If the water was in a cylinder of radius 5.0 cm, would the falling ball create a turbulent flow? Explain your reasoning.
   iii If the water was warmed up, what would you expect to happen to the terminal velocity of the sphere?

15 Vegetable oil in a factory flows through a pipeline of radius 5.0 cm at a speed of 2.0 m s^{-1}. Its viscosity is 3.5×10^{-2} Pa s and its density is 750 kg m^{-1}.

    a Determine if the flow is laminar or turbulent.

    b What is the maximum speed at which the oil can flow through the pipe, so that its flow remains laminar?

HL Exercise B.4 – Forced vibrations and resonance

1 Define the following terms.

    a Free oscillations.

    b Forced oscillations.

    c Resonance.

2   **a** Explain what is meant by *damping*.

    b Outline the difference between an oscillating system being overdamped, underdamped and critically damped.

    c Sketch a graph to show how the amplitude of an oscillator would vary with time if the oscillations are:

      i critically damped; label this C

      ii over damped; label this O.

3 Jo is on a playground swing. The amplitude of her free oscillations decreases by a factor of 0.80 for each swing.

    a Calculate the Q factor for the swing.

    b How many swings will the swing make before Jo comes to a rest?

4 You hold a long spring of spring constant 10 N m^{-1} with a 200 g mass attached to it. You make the mass on the spring bounce up and down by applying a periodic force, of varying frequency, to the spring.

    a Sketch a graph to show how the amplitude of the oscillations will vary with the frequency of your periodic force.

    b At what frequency will the amplitude of the oscillations be a maximum?

    c One of your friends suggests that you try damping your oscillations.

      i Suggest how you might be able to do this.

      ii Add another line to your sketch to show how the amplitude of the oscillations varies if your damping is heavy.

      iii What has happened to the forcing frequency at which the maximum amplitude occurs?

    d What is the phase relationship between the forcing oscillations and the oscillations of the mass–spring system when:

      i the forcing frequency is much less than the natural frequency

      ii resonance occurs

      iii the forcing frequency is much greater than the natural frequency?

1   The hard drive of a laptop rotates with an angular speed of 7200 revolutions per
    minute. The laser reading head is positioned 3.0 cm from the axis of rotation.
    a Calculate the angular speed of the hard drive in radians s^{-1}. **[2]**
    b Calculate the linear speed at which the hard drive moves past the laser reading head. **[2]**
    c To read one byte of information, 4.00 μm of the hard drive has to pass the laser reading
        head. Calculate the reading speed from the hard drive in Mb s^{-1}. **[2]**

2   A 20.0 kg circular disc, with a radius of 0.40 m, is made to spin, from rest, by
    exerting a tangential force of 150 N for one complete turn of the disc. There are no
    frictional forces. Calculate the:
    a amount of work is done on the disc **[2]**
    b final angular speed of the disc **[2]**
    c average power required if the whole process takes 2.5 s. **[2]**

3   Figure B.18 shows a $p–V$ diagram for 2.0×10^{-3} moles of ideal gas. It shows four
    thermodynamic processes, A, B, C and D, each acting on the thermodynamic state X.

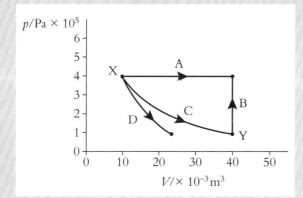

Figure B.18

    a Identify which of the thermodynamic processes are represented by A, B, C and D. **[4]**
    b For process A, determine how much work the gas has done on its surroundings. **[2]**
    c For process C, determine the temperature of the gas at:
        i X
        ii Y. **[3]**
    d For process C, estimate how much heat the gas has exchanged with its surroundings. **[2]**

4   The first law of thermodynamics can be written as: $Q = \Delta U + W$
    a Identify what each of the terms represents and, for each, state the conditions under which
        the term is a positive value. **[3]**
    b A system exchanges 50 J of heat with its hotter surroundings, whilst doing 35 J of work on
        its surroundings. Calculate the change in the system's internal energy. **[1]**
    c In an isothermal process a system does 25.0 J of work on its surroundings.
        i How much heat is transferred?
        ii Is the heat transferred to or from the surroundings? **[2]**

5   Figure B.19 shows a *p*–V diagram for the expansion of a fixed sample of ideal gas. The temperature of the gas at X is 300 K.

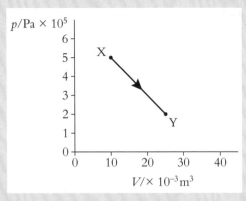

Figure B.19

a   Calculate the number of moles of gas present. **[2]**
b   Show that the temperature of Y is also 300 K. **[2]**
c   Calculate the work done by the gas during its expansion. **[2]**
d   State the value of the heat exchanged between the gas and its surroundings. **[1]**
e   i   Copy Figure B.19 and draw on it the isothermal expansion from X to Y. **[2]**
    ii   Will the amount of heat exchanged between the gas and its surroundings be more or less than before? Explain your answer. **[2]**

6   **HL**
a   Suggest why simple harmonic oscillations are not encountered in real life. **[2]**
b   A simple pendulum in oscillation has an amplitude that decreases exponentially.
    i   Explain the term *exponentially*. **[2]**
    ii   Outline an easy test you could do to check that the amplitude of the oscillations was decreasing exponentially. **[3]**
    iii If the amplitude of the pendulum's oscillations decreases by a factor of 0.9 for each oscillation, how many oscillations will the pendulum have to make before its amplitude has halved? **[2]**

7   **HL**
a   State how the energy of an oscillator depends on its amplitude. **[1]**
b   Suppose that, in each oscillation, 10% of the oscillator's energy is lost. How many oscillations would it take for the oscillator to lose 99.9% of its energy? **[2]**
c   Calculate the Q factor for the oscillations given in part **b**. **[2]**
d   By comparing your answers to parts **b** and **c**, suggest how you might be able to describe what the Q factor means? **[2]**
e   State what the maximum value for the Q factor is for a critically damped oscillator. **[1]**

Option C: Imaging

Chapter outline

In this chapter, you will:
- Describe how a thin lens modifies the shape of an incident wavefront.
- Identify the principal axis, the focal points and the focal length of a simple converging or diverging lens on a scale diagram.
- Understand the concept of a real and a virtual image.
- Solve problems involving two lenses by constructing a scaled ray diagram and problems involving two mirrors by constructing a scaled ray diagram.
- Use the thin lens equation and be able to use it to solve problems involving linear and angular magnification.
- Identify the causes of spherical and chromatic aberration and describe the effect they have on an image.
- Construct and interpret a ray diagram of an optical compound microscope at normal adjustment.
- Solve problems involving angular magnification and resolution of an optical compound microscope and investigate an optical compound microscope experimentally.
- Construct and interpret a ray diagram for a simple optical astronomical refracting telescope at normal adjustment and solve problems involving angular magnification of a simple optical astronomical telescope.
- Construct and interpret a ray diagram for a simple astronomical reflecting telescope.
- Describe the main features and operation of a single radio telescope dish and a radio interferometer array.
- Compare the performance of Earth-based and satellite-borne telescopes.
- Understand the structure of an optical fibre and solve problems involving total internal reflection and critical angle in an optical fibre.
- Describe and distinguish between graded index and step index optical fibres and describe how waveguide (or modal) and material dispersion leads to attenuation and describe the advantages of fibre optic cables over twisted pair and coaxial cables.
- **HL** Explain the main features of X-ray imaging in medical contexts, including attenuation coefficient, half thickness value, linear and mass absorption coefficient and techniques for improving sharpness and contrast; solve problems involving X-ray attenuation.
- **HL** Explain the main features of imaging using ultrasound in medicine, including acoustic impedance, speed of ultrasound through tissue and air and relative intensity levels.
- **HL** Identify and explain the use of gel and choice of frequency and the difference between A and B scans in ultrasound imaging.
- **HL** Describe the basic features of how an MRI scan works, including the origin of relaxation of proton spin, explain the use of a gradient field in nuclear magnetic resonance and discuss the advantages and disadvantages of ultrasound and NMR imaging and their relative risks.

Linear magnification, *m*: $m = \dfrac{\text{height of image}}{\text{height of object}} = \dfrac{v}{u}$

Angular magnification, *M*: $M = \dfrac{\text{angle subtended by image}}{\text{angle subtended by object}}$

Thin lens equation: $\dfrac{1}{f} = \dfrac{1}{u} + \dfrac{1}{v}$, where f is the focal length of the lens, u the distance from the object to the lens and v the distance from the image to the lens.

Resolution: $\sin\theta = 1.22\dfrac{\lambda}{d}$ for a circular aperture of diameter, d.

Angular magnification of an astronomical telescope:
$M = \dfrac{\text{focal length of objective lens}}{\text{focal length of eyepiece lens}} = \dfrac{f_\text{o}}{f_\text{e}}$

Attenuation and dispersion: attenuation: the reduction of energy in a pulse – made up of a combination of scattering and absorption. Dispersion: when a pulse changes shape and spreads out as it travels along the optical fibre. Attenuation in bels $= \log_{10}\dfrac{I}{I_0}$, attenuation in decibels $= 10\log_{10}\dfrac{I}{I_0}$

Linear absorption coefficient, *μ*: the constant in the equation, $I = I_0\, e^{-\mu x}$ that describes how effective an absorber is.

Larmor frequency: The required frequency to make protons flip their energy state, given by $f_\text{Larmor} = 4.26 \times 10^7 \times B$, where B is the magnetic flux density of the magnetic field in tesla.

Exercise C.1 – Introduction to imaging

1   Figure C.1 shows a thin lens and four rays of light passing through the lens.

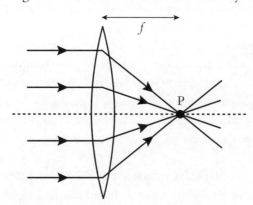

Figure C.1

  a What kind of lens is this?
  b What does the dotted line represent?
  c What is point P?
  d What is distance f?

2 **a** Look at Figure C.1. How does distance, f, vary with the power of the lens?

  b Calculate the power of the lens when f equals:

    i 1.0 m

    ii 0.6 m

    iii 25.0 cm.

  c Calculate the focal length, f, of a lens with power of:

    i +10 D

    ii +17 D

    iii +4 D.

3 Figure C.2 shows a thin lens with four rays of light passing through it.

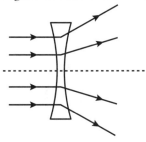

Figure C.2

  a What kind of lens is this?

  b Copy Figure C.2 and label the:

    i focal point of the lens

    ii focal length, f, of the lens.

  c Do any rays of light actually come from the focal point?

  d **i** If this lens has a power of −6 D, what is its focal length?

    ii What does your answer *mean*?

4 Sketch a diagram to show three rays of light that begin at one of the focal points of a thin convex lens, incident on the lens. Show what happens to the three rays of light.

5 Figure C.3 shows a thin convex lens; it is a vertical line only. The focal points on either side of the lens are also shown.

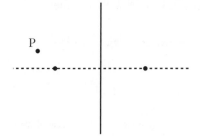

Figure C.3

Copy Figure C.3 and add a:

  a ray passing along the principal axis of the lens and through the lens and the focal point; label this R_1

  b second ray that starts at the point P, is parallel to the principal axis and passes through the lens; label this R_2

  c third ray that starts at the point P and passes through the optical centre of the lens; label this R_3.

6 Figure C.4 shows a thin convex lens and a distance scale, drawn along the principal axis from the optical centre of the lens out beyond twice the focal length. Also shown is an object (represented by a vertical arrow) placed at a distance, *u*, equal to twice the focal length, 2*f*.

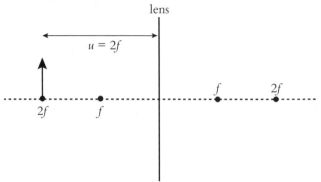

Figure C.4

  a Copy Figure C.4 and add:

    i a ray that starts at the object arrow tip and travels parallel to the principal axis before passing through the lens

    ii a ray that starts at the object arrow tip and passes through the optical centre of the lens

    iii a ray that starts at the object arrow tip and passes through the focal point onto the lens and then through the lens.

  b **i** The image of the arrow tip is the point at which the three rays intersect. Draw a vertical line to represent the image of the arrow.

    ii How far away from the lens is the image? Label this distance, *v*.

  c **i** If you put a screen at this distance, *v*, would you see an image on it?

    ii Hence, is this image real or virtual?

    iii How large is this image compared with the size of the object?

    iv Is the image inverted or upright?

7 Repeat the steps from question **6** two more times, but with these changes:

  a When copying Figure C.4, replace the object arrow at 2*f* with an object arrow that is greater than 2*f* from the lens.

  b When copying Figure C.4, replace the object arrow at 2*f* with an object that is between *f* and 2*f* from the lens.

8 Use your answers to questions **6** and **7** to copy and complete Table C.1.

Position of object	Position of image	Real or virtual image?	Upright or inverted image?	Size of image of object
u > 2*f*				
u = 2*f*				
f < *u* < 2*f*				

Table C.1

9   An object is placed on the principal axis at a distance of 20 cm from a lens of power +10 D.
    a   How far from the lens will the image of the object be?
    b   Will the image be real or virtual?
    c   How large will the image be compared to the size of the object?
    d   Will the image be inverted or upright?

10 Figure C.5 shows an object at a distance from a thin convex lens equal to the lens's focal length.

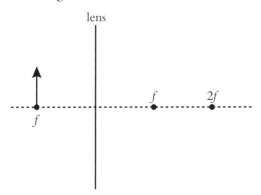

Figure C.5

    a   Copy and complete Figure C.5 to show where you would expect the image of the object to be.
    b   State whether the image is:
        i   upright or inverted
        ii   magnified or diminished
        iii real or virtual.

11 a   i   State the thin lens equation that relates u, v, and f.
        ii What are u, v and f?
    b   An object is placed on the principal axis of a lens of focal length 15.0 cm at a distance of 20.0 cm from the centre of the lens.
        i   Calculate the image distance, v.
        ii State the size and nature of the image.

12 An object is placed on the principal axis of a thin convex lens of focal length 20.0 cm, 15.0 cm from the centre of the lens.
    a   Use the thin lens equation to determine the position of the image.
    b   i   Is the image upright or inverted?
        ii Is the image real or virtual?
        iii What can you say about the size of the image compared to the size of the object?

13 Determine the position and size of an image formed by a thin converging lens of focal length 10.0 cm if an object that is 1.0 cm tall is placed 14 cm away from the lens.

14 An object is placed at a distance of 10.0 cm from a converging lens of focal length 15.0 cm.
   a Use the thin lens equation to determine the image distance, v.
   b State whether the image is:
      i real or virtual
      ii magnified or diminished
      iii upright or inverted.
   c Calculate the linear magnification, m of the image.

15 Consider some plane wavefronts incident on a convex lens.
Sketch a diagram to show how the lens adds curvature to the wavefronts and to show the significance of the principal focus of the lens.

16 Consider some plane wavefronts incident on a concave lens.
Sketch a diagram to show how the lens adds curvature to the wavefronts.

17 **a** When plane wavefronts (i.e. wavefronts that have come from an object a long way away) are incident on the lens, where does the light come to a focus?
   b Now suppose that diverging wavefronts are incident on the lens – because they have come from a nearby object. Where will the light now come to a focus?
   c **i** In your eye, all wavefronts need to come to a focus on your retina, which is a fixed distance from your eye's lens. Suggest what happens in your eye when you look at something far away, and then look at something close up.
      ii Try doing this. What do you feel?

18 Figure C.6 shows three rays of light incident on a concave spherical mirror of radius of curvature, r. Assume that the size of the mirror is small compared to its radius of curvature – i.e. a small arc length of the circle of radius r.

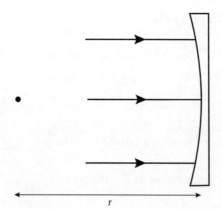

Figure C.6

   a Copy and complete Figure C.6 to show where the rays of light come to a focus.
   b What is the relationship between r and f, the focal length of the mirror?

19 Figure C.7 shows a spherical concave mirror of radius, r, and focal length, f. There is an object between r and f. The mirror is shown as a vertical line, using the same representation as with lenses.

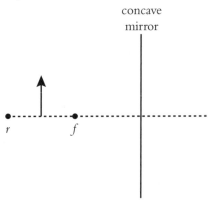

Figure C.7

    a Copy and complete Figure C.7 to show the position of the image of the object.
    b **i** Is the image real or virtual? Explain your answer.
       ii Is the image inverted or upright?
       iii Is the image magnified, diminished or the same size as the object?

20 **a** Draw a ray diagram for the image produced by an object placed on the principal axis of a concave spherical mirror at a distance greater than the radius of curvature of the mirror.
    b Is the image inverted or upright?
    c Is the image real or virtual?

21 An object of height 1.5 cm is placed 8.0 cm in front of a spherical concave mirror with a radius of curvature of 25.0 cm.
    a Without drawing a scale diagram, calculate the distance of the image from the mirror.
    b Calculate the size of the image.

22 Consider three parallel rays of light incident on a convex spherical mirror of radius of curvature, r. Assume that the size of the mirror is small compared to its radius of curvature – i.e. a small arc length of the circle of radius r.
    a Sketch a diagram to show what happens to the rays of light and how the focal point of the mirror can be found.
    b What is the relationship between r and the focal length of the mirror, f?

23 The side mirrors of cars are fitted with convex mirrors so the driver can see behind the car.
    A car side mirror has a radius of curvature of 15.0 m. If another car is approaching 12 m from the mirror, calculate the:
    a position of the image of the approaching car
    b size of the image, if the approaching car is 1.5 m high.

24 When two lenses of power D_1 and D_2 are placed next to each other, their combined power is $D_{total} = D_1 + D_2$.

Show that the focal length of the arrangement of the two lenses is given by:

$$f = \frac{f_1 f_2}{f_1 + f_2}$$

25 Calculate the focal length of the following arrangements of two lenses.

   a Two identical convex lenses of focal length 25.0 cm.

   b Two convex lenses, of focal lengths 10.0 cm and 15.0 cm.

   c A convex lens of focal length 12 cm and a concave lens of focal length −15 cm.

26 a Explain what is meant by *spherical aberration* when applied to a spherical mirror.

   b How can spherical aberration be avoided when using mirrors?

27 a Explain what is meant by *chromatic aberration* when using lenses to form images of objects.

   b How can the problems of chromatic aberration be avoided or reduced?

   c Explain why mirrors do not suffer from chromatic aberration.

28 a Outline what is meant by *near point*.

   b What is the accepted value of near point for a healthy eye?

29 An object is placed just closer than the focal length from a convex magnifying glass lens.

   a Will the image of the object be:

      i   real or virtual

      ii upright or inverted?

   b Define the angular magnification of the eyepiece in terms of the near point of the eye, D and the focal length of the lens, f.

   c i   If the image is formed at the near point of an eye, show that the object must be placed at a distance $u = \dfrac{fD}{f + D}$ from the lens.

      ii How is the angular magnification modified in this case?

30 A converging lens of focal length 6.0 cm is used to produce a magnified image of a 1.5 mm insect at the near point.

   a Determine the distance from the lens to the insect.

   b Calculate the size of the image.

31 Figure C.8 shows a convex lens used by an elderly gentleman as a magnifying glass to read his newspaper.

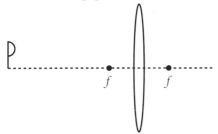

Figure C.8

a The gentleman is confused because he does not see what he was expecting. Complete Figure C.8 to show the image of the letter P that the gentleman sees.
b Outline why he is confused.
c What must the gentleman do to produce an image that he wants – i.e. an image that is magnified, and upright?

Exercise C.2 – Imaging instrumentation

1 Figure C.9 shows two convex lenses, separated by a distance, L. They are used as a compound microscope to observe very small objects. The focal lengths, f_o and f_e, of the lenses are shown. The magnified image is produced at the near point from the observer's eye

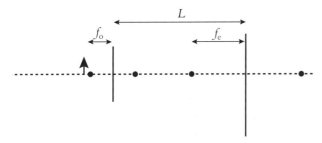

Figure C.9

a i Identify the objective lens and the eyepiece lens.
  ii Which of the two lenses has the smaller focal length?
b Copy Figure C.9, and:
  i use the standard technique to find the position of the image formed by the objective lens
  ii taking the image to be the object in front of the eyepiece lens, use the standard technique to find the position of the virtual image produced by the microscope.
c If the angular magnification of the eyepiece lens is $M_e = \dfrac{25}{f_e}$ and the angular magnification of the objective lens is $M_o = \dfrac{L}{f_o}$, what is the total magnification of the microscope?

2 In a compound microscope in normal adjustment, the objective lens has a focal length of 0.75 cm and eyepiece has a focal length of 4.0 cm. A small object is placed 0.80 cm from the objective lens.
Calculate the:
  a distance from the objective lens to the intermediate image
  b linear magnification for the objective lens
  c distance between the intermediate image and the eyepiece lens
  d angular magnification of the microscope.

3 An astronomical refracting telescope is constructed from two convex lenses of focal lengths, f_o and f_e. It is designed to produce a magnified image of a distant object in normal adjustment.
  a Explain what is meant by *normal adjustment* when applied to a refracting telescope.
  b Because the observed object is distant, what can you say about the rays of light that come from any part of the object to the objective lens?
  c Suggest a reason for the objective lens being as large as possible.
  d How far apart must the two lenses be placed?
  e Is the image produced by the telescope real or virtual?
  f Is the image produce by the telescope upright or inverted?

4 Draw a ray diagram to show how a magnified virtual image is produced in normal adjustment by an astronomical refracting telescope.

5 Figure C.10 shows two convex lenses used as an astronomical refracting telescope. The passage of four possible rays of light are shown.

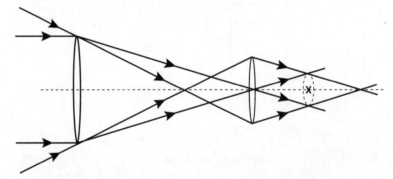

Figure C.10

  a What is the significance of the region labelled X?
  b Suggest two reasons why it is advantageous to observe the image from within this eye ring.

6 **a** Draw a ray diagram to show the construction of a Newtonian reflecting telescope.
  b Suggest two reasons why astronomers prefer to use reflecting telescopes rather than refracting telescopes.

7 **a** Draw a ray diagram to show the construction of a Cassegrain reflecting telescope.
  b **i** What shape is the primary mirror?
     ii Why is the primary mirror this shape?
  c **i** What shape is the secondary mirror?
     ii What purpose does this shape of secondary mirror have?

8   a   i   Explain what is meant by the *resolution* of a telescope.
        ii Outline what is meant by the *Rayleigh criterion*.
    b   i   What is the minimum angle that two distant objects can subtend for the 6.0 m
            diameter reflecting telescope in Zelenchukskaya, Russia in order for them to
            be resolved in light of wavelength 500 nm?
        ii What is the smallest size of object on the Moon's surface that could be seen
            clearly using this telescope? (The Moon is 3.8×10^8 m from the Earth.)

9   a   i   Why is a radio telescope so much larger than an optical telescope?
        ii Suggest the engineering difficulty when building a very large diameter radio
            telescope.
    b   Compare the resolving ability of:
        •   a 1.0 m diameter optical telescope observing in a wavelength region of 500 nm, and
        •   a 50.0 m diameter telescope observing microwaves in the wavelength region
            of 10 cm.

10 a   Outline what is meant by an *interferometer*.
    b   How does an interferometer produce a better resolving power than a single large dish?
    c   If all the radio telescopes on the Earth's surface could be used as an interferometer,
        they could provide the best possible resolution. If the Earth's radius is 6.4×10^6 m,
        calculate the smallest angle that two separate distant astronomical objects could
        subtend for them to be just resolved in a wavelength of 12 cm.

11 The Hubble Space Telescope has produced well-resolved images of distant galaxies
    and nebulae.
    a   Explain why distant stars observed by the Hubble telescope do not twinkle.
    b   Explain why the Hubble telescope is able to map the universe in a range of
        wavelengths not possible from the Earth's surface.
    c   Suggest a disadvantage of a satellite-borne telescope, such as the Hubble telescope.

Exercise C.3 – Fibre optics

1   Figure C.11 shows a section of an optical fibre. It is made from a central glass core of
    refractive index 1.50 and a cladding of refractive index 1.40.

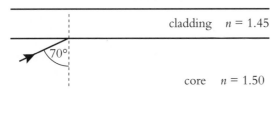

cladding $n = 1.45$

70°

core $n = 1.50$

cladding $n = 1.45$

Figure C.11

    a   Calculate the speed at which light travels through the core of the optical fibre.
    b   Calculate the critical angle for the boundary between the core and the cladding.
    c   i   Copy and complete Figure C.11 to show what you would expect the ray of
            light to do.
        ii What is the name of the optical phenomenon occurring here?

2 Figure C.12 shows a ray of light entering an optical fibre. The fibre has a core with a refractive index of n_1 at an angle of θ_A to the normal. The ray refracts when it enters the optical fibre and is totally internally reflected at the core-cladding boundary at the critical angle.

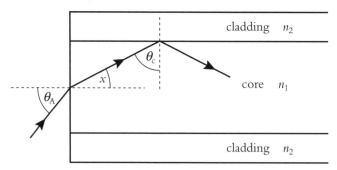

Figure C.12

a How is the angle x related to θ_A?
b Show that $\sin x = \cos \theta_c$
c Show that $\sin (90 - \theta_c) = \sqrt{1 - \sin^2 \theta_c}$

d Show that $\theta_A = \sin^{-1} \sqrt{n_1^2 - n_2^2}$

e What does θ_A represent?

3 An optical fibre is constructed from a central glass core of refractive index 1.53 and some cladding of refractive index 1.47. Will a ray that is incident on the end of the optical fibre at an angle of incidence of 23° be propagated through the optical fibre by total internal reflection?

4 Figure C.13 shows two rays that have entered one end of an optical fibre. The critical angle at the core-cladding boundary is 68° and the refractive index of the core material is 1.52.
The optical fibre is 25.0 km long.

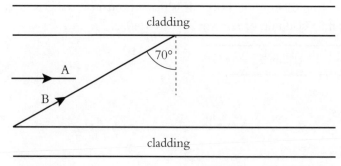

Figure C.13

Calculate the:
a time taken for ray A to travel through the optical fibre
b time delay between rays A and B when they appear at the other end of the optical fibre.

5 **a** Outline what is meant by:

    i *material dispersion*

    ii *waveguide dispersion*.

  b Explain why dispersion limits the rate at which an optical fibre can transmit information.

  c Figure C.14 shows a graph of the power input of a pulse of light with a spread of wavelengths on entering an optical fibre (left), and the graph of the power of the pulse as it emerges from the other end of the optical fibre (right).

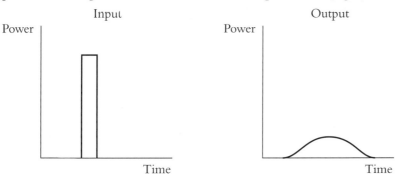

Figure C.14

    i Explain why the power output graph from the optical fibre has a smaller area than the power input graph.

    ii Suggest two reasons why the power output graph is wider than the power input graph.

  d Suggest two ways in which waveguide dispersion can be reduced.

6 **a** Explain why some electrical cables consist of two or more smaller cables that are twisted together.

  b Outline why an optical fibre does not suffer from the same problems as a twisted pair cable.

7 **a** Sketch the construction of a coaxial cable, labelling the various components.

  b Suggest why optical fibres are preferred over coaxial cables.

8 List some of the advantages that optical fibres have over other ways of transmitting signals securely.

9 A signal is transmitted along an optical fibre with an initial power of P_i. The output power of the signal is P_o.

  a In what units will the amount of attenuation be measured?

  b State the equation used to calculate the amount of attenuation in terms of P_i and P_o.

  c Calculate the following amounts of attenuation;

    i $P_i = 100$ mW and $P_o = 1$ mW

    ii $P_i = 100$ mW and $P_o = 10$ mW

    iii $P_i = 100$ mW and $P_o = 50$ mW

  d What is meant by *specific attenuation*?

  e If the specific attenuation of an optical fibre is 0.35 dB km^{-1}, what will the ratio of the output power to the input power be for an optical fibre of length 25 km?

10 Calculate the following output powers.

  a $P_i = 30.0$ mW; specific attenuation $= 0.5$ dB km^{-1}; length of optical fibre $= 8.0$ km.

  b $P_i = 50.0$ mW; specific attenuation $= 0.40$ dB km^{-1}; length of optical fibre $= 2.5$ km.

  c $P_i = 20.0$ mW; specific attenuation $= 1.5$ dB km^{-1}; length of optical fibre $= 12.0$ km.

11 a Define the term *gain* for an amplifier.

  b A signal from an optical fibre is fed into an amplifier with a gain of 5 dB. By what factor will the output power be increased?

  c A repeater amplifier of gain 2.4 dB is used 8.0 km along an optical fibre with a specific attenuation of 0.3 dB km^{-1}. Show that no net loss of signal occurs.

HL Exercise C.4 – Medical imaging

1 a Outline how X-rays are produced for use in medical imaging.

  b Suggest why it is advisable for the anode of an X-ray tube to rotate.

  c When referring to X-rays, explain what is meant by the terms:

    i soft

    ii hard.

2 The transmission of X-rays through materials is affected by attenuation. Outline how each of the following processes contribute to attenuation.

  a Beam divergence.

  b The photoelectric effect.

  c Coherent scattering.

  d Compton scattering.

  e Pair production.

3 The intensity of X-rays passing through a material is given by the equation:
$I = I_0 e^{-\mu x}$, where x is the distance through the material that the X-rays have passed.

  a i What is μ?

    ii What units does μ have?

  b How does μ relate to materials of different densities?

4 a X-rays of a constant energy pass through 10.0 cm of tissue with a linear absorption coefficient of 0.04 cm^{-1}. Calculate the fraction of X-rays that are transmitted.

  b Calculate the mass absorption coefficient for a metal with density of 4500 kg m^{-3} and linear absorption coefficient of 65 m^{-1}.

  c For monochromatic X-rays passing through a material of linear absorption coefficient 0.030 cm^{-1}:

    i calculate the thickness of material required to reduce the intensity by half

    ii state how thick the material will have to be to reduce the intensity by 75%.

5 Monochromatic X-rays are directed at a metal sheet of thickness 5.0 mm and half-value thickness 4.0 mm.

  a Calculate the linear absorption coefficient for the metal.

  b Calculate the percentage of X-rays that are transmitted through the metal.

6 X-rays used to detect breaks in bones have energy of about 30 keV. Such X-rays provide good contrast on a radiogram.

   a Outline what is meant by *contrast* in this context.

   b On passing through human flesh, such X-rays are attenuated. What is the most significant process contributing to attenuation for X-rays of this energy?

   c **i** Suggest why X-rays of this energy will not produce a good contrast on a radiogram if used to examine a problem in the stomach.

     ii Suggest what a radiographer might do to improve the contrast on a radiogram of a patient's stomach.

7 Figure C.15 shows how the fraction of transmitted monochromatic X-rays varies with distance through a material.

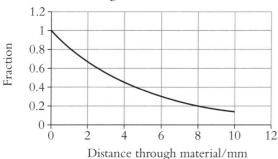

Figure C.15

   a Explain the term *monochromatic*.

   b Use the graph to find the half thickness of the material.

   c Find the value of the linear absorption coefficient of the material.

8 **a** Outline what an intensifying screen is, and explain how it enhances the brightness of a radiogram.

   b Outline what a collimating grid is, and explain how it enhances the contrast of a radiogram.

9 Outline what is meant by computer aided tomography (CAT) and how this technique can provide more detailed information than a normal X-ray.

10 **a** What is *ultrasound*?

   b What range of ultrasound frequencies are typically used in medical diagnostics?

   c Suggest three advantages and three disadvantages of using ultrasound diagnostically.

11 **a** Define the term *acoustic impedance, Z*.

   b State the units of Z.

   c Explain what is meant by *impedance matching*.

   d Suggest why a medical practitioner uses gel between an ultrasound emitter/receiver and a human's skin when conducting an ultrasound scan.

12 Outline the difference between an A scan and a B scan in ultrasound imaging.

13 A Magnetic Resonance Image (MRI) scan involves the physics of nuclear magnetic resonance (NMR).

    a Which sub-atomic particles are used in NMR?

    b There are two hydrogen atoms in every water molecule – so there are lots of them in the human body. Which parts of the body are particularly good for imaging with the NMR technique?

    c Which aspect of a proton's behaviour is utilised in NMR?

    d What does applying a radio frequency signal do to the protons in the nuclei of the material's atoms?

    e When the radio frequency signal is switched off, what happens to the protons?

    f Explain the significance of the *Larmor frequency*.

    g If a strong magnetic field with a linearly changing strength – a gradient field – is applied across a body, what will happen to the Larmor frequency across the body?

    h Explain, therefore, why a gradient field will reveal detail in a two-dimensional slice through a patient.

14 Complete Table C.2.

Imaging technique	Resolution	Advantages	Disadvantages
X-ray			
CT scan			
Ultrasound scan			
MRI scan			

Table C.2

? Exam-style questions

1 **Figure C.16 shows a spherical concave mirror. An object is at a distance smaller than the focal length of the mirror.**

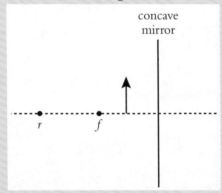

concave mirror

r   *f*

Figure C.16

    a Copy and complete Figure C.16 to show the position and nature of the image produced. **[3]**

    b **i** Is the image real or virtual? Explain your reasoning.

        ii Is the image magnified or diminished?

        iii Is the image upright or inverted? **[4]**

    c Suggest a use for this kind of mirror in your home. **[1]**

2 Consider a spherical convex mirror of radius of curvature, r, and an object placed on the principal axis in front of the mirror at a distance just larger than f.
  a Sketch a diagram to show the position of the image of the object. [3]
  b Is the image:
    i   real or virtual? (Explain your reasoning.)
    ii upright or inverted?
    iii magnified or diminished? [4]

3 Figure C.17 shows two convex lenses, A and B, used in a compound microscope to observe an object, O. The principal focal points for lens A are shown, along with two standard rays that form the image from lens A.

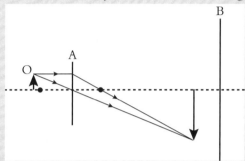

Figure C.17

  a Add a possible position for the principal focal points of lens B either side of lens B. [2]
  b The microscope is set to normal adjustment. Explain what this means. [1]
  c Is the image produced by the microscope real or virtual? Explain your reasoning. [2]

4 Two lenses, of focal length 1.80 cm and 3.0 cm, are used to make a compound microscope. The microscope's image is produced 25.0 cm from the eyepiece.
  a Suggest which of the lenses should be used as the objective. [1]
  b If a small object is placed 2.0 cm from the objective, calculate the position of the intermediate image produced by the objective lens. [2]
  c Calculate how far apart the two lenses need to be. [2]
  d Calculate the overall magnification of the microscope. [2]

5 a Which feature of an astronomical refracting telescope most limits its ability to view the furthest objects? [1]
  b Another problem suffered by an astronomical telescope is spherical aberration.
    i   Explain how spherical aberration occurs.
    ii Suppose that the image from a telescope that does not suffer from spherical aberration is a square with a simple cross – like an x – inside it. Sketch a diagram to show what the image might look like if a telescope is used that *does* suffer from spherical aberration. [3]
  c Outline one other problem suffered by a refracting telescope. [2]

6   **A refracting telescope in normal adjustment is made from two lenses of focal lengths 84.0 cm and 12.0 cm.**
    a   Which of the lenses, the objective or the eyepiece, has the focal length 84.0 cm? **[1]**
    b   Calculate how far apart the two lenses are. **[2]**
    c   Calculate the angular magnification of the telescope. **[2]**
    d   If the telescope is used to observe the Moon, the angle subtended by the Moon is 0.40°. Calculate the angle subtended by the image of the Moon. **[2]**

7   a   What are the two main contributors to attenuation in an optical fibre? **[2]**
    b   Figure C.18 shows how the contribution of absorption of energy varies with wavelength for a typical optical fibre.

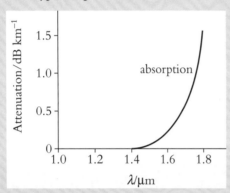

Figure C.18

Add a line to show the contribution to attenuation of Rayleigh scattering. [2]
    c   i   Outline how Rayleigh scattering occurs.
        ii How does the amount of Rayleigh scattering vary with wavelength?
        iii What does this dictate about the quality of the glass that makes the optical fibre core? **[4]**
    d   In order to counteract the effect of attenuation, it is sometimes necessary to boost the signal being transmitted. This is done with a repeater at a mid-way point along the length of the optical fibre. State two aspects of the transmitted pulses that the repeater must fix. **[2]**

8   **HL** The speed of ultrasound in soft human tissue is about 1.55 km s^{-1}.
    a   Calculate the wavelength of ultrasound waves of frequency 3.0 MHz. **[2]**
    b   State the smallest feature that can be distinguished using these ultrasound waves. **[1]**
    c   How far into a human will these ultrasound waves penetrate in order to produce useful diagnostic images? **[2]**

9   **HL** The density of air is 1.3 kg m^{-3} and the speed of sound in air is 330 m s^{-1}. The density of human flesh is very similar to that of water (1000 kg m^{-3}); sound travels through at 1550 m s^{-1}.
    a   Calculate the acoustic impedance of:
        i   air
        ii human flesh. **[3]**
    b   Show that the percentage of ultrasound intensity transmitted through an air–flesh boundary is less than 1%. **[2]**
    c   Hence explain how the use of gel between the skin and the ultrasound emitter/receiver increases the amount of transmitted ultrasound. **[2]**

Option D: Astrophysics

Chapter outline

In this chapter, you will:
- Identify objects in the universe, understand and describe qualitatively the conditions for equilibrium between pressure and gravitational forces in stars.
- Use the units of distance: astronomical unit (AU), light year (ly) and parsec (pc).
- Understand the concept of stellar parallax and use it to determine the distance to stars that are less than 100 pc from the Earth.
- Use the concepts of luminosity and apparent brightness to solve problems involving the distance to stars that are between 100 pc and 10,000 pc from the Earth.
- Explain how the temperature of a star's surface can be found from its emission spectrum and explain how the composition of a star can be determined from its emission spectrum; solve problems involving the mass–luminosity relationship for main sequence stars.
- Use and interpret a Hertzsprung–Russell (HR) diagram.
- Understand what a Cepheid variable star is, explain why its luminosity varies and use Cepheid variable stars to determine the distance to stars.
- Identify the main characteristics of red giants, white dwarfs, neutron stars and black holes, and know how to plot an evolutionary track for stars on the HR diagram.
- Describe the evolution of stars when they move off the main sequence.
- Describe the relevance of the Chandrasekhar limit and the Oppenheimer-Volkoff limit in a heavy star's evolution.
- Describe the Big Bang model of the universe and explain how the characteristics of cosmic microwave background radiation provide evidence for the hot Big Bang model of the universe.
- Describe the significance of Hubble's law, determine the age of the universe using the Hubble constant, H and solve problems using the cosmological redshift (z), the cosmic scale factor (R) and Hubble's law.
- **HL** Apply the Jeans criterion to a star's formation from an interstellar cloud, describe the various ways in which nuclear fusion takes place in stars off the main sequence and compare lifetimes of stars on the main sequence with that of our Sun, by using the mass-luminosity relationship.
- **HL** Describe the processes of nucleosynthesis of heavy elements in stars, describe qualitatively the r and s processes for neutron capture and distinguish between type 1a and type 2 supernovae.
- **HL** Describe the cosmological principle and its role in different models of the universe.
- **HL** Describe how a rotation curve can provide evidence for dark matter.
- **HL** Derive rotational velocity using ideas from Newtonian gravitation.
- **HL** Describe and interpret anisotropies in the CMB, derive a critical density for the universe from ideas from Newtonian gravitation, sketch and interpret graphs showing the variation of cosmic scale factor with time and describe qualitatively the effect of dark matter on the cosmic scale factor.

KEY TERMS

Apparent brightness, b: The amount of energy incident per unit area per second at a distance, d, from a star of luminosity, L; $b = \dfrac{L}{4\pi d^2}$

Stefan–Boltzmann law: The luminosity of a star, $L = \sigma A T^4$, where σ is the Stefan–Boltzmann constant, A is the surface area of the star and T is its absolute temperature.

Wien's displacement law: $T = \dfrac{2.9 \times 10^{-3}}{\lambda_{max}}$

Mass–luminosity relationship for a main sequence star: $L \propto M^{3.5}$

Chandrasekhar limit: The maximum mass of a white dwarf is 1.4 solar masses. Above this mass, the star will collapse into a neutron star.

Oppenheimer–Volkoff limit: The maximum mass of a neutron star is between 1.4 and 3.0 solar masses. Above this mass and the star will collapse into a black hole.

Hubble's law: $v = H d$ (note that $\dfrac{1}{H}$ gives an approximation for the age of the universe).

Cosmic scale factor, R: The factor by which all distances are stretched because of cosmological expansion; $z = \dfrac{\Delta \lambda}{\lambda} = \dfrac{R}{R_0} - 1$

Critical density: $\rho_c = \dfrac{3H^2}{8\pi G}$ and $\Omega_0 = \dfrac{\rho}{\rho_c}$. So, when: $\Omega_0 > 1$ closed universe, $\Omega_0 = 1$ flat universe and $\Omega_0 < 1$ open universe.

Exercise D.1 – Stellar quantities

1   Describe the following terms.
   a   Planet
   b   Asteroid
   c   Comet
   d   Moon
   e   Galaxy
   f   Cluster
   g   Constellation
   h   Nebula

2   State what is meant by *light year*, then calculate the distance of one light year (1 ly) in metres.

3   With the use of a suitable diagram, explain what is meant by *parsec*.

4   Given that the average orbital radius of the Earth about the Sun is 1 AU ($= 1.5 \times 10^{11}$ m) convert one parsec (1 pc) into metres, and show that 1 pc $\approx$ 3.26 ly.

5   Calculate the distance (in metres) equivalent to 800 pc.

6   The distance between the Earth and the Sun is 1.5×10^{11} m. Show that this can be expressed as 8.33 light minutes.

7   A star exhibiting a parallax angle of one second of arc is, by definition, 1 pc from the Sun. Explain why it is not necessary for us to consider the distance of the Earth from the Sun if we would like to know how far the star is from the Earth.

8   An observed star has a parallax angle of five seconds of arc. How far is the star from the Sun?

9   The smallest parallax angle that we can measure accurately from the Earth is about $\frac{1}{100}$ of a second of arc. What is the farthest distance away a star can be for us to measure how far it is from the Sun using the parallax angle method?

10 Explain what is meant by the following terms used to describe and classify stars.
    a *Luminosity*
    b *Apparent brightness*

11 If we make the assumption that a star radiates like a black body (its emissivity is one), on what factors does a star's luminosity depend? Write an equation for the luminosity of a star.

12 Using the Stefan–Boltzmann constant of $\sigma = 5.67 \times 10^{-8}\,\mathrm{W\,m^{-2}\,K^{-4}}$, calculate the luminosities of the following stars.
    a Star A, radius 7×10^{8} m, surface temperature 5700 K.
    b Star B, radius 8.2×10^{11} m, surface temperature 3500 K.
    c Star C, radius 4.9×10^{10} m, surface temperature 11 200 K.

13 Procyon A, a star in the constellation Canis Minor, has a surface temperature of 6530 K and a radius that is twice that of our Sun. If the surface temperature of our Sun is 5700 K, calculate the ratio of their two luminosities, $\frac{L_{\mathrm{Procyon}}}{L_{\mathrm{Sun}}}$.

14 Sirius A, a main sequence star, has a luminosity that is 25.4 times that of our Sun. If the surface temperature of Sirius A is 9940 K and the surface temperature of our Sun is 5700 K, calculate the ratio of the radii of the two stars, $\frac{r_{\mathrm{Sirius\,A}}}{r_{\mathrm{Sun}}}$.

15 Two stars, X and Y, have luminosities in the ratio $L_{\mathrm{X}} : L_{\mathrm{Y}} = 500$. If the ratio of their surface temperatures, $T_{\mathrm{X}} : T_{\mathrm{Y}} = 20$, calculate the ratio of their radii, $R_{\mathrm{x}} : R_{\mathrm{y}}$.

16 The star Rigel, in the constellation of Orion, is about 70 times the radius of our Sun. The star Betelgeuse, also in Orion, has a radius about 1100 times that of our Sun. The surface temperature of Rigel is about twice that of our Sun and the surface temperature of Betelgeuse is about three fifths that of our Sun. Show that the luminosity of Betelgeuse is about twice that of Rigel.

17 Calculate the apparent brightness, b_{Sun}, of our Sun. Our Sun has luminosity 3.8×10^{26} W and is 1.5×10^{11} m away from the Earth.

18 Calculate the apparent brightness of a star that has a luminosity of 5.0×10^{28} W if it is four light years away.

19 Alpha Centauri, a triple star in the constellation of Centaurus, has a luminosity that is 152 times that of our Sun and it is 4.3 light years from the Earth. Our Sun is 8.33 light minutes from the Earth. Calculate the ratio of the apparent brightness of Alpha Centauri to that of our Sun, $\frac{b_{\alpha}}{b_{\mathrm{Sun}}}$.

Exercise D.2 – Stellar characteristics and stellar evolution

1 **a** Sketch the black body emission spectrum for a star with a:
   i   very hot surface temperature, such as the star Spica
   ii low surface temperature, such as the star Betelgeuse.
   b How can you tell the difference between the surface temperatures of two stars by examining their black body emission spectra?

2 Suggest why the spectrum from a star contains a number of dark lines superposed on top of a continuum.

3 In the emission spectrum of Vega (a star in the constellation of Lyra) there is a strong set of absorption lines that occur at wavelengths 656 nm, 486 nm, 434 nm and 410 nm. Though these absorption lines also appear in the spectrum of our Sun, they are very much less prominent.
   a Which element in the outer layers of Vega is responsible for these absorption lines?
   b What is the usual name given to this series of lines?
   c What electron energy level transitions are responsible for these four absorption lines?
   d How does this suggest that the temperature of the surface of Vega is hotter than the temperature of the surface of our Sun?
   e Sketch the emission spectra of Vega and our Sun. Use your sketch to show that Vega's surface is hotter than the Sun's surface.

4 Star X has a surface temperature higher than Vega. It does not display the same set of absorption lines as Vega, even though its outer layers contain a significant amount of hydrogen.
   a Suggest why.
   b How has this helped astronomers to classify stars?

5 **a** The Sun has a surface temperature lower than that Vega. It does display the same set of absorption lines as Vega (albeit very much less prominently). Suggest why.
   b In which part of the electromagnetic spectrum would you expect there to be prominent absorption lines in the spectrum from our Sun? Explain your reasoning.

6 Use Wien's displacement law to calculate the surface temperature of a star whose peak wavelength in its emission spectrum is at 650 nm.
   (Wien's constant = 2.9×10^{-3} m K.)

7 Arcturus is a star in the constellation of Bootes. Its surface temperature is about 4300 K.
   a Use Wien's displacement law to calculate the peak wavelength in its emission spectrum.
   b Suggest why astronomers consider the luminosity of Arcturus to be larger than the calculated value of 110 L_{Sun}.

8   a   Outline what is meant by *Hertzsprung–Russell diagram*.
    b   Sketch a Hertzsprung–Russell (HR) diagram, showing an approximate scale for
        the two axes.
    c   Indicate what is meant by *main sequence*.
    d   Indicate where you would expect to find the following stars.
        i   Our Sun, $T = 5700$ K.
        ii   Vega, $T = 9600$ K.
        iii Betelgeuse, a red supergiant of $T = 3500$ K.
        iv   Sirius B, a white dwarf of $T = 25\,000$ K.

9   Outline, in terms of their luminosity and their surface temperatures, the main
    features of a:
    a   main sequence star
    b   red giant star
    c   supergiant star
    d   white dwarf star.

10 How is the luminosity of a main sequence star affected by its mass?

11 Show that a main sequence star with a mass 10 times that of our Sun will have a
    luminosity that is about 3200 times that of our Sun.

12 Use the relationship between luminosity and mass for a star on the main sequence
    to find the luminosity of a main sequence star that is five times the mass of our Sun.
    ($L_{Sun} = 3.8 \times 10^{26}$ W.)

13 Stars form when large clouds of gas and dust come together to form a concentrated
    region of matter called a protostar. What is the main energy transformation taking
    place as this occurs?

14 Once the protostar becomes massive enough to initiate *thermonuclear fusion*, it will
    become a star, producing energy from its core.
    a   What is meant by *thermonuclear fusion*?
    b   What is/are the end product(s) of thermonuclear fusion for a main sequence star?

15 What happens in the core of a main sequence star to cause it to move off the main
    sequence?

16 Outline what will happen to a main sequence star (with similar mass to our Sun)
    after it has moved off the main sequence until it becomes no longer visible.

17 Explain what prevents the gravitational collapse of a white dwarf star into a neutron
    star.

18 Which of the following is the best estimate for the density of a white dwarf?
    A 10^3 kg m^{-3}
    B 10^6 kg m^{-3}
    C 10^9 kg m^{-3}
    D 10^{12} kg m^{-3}

19 Outline what will happen to a star that is much heavier than our Sun once it leaves the main sequence.

20 Explain what is meant by the term *Chandrasekhar limit* and why it is important in defining the eventual fate of a heavy main sequence star.

21 What opposes the gravitational force in a neutron star to allow the star to have hydrostatic equilibrium?

22 Explain what is meant by the *Oppenheimer–Volkoff limit* and why it is important in defining the eventual fate of a heavy main sequence star.

23 **a** Sketch a Hertzsprung–Russell diagram and indicate the path that our Sun will follow during its lifetime.
 b State what happens to the luminosity of the Sun, and what causes the luminosity to change, as it proceeds along this path on the HR diagram.

24 It is not possible to *see* a black hole. What observational evidence *do* astronomers have for their existence?

Exercise D.3 – Cosmology

1 **a** What three features did Newton consider in his early model of the universe?
 b What is meant by *Olbers' paradox* and how does this help to show that Newton's model of the universe was flawed?

2 Explain what is meant by *redshift* when applied to the observation of spectral lines in the emission spectrum of a distant star.

3 The redshift measured from a distant galaxy has a value of 0.04. Calculate the recessional speed of the galaxy from the Earth.

4 State Hubble's law and suggest how this leads to the idea of the Big Bang model of the universe.

5 A spectral line of proper wavelength 5.3×10^{-7} m is observed from a distant star to have a wavelength of 5.7×10^{-7} m. Find:
 a z
 b the recessional speed of the star
 c the distance between the star and the Earth in pc ($H = 72$ km s^{-1} Mpc^{-1}).

6 In a distant quasar, a spectral line is observed at a wavelength of 750 nm. The wavelength of the same line observed in the laboratory is 660 nm. Taking H to be 72 km s^{-1} Mpc^{-1}, calculate the distance, in Mpc, of the quasar from the Earth.

7 **a** Show that the reciprocal of the Hubble constant, $\frac{1}{H}$, can be used as a measure of the age of the universe.
 b Using $H = 72$ km s^{-1} Mpc^{-1}, show that the age of the universe is a little less than 14 billion years.

8 Astrophysicists have estimated that the value of H may lie somewhere between 60 and 90 km s^{-1} Mpc^{-1}. Suggest two reasons why there is such a large uncertainty.

9 The Big Bang model is supported by two other pieces of observational evidence. Outline what these are and why they support the Big Bang model.

10 What feature of the cosmic microwave background (CMB) radiation supports the idea that the universe is:
   a cooler now than it used to be
   b essentially isotropic
   c structured, on a small scale (i.e. it contains regions in which the density of material is relatively large and other regions in which the density of material is relatively small).

11 Use Wien's displacement law to find the temperature of the universe if the peak wavelength in the spectrum of CMB is 1.1 mm.

12 Explain what is meant by *cosmological redshift* and why this is different to the redshift caused by the Doppler effect of objects moving away from the Earth.

13 Explain what is meant by the cosmic scale factor, R, and show how R is related to z, the redshift.

14 If a distant quasar is seen to have a redshift of $z = 3.5$, calculate:
   a what the apparent speed of the quasar is relative to the Earth
   b how many times bigger the universe is now than when the photons were emitted by the quasar.

15 **a** Explain how the observation of type 1a supernovae at distances of up to 1 Gpc has led to the realisation that the universe is expanding at an increasing rate.
   b How have scientists suggested our model of the universe needs to be changed to account for this increasing rate of expansion?

HL Exercise D.4 – Stellar processes

1 By considering the two kinds of energy that are possessed by a collapsing cloud of gas, explain what is meant by the *Jeans criterion* for star formation. Why, therefore, is it easier for a cold, dense cloud of gas to form a star than it is for a hot, low-density cloud of gas?

2 In main sequence stars, one of the fusion processes is called the proton–proton (p–p) chain. It involves six protons to produce a helium nucleus and two surplus protons. Complete the following equations to show the three stages in the p–p chain.
   a $^1_1p + ^1_1p \rightarrow$ _____ + _____ + _____
   b $^1_1p +$ _____ $\rightarrow$ _____ $+ \gamma$
   c $^3_2He +$ _____ $\rightarrow$ _____ $+ 2^1_1p$

3 Explain why the production of helium nuclei from protons produces energy.

4 Stars with a mass much larger than the Sun on the main sequence can produce energy by the carbon–nitrogen–oxygen (CNO) cycle. Complete the following reaction equations that show the complete CNO cycle:

a $\quad {}^1_1p + {}^{12}_6C \rightarrow \underline{\quad\quad} + \gamma$

b $\quad \underline{\quad\quad} \rightarrow {}^{13}_6C + \underline{\quad\quad} + {}^0_0\nu$

c $\quad {}^1_1p + {}^{13}_6C \rightarrow \underline{\quad\quad} + \gamma$

d $\quad {}^1_1p + \underline{\quad\quad} \rightarrow {}^{15}_8O + \underline{\quad\quad}$

e $\quad {}^{15}_8O \rightarrow {}^{15}_7N + \underline{\quad\quad} + \underline{\quad\quad}$

f $\quad {}^1_1p + {}^{15}_7N \rightarrow {}^{12}_6C + \underline{\quad\quad}$

5 Explain why main sequence stars producing energy by the CNO cycle must have a hotter core temperature than main sequence stars producing energy by the p–p chain.

6 Outline how a star that has moved off the main sequence and become a red giant can produce:

a unstable beryllium $\left({}^8_4Be\right)$

b carbon $\left({}^{12}_6C\right)$

c oxygen $\left({}^{16}_8O\right)$.

7 Further reactions are possible in red giant stars that can produce elements up to iron-56. Explain why it is not possible to produce elements heavier than iron-56 by the continued fusion of lighter elements in red giant stars.

8 Very heavy stars can produce nuclides up to bismuth-209 by the *slow neutron capture* process, or *s-process*. Explain what this process requires and why it produces nuclides of higher atomic number.

9 Another process involved in the production of heavier elements is the *rapid neutron capture process*, or *process*. Explain how this process is different to the s–process and why it can produce heavier isotopes of the same element.

10 Outline how a type 1a supernova occurs and why this implies that they can be used as *standard candles*.

11 Outline how a type 2 supernova occurs and contrast how the relative luminosity of the type 2 supernova is different to that of the type 1a supernova.

🅗🅛 Exercise D.5 – Further cosmology

1 a Explain what is meant by the term *cosmological principle*, as suggested by Einstein.
b How have detailed observations of the CMB shown the cosmological principle to be generally true, though on a smaller scale inappropriate?

2 Use your ideas about gravitational potential energy, kinetic energy and Hubble's law to derive an algebraic expression for the critical density of the universe.

3 Calculate the critical density of the universe, using the value 72 km s^{-1} Mpc^{-1} for the Hubble constant. How many nucleons does this correspond to?

4 Suggest two reasons why the density of the universe is difficult for astronomers and astrophysicists to measure accurately.

5 By referring to the current density parameter, Ω_0, and the fact that $\Omega_0 = 0$, outline the conditions necessary for three possible fates for the universe.

6 Sketch a diagram to show how the cosmic scale factor, R, varies with time for these three possible fates of the universe.

7 a Sketch a diagram of a rotation curve for a typical spiral galaxy that does not contain any dark matter. Make sure you label the axes correctly.
  b Sketch a diagram of what we *actually* observe when we look at the rotation curve of a spiral galaxy.
  c How do your two diagrams differ? What aspect of your second diagram indicates the presence of dark matter forming a halo around the galaxy?

8 MACHOs and WIMPs are examples of astronomical objects that scientists think make up dark matter.
  a State what the acronyms MACHOs and WIMPs mean.
  b Suggest what known astronomical objects might be MACHOs.
  c Suggest what kinds of particles might be WIMPs.

? Exam-style questions

1 **Figure D.1 shows a star that is subject to two different forces.**

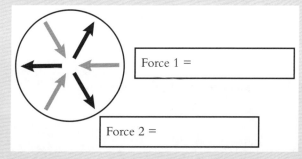

Force 1 =

Force 2 =

Figure D.1

  a Complete the labels of the two forces to show what is causing them. **[2]**
  b Explain what is meant by *hydrostatic equilibrium*. **[2]**
  c Suggest what you would expect a star to do if it lost its hydrostatic equilibrium. **[2]**

2 **In 1987, a supernova in the Large Magellanic Cloud (LMC) galaxy was observed.**
  a State which region of the Hertzsprung–Russell (HR) diagram the star would have been in before it turned into a supernova. **[1]**
  b Suggest whether this star would have been less massive, the same mass or more massive than our Sun. **[1]**
  c State the minimum mass there must be in the core of this star for it to become a neutron star. **[1]**
  d Suggest what might eventually happen to the material that has been ejected from the star during the supernova event. **[2]**

3 **Polaris, a star much-used for navigation, is a population 1 *Cepheid variable* star.**
   a Explain what is meant by *Cepheid variable*. [2]
   b Sketch a graph to show how the luminosity of a typical Cepheid variable varies in time. [2]
   c Suggest a reason why the luminosity of the Cepheid variable varies like this. [1]
   d State the special relationship that Cepheid variables possess that helps astronomers use calculate distances to faraway galaxies. [1]
   e Outline the method and measurements required to use a Cepheid variable star as a *standard candle* to find the distance to a faraway galaxy. [2]

4 **HL For protons to fuse together, they must approach each other to within a distance of about 3×10^{-5} m (3 fm).**
   a State what force becomes the dominant force experienced by protons when the two protons are 3 fm apart, thus allowing the protons to fuse. [1]
   b Calculate the electrical potential energy that the two protons will have when they are 3 fm apart. [2]
   c If the protons transform kinetic energy into electrical potential energy to get this close, calculate the effective temperature that the protons must have. [2]
   d Stars that produce energy by the p–p chain usually have temperatures of about 10 MK. With reference to your answer to part **c**, suggest what you can conclude. [2]
   e Explain how the protons are able to fuse. [3]

5 **HL Detailed studies of the anisotropies in the CMB undertaken by the COBE, WMAP, Boomerang and the Planck satellite have shown that $\Omega_m + \Omega_\Delta \approx 1$, where $\Omega_m = \dfrac{\rho_m}{\rho_c} = 0.32$ and $\Omega_\Delta = \dfrac{\rho_\Lambda}{\rho_c} = 0.68$.**
   a Explain what this equation states about the universe and its expected fate. [3]
   b If 84% of Ω_m is dark matter, determine how much of the universe we can actually observe. [2]

6 **HL A main sequence star has a luminosity that is 3000 times that of our Sun.**
   a State what is meant by:
      i a main sequence star
      ii *luminosity*. [2]
   b Using the relationship between the masses and their luminosities for stars on the main sequence, show that the mass of the star is about 10 times the mass of our Sun. [2]
   c Outline how this star is most likely to develop after it leaves the main sequence. [3]

7 **HL This question is about how observational evidence contributes to our big bang model of the universe.**
   Some fifty years ago, Penzias and Wilson showed that the universe was full of cosmic microwave background (CMB) radiation with a spectrum of peak wavelength at 1.1 mm.
   a Use Wien's law to determine the black body temperature of the CMB. [2]
   b Explain how your answer to part **a** provides observational evidence to support the big bang model of the universe. [2]
   c The shift in wavelength of spectral lines observed from distant galaxies also provides observational evidence to support the Big Bang model. Outline how. [2]

Glossary

absolute uncertainty a quantity giving the extremes a measured value falls within

absolute zero the temperature at which all random motion of molecules stops

absorption spectra the set of wavelengths of photons absorbed by a substance

ac generator a rotating coil in a magnetic field that generates ac voltage

acceleration of free fall the acceleration due to the pull of the Earth on a body

accurate a measurement where the systematic error is small and so close to the 'true' value

acoustic impedance, Z a factor that determines how easy it is to transmit ultrasound through a material. $Z = \rho c$, in units of $kg\ m^{-2}\ s^{-1}$, where ρ is the density of the material and c is the speed of sound in the material

activity the rate of decay of a radioactive sample

adiabatic process a process in which no thermal energy is exchanged

albedo the ratio of scattered to incident intensity of radiation

alpha decay a decay producing an alpha particle

alpha particle the nucleus of helium-4

alternating current (ac) current in which electrons oscillate instead of moving with same drift speed in the same direction

alternating voltage voltage that takes positive as well as negative values

ammeter an instrument that measures the electric current through it

amplitude the largest value of the displacement from equilibrium of an oscillation

angular frequency same as angular speed

angular momentum the product of mass, speed and orbit radius of a particle

angular separation the angle that the distance between two objects subtends at the observer's eye

angular speed the ratio of angle turned to time taken

antinode a point in a medium with a standing wave where the displacement is momentarily a maximum

anti-particle a particle with the same mass as its particle but with all other properties opposite, such as electric charge

Archimedes' principle any object wholly or partly submersed in a fluid is subject to an upward buoyancy force which is equal to the weight of the fluid that has been displaced by the object

atmosphere a non-SI unit of pressure

atomic (or proton) number the number of protons in a nucleus

atomic mass the mass of an atom measured in units of u

atomic mass unit a unit of mass equal to $\frac{1}{12}$ of the mass of a neutral atom of carbon-12

attenuation the loss of energy in a transmission caused by the combination of scattering and absorption

average another word for mean

average power for sinusoidally varying voltages and currents the average power in a conductor is half the peak value

average speed the ratio of distance travelled to total time taken

average velocity the ratio of displacement to total time taken

Avogadro constant the number of particles in one mole

background radiation radiation from natural sources

Balmer series the set of emission lines from a hydrogen atom where the end electron energy level is $n = 2$

bar magnet a rectangular piece of iron that has a magnetic field

baryon a particle made up of three quarks

baryon number a conserved quantum number; it is assigned to each quark and by extension to baryons

battery a source of emf

best estimate the average value of a set of measurements of a given quantity that will serve as the quoted value for that quantity

beta minus decay a decay producing an electron and an anti-neutrino

beta particle an electron

beta plus decay a decay producing a positron and a neutrino

binding energy the minimum energy that must be supplied to completely separate the nucleons in a nucleus or the energy released when a nucleus is assembled

black body a theoretical body that reflects none of the radiation incident on it and so absorbs all of it

black hole the final evolutionary state of a star whose mass is greater than the Oppenheimer-Volkoff limit and whose gravitational field is so strong that its escape velocity is greater than the speed of light

blue-shift an decrease in the observed wavelength

boiling the change from the liquid to the vapour state at a specific constant temperature

bottom a flavour of quark with electric charge $-\frac{1}{3}$, but heavier than the strange quark

Boyle's law the relation between pressure and volume of a fixed quantity of an ideal gas when the temperature is kept constant

capacitance the charge that can be stored on a capacitor per unit voltage

capacitor a device that can store electric charge

carbon brushes conducting, soft material that joins the slip rings to the external circuit in an ac generator

centripetal acceleration   the acceleration due to a changing direction of velocity

centripetal force   a force pointing to the centre of a circular path

cepheid variable   a kind of highly luminous star whose luminosity varies periodically such that its period is related to its maximum luminosity

chain reaction   a self-sustaining reaction

charge carrier   charged particles that are able to move, creating an electric current

charge polarisation   the separation of charge when a dielectric is exposed to an external electric field

Charles' law   the relation between volume and temperature of a fixed quantity of an ideal gas when the pressure is kept constant

charm   a flavour of quark with electric charge $+\frac{2}{3}$, but heavier than the up quark

chromatic aberration   a problem (caused by dispersion) encountered by lenses where different colours of light have slightly different focal lengths, leading to coloured images not being focused sharply

circular slit   an opening in the shape of a circle through which diffraction takes place

closed system   any system in which mass cannot enter or leave

coefficient of dynamic friction   the ratio of the force of friction to the normal reaction force on a body while the body is sliding on a surface

coefficient of static friction   the ratio of the maximum force of friction that can develop between two bodies to the normal reaction force on a body while the body is at rest

coherent   sources whose phase difference is constant in time

compression   a point in a medium through which a wave is travelling that has maximum density

Compton scattering   a process in which an x-ray or gamma ray photon interacts with an electron (usually in one of the outer energy levels within an atom) so that the electron gains some of the photon's energy, thereby changing the direction of motion of the photon. This may result in the electron gaining enough energy to leave the atom

computer aided tomography (CAT)   or Computed Axial Tomography - a body-imaging process that combines a number of x-ray images taken from a range of angles to produce a three dimensional, highly detailed picture of a given volume of a body

condensation   the change from the vapour to the liquid state

conduction   the transfer of heat through electron and molecular collisions

conductor   an object or material through which electric current can pass

conservation of energy   the principle that energy cannot be destroyed or created but can only be changed from one form into another

conservation of momentum   when the net force on a system is zero, the total momentum of the system is constant

conservative forces   forces for which work done is independent of the path followed.

conserved   a quantity that stays the same before and after an interaction

constructive interference   the superposition of two identical waves that arrive at a point in phase

contact force   another name for a reaction force

continuity principle   a feature of the incompressibility of a fluid that states that the volume of fluid flowing in a given time must remain constant in any pipe or conduit

control rod   a rod that regulates the rate of energy release in a nuclear fission reactor by regulating the absorption of neutrons

convection   the transfer of heat in fluids through differences in fluid density

convection current   motion of a fluid as result of differences in fluid density

cosmological constant   a factor introduced by Einstein into his equations of Relativity that allowed his model of the universe to be static, whilst not contradicting his earlier result that the size of the universe had to change in time

Coulomb's law   the electric force between two point charges is proportional to the product of the charges and inversely proportional to the square of their separation;
$$F = \frac{1}{4\pi\varepsilon_0} \times \frac{q_1 q_2}{r^2}$$

couple   a pair of equal and opposite forces not acting along the same line whose effect is to cause angular acceleration but not linear acceleration

crest   a point on a wave of maximum displacement

critical angle   the angle of incidence for which the angle of refraction is a right angle

critical density of the universe   the density of the universe that would cause the universe to be flat. That is, the density of matter that allows the universe to continue to expand, at a decreasing rate, until a maximum size

critical damping   damping that forces an oscillating system to return to its equilibrium position in the shortest possible time

critical mass   the smallest mass of fissionable material that can sustain fission reactions

damping   any form of resistive force that causes an oscillating system's amplitude to decay

decay constant   the probability per unit time for a nucleus to decay

decay series   the sequence of decays that occurs until a radioactive element reaches a stable nuclide

derived unit   a unit that is made up of a combination of two or more of the SI base units

destructive interference   the superposition of two identical waves that arrive at a point 180° out of phase

dielectric   an insulator that shows charge polarisation

diffraction   the spreading of a wave past an aperture or an obstacle

diffraction grating   a series of very many and very narrow slits

diode a device that lets current through it only in one direction

diode bridge rectifier a circuit that achieves full-wave rectification

dipole a pair of two equal and opposite electric charges

direct current (dc) current in which electrons move in the same direction with the same average drift speed

discrete energy that can take a set of specific values as opposed to a continuous range of values

dispersion the dependence of refractive index on wavelength

displacement the change in position; for an oscillation, the difference between the position of a particle and its equilibrium position

distance of closest approach the smallest distance between an incoming particle and the target in a scattering experiment

distance the length of the path followed by a particle or object

Doppler effect the change in measured frequency when there is relative motion between source and observer

down a flavour of quark with electric charge $-\frac{1}{3}$

drag force a force of resistance to motion

dynamic or kinetic friction a force opposing motion when a body moves

eddy currents small induced currents in a conductor where the flux is changing that dissipate energy

efficiency the ratio of useful work or power to input work or power

elastic potential energy the energy stored in a spring when it is compressed or stretched

electric charge a conserved property of matter

electric field the field produced by electric charges

electric field strength the electric force per unit charge experienced by a small point positive charge

electric potential the work done per unit charge by an external agent in bringing a small point positive charge from infinity to a point

electric potential energy the work that needs to be done by an external agent in order to bring a set of charges from where they were separated by an infinite distance to their current position

electric resistance the ratio of the voltage across a device to the current through it

electrical conductor a material that allows electrons (or in some cases ions) to move freely within it

electrical energy same as electric potential energy

electromagnetic an interaction mediated by the exchange of photons

electromagnetic waves transverse waves moving at the speed of light in vacuum consisting of oscillating electric and magnetic fields at right angles to each other

electroweak interaction the interaction that is the unification of the electromagnetic and the weak nuclear interactions

elementary particles particles that have no constituents

emf the work done per unit charge in moving charge across the terminals of a battery

emission spectrum the set of wavelengths of photons radiated by a substance

emissivity the ratio of the intensity radiated by a body to the intensity radiated by a black body of the same temperature

energy something that can be stored and which can be used in order to do things

energy balance equation an equation expressing the equality of incoming and outgoing intensities of radiation

energy density the energy that can be obtained from a unit volume of fuel

energy level diagram a diagram showing the discrete energies a system can take

equation of state the equation relating pressure, volume, temperature and number of moles of a gas

equilibrium the state when the net force on a system is zero

equilibrium position a position for an oscillator where all the forces that may be acting on it are balanced, giving a zero net force

equipotential surfaces set of points that have the same potential

error bar the representation of absolute uncertainty in a graph of plotted points

escape velocity the minimum speed at launch so that a particle can move to infinity and never return

exchange particle an elementary particle used as the intermediary of an interaction

excited state a state of energy higher than the ground state energy

expanding universe the distance between distant galaxies is increasing as space between them stretches

expansion another name for rarefaction

exponentially a term referring to the way that a dependent variable changes by a constant factor for each linear increment of the independent variable

family lepton number a quantum number assigned to each lepton in each family

Faraday's law the induced emf in a loop is the rate of change of magnetic flux linkage through the loop

Feynman diagram a pictorial representation of an interaction

first harmonic the mode of vibration of a standing wave of lowest frequency

first law of thermodynamics a law that states that, for a closed system, an internal energy change (ΔU) is the result of work done on the system (ΔW) and thermal energy (ΔQ) exchanged with the system, sometimes written in the form $\Delta Q = \Delta U + \Delta W$

first postulate of special relativity the laws of Physics are the same in all inertial frames of reference

flavour a type of quark

fluid resistance force a force of resistance to motion when a body moves through a fluid

flux linkage the magnetic flux in a loop times the number of turns in the loop

force something that accelerates a body

force of reaction a force that develops as a result of two bodies being in contact

force pair two forces acting on different bodies that are equal and opposite according to Newton's third law

forced oscillations oscillations occurring because of the application of a periodic external force

fractional uncertainty the ratio of the absolute uncertainty to the mean value of a quantity

frame of reference a co-ordinate system and a way of measuring time so that a value of position and time can be given to any particle anywhere and at any time

free-body diagram a diagram showing a body in isolation with all forces acting on it drawn as arrows

free oscillations oscillations of a system that has been displaced from its equilibrium position and left to oscillate without any external forces acting

freezing the change from the liquid to the solid state at a specific constant temperature

frequency the number of full oscillations or waves in unit time

friction laws empirical 'laws' about frictional forces

fuel a source of energy

fuel rods containers of nuclear fuels, e.g. oxides of uranium-235 or plutonium-239, in a nuclear fission reactor

full-wave rectification the turning of ac current into dc current during both halves of the cycle

fundamental particle a particle that has no internal structure and is not made up of anything else

fundamental unit in the SI system, the kilogram, metre, second, kelvin, mole, ampere and candela are fundamental units; all other units are combinations of these and are called derived units

gamma decay a decay producing a gamma ray photon

gamma ray a photon

global warming a gradual increase in the temperature of the Earth's surface and its oceans, observed over a period of time and considered to be the cause of changes to the climate

gravitational field the field produced by mass; its strength is the gravitational force per unit mass experienced by a small point mass

gravitational field strength the gravitational force per unit mass experienced by a small point mass

gravitational interaction an interaction mediated by the exchange of gravitons

gravitational mass the property of a body that defines the effect of a gravitational force acting upon it

gravitational potential the work done per unit mass by an external agent in bringing a small point mass from infinity to a point

gravitational potential energy the work that must be performed by an external agent to raise a mass to certain height from a position where the height is zero, or to bring a set of masses to their current position from when they were separated by an infinite distance

greenhouse effect the phenomenon in which infrared radiation emitted by the Earth's surface is absorbed by greenhouse gases in the atmosphere and then re-radiated in many directions, including back down to Earth

greenhouse gas a gas in the atmosphere that absorbs infrared radiation

ground state the state of lowest energy

hadron a particle made up of quarks

half-life the time for the activity of a radioactive sample to be reduced to half its initial value

half-wave rectification the turning of ac current into dc current by allowing the passage of current during one half of the cycle only

heat the energy transferred as a result of a temperature difference

heat exchanger system that extracts thermal energy from the moderator of a nuclear reactor

Hertzsprung–Russell diagram a diagrammatic way of showing the relationship for stars between their luminosities and their surface temperatures

Higgs particle the particle whose interactions with other particles gives mass to those particles

Hooke's law the tension in a spring is proportional to the extension or compression

hydroelectric power plant producing power by converting the potential or kinetic energy of water

ideal fluid a fluid that is incompressible, non-viscous and that undergoes laminar flow

ideal gas an idealised version of a gas obeying the gas laws at all pressures, volumes and temperatures

ideal transformer a transformer that obeys the transformer equation $\frac{V_s}{V_p} = \frac{N_s}{N_p}$ or a transformer in which the input power is equal to the output power

impulse the product of force and the time interval for which the force acts; it equals the change in momentum

inertia the tendency of a massive body to remain in its current state of motion

inertial frame of reference any frame of reference in which Newton's first law of motion is obeyed

inertial mass the property of a body that defines its acceleration when subjected to an unbalanced force

instantaneous speed the speed at an instant of time; the rate of change of distance with time

instantaneous velocity the velocity at an instant of time; the rate of change of displacement with time

insulator an object or material which electric current cannot pass through

intensity power of radiation per unit area; power per unit area carried by a wave – intensity is proportional to the square of the amplitude of the wave

interaction vertex a building block of Feynman diagrams representing a fundamental interaction process

interferometer an array of two or more radio telescopes, whose signals can be added (with any appropriate time delays) to produce an amalgamated signal that allows for better resolution

internal energy   the total random kinetic energy and intermolecular potential energy of the molecules of a substance

invariant   a quantity that is the same for all observers in all inertial frames of reference

inverse square law   a relationship between two variables, x and y, in which y varies with $\dfrac{1}{x^2}$

ionising   the ability to knock electrons off atoms

isolated   a system whose total energy stays constant

isotopes   nuclei of the same element containing the same number of protons but different numbers of neutrons

Jeans criterion   a statement that defines whether a star can be formed from a cloud of gas and dust; the magnitude of the gravitational potential energy of the matter in the cloud must be greater than the magnitude of the kinetic energy of all the particles in the cloud for the cloud to contract into a star

kinetic energy   the energy a body has as a result of its motion

Kirchhoff's current law $\Sigma I_{in} = \Sigma I_{out}$

Kirchhoff's loop law $\varepsilon = \Sigma IR$

Larmor frequency   the forcing frequency of a radio signal that will cause a proton's spin to flip from one state to the other

length contraction   a decrease in the measured value of the length of an object caused by a non-zero relative motion between the observer and the object

Lenz's law   the direction of the induced emf is such as to oppose the change in flux that created it

lepton   an elementary particle

light year   the distance travelled by light in 1 year ($= 9.46 \times 10^{15}$ m)

linear momentum   the product of mass and velocity

longitudinal wave   a wave where the displacement is parallel to the direction of energy transfer

luminosity   the total power emitted by a star (across all wavelengths of the electromagnetic spectrum)

Lyman series   the set of emission lines of ultra-violet radiation from a hydrogen atom where the end electron energy level is n = 1

magnetic field   a field created by electric currents and moving charges

magnetic field lines   imaginary curves whose tangents give the magnetic field

magnetic flux   the product of the component of the magnetic field strength normal to an area

magnetic flux density   another name for the magnetic field strength B; it is the force per unit charge on a charge moving with unit velocity at right angles to the field

magnetic flux linkage   the product of the magnetic flux, Φ, and the number of turns of the conductor, N. Magnetic flux linkage = NΦ

magnetic force   the force experienced by a magnetic field on a moving charge or an electric current

magnetic hysteresis   the lagging of an effect behind its cause, as when the change in magnetism of a body lags behind changes in the magnetic field

magnitude   the length of a vector; the size of a quantity

Malus's law   the transmitted intensity of polarised light through a polariser is reduced by a factor of $\cos^2 \theta$

mass (or nucleon) number   the number of protons plus neutrons in a nucleus

mass defect   the difference in mass between the mass of the nucleons making up a nucleus and the nuclear mass

massive compact halo objects (MACHOs)   one of the possible sources of dark mass in the universe, perhaps comprising of black holes, neutron stars, brown and black dwarfs

mean   the sum of a set of measurements divided by the number of measurements

mean value   the average value of a set of measurements of a given quantity that will serve as the quoted value for that quantity

melting   the change from the solid to the liquid state at a specific constant temperature

meson   a particle made up of one quark and one anti-quark

method of mixtures   a method to measure specific heat capacity by measuring the temperature increase when a hot body is put into a liquid in a calorimeter

Minkowski diagram   another name for a spacetime diagram. This is a diagram that represents events occurring in spacetime and the world lines of objects

moderator   body whose molecules slow down the fast neutrons produced in a fission reaction through collisions with the neutrons

modulated   the change in the two-slit intensity pattern when the single-slit diffraction effect is taken into account

molar mass   the mass of one mole of a substance

mole   a quantity of a substance containing as many particles as atoms in 12 g of carbon-12

moment of inertia   the property of a body that resists angular acceleration – it is analogous to the concept of inertial mass resisting linear acceleration and is defined as $I = \sum_i m_i r_i^2$, where m is the mass of a small part of an object and r is its distance from the axis of rotation

monochromatic   of one wavelength only. Literally translated this means one colour

motional emf   the emf generated when a conductor moves in a region of magnetic field

natural frequency   also called the resonant frequency. This is the frequency of free oscillations of a body

net force   the one force whose effect is the same as that of a number of forces combined

neutrino   a neutral particle with very small mass that interacts very weakly

Newton's first law   particle moves with a constant velocity (which may be zero) when no forces act on it

Newton's law of gravitation   there is a force of attraction between any two point masses that is proportional to the product of the masses and inversely proportional to the square of their separation; the force is directed along the line joining the two masses

Newton's second law the net force on a body is the rate of change of the body's momentum

Newton's third law when a body A exerts a force on body B, body B will exert an equal but opposite force on body A

node a point in a medium with a standing wave where the displacement is always zero

non-renewable sources of energy that are being used at a much faster rate than that at which they are being produced and so will run out

nuclear fission the reaction in which a heavy nucleus splits into two medium-sized nuclei plus neutrons, releasing energy

nuclear fusion the reaction in which two light nuclei join to form a heavier nucleus, releasing energy

nuclear magnetic resonance (NMR) a process by which the spin state of protons can be flipped by the application of an oscillating radio frequency signal. The frequency of this signal is dependent on the strength of the applied magnetic field and the induced emfs created can be used to make highly detailed images in the medical and spectroscopic industries

nucleon a proton or neutron

nuclide a nucleus with a specific number of neutrons and protons

Ohm's law at constant temperature the current through most metallic conductors is proportional to the voltage across the conductor

Olbers' paradox a question that asks, "Why is the night sky dark?" and which contradicts Newton's views that the universe was both static and infinite

open system a system that allows mass to enter or leave

order of magnitude an estimate given as just a power of 10

pair annihilation the disappearance of a particle and its anti-particle when they collide

pair creation the production of a particle and its anti-particle from a vacuum

parallel connection resistors connected so that they have the same potential difference across them

parallel plates two parallel and equally but oppositely charged plates

parsec the distance away required for 1 astronomical unit to subtend a parallax angle of 1 second of arc. 1 pc = 3.26 light years = 3.086×10^{16} m

Pascal's principle for an incompressible fluid, a pressure applied to any part of the fluid will be transmitted to all parts of the fluid and to its container

path difference the difference in the distance from a point to two sources of waves

penetrating the ability to move deep into a material

period the time needed to produce one full oscillation or wave

periodic motion that repeats

permittivity of vacuum the constant ε appearing in Coulomb's law when the charges are situated in a vacuum

phase the state of a substance depending on the separation of its molecules; we consider the solid, liquid and vapour phase in this course

phase change the phase of a wave increases by π (radians) upon reflection from a medium of higher refractive index

phase difference the quantity $\dfrac{\text{shift}}{\text{period}} \times 360°$ or $\dfrac{\text{shift}}{\text{wavelength}} \times 360°$

photoelectric effect the phenomenon in which electromagnetic radiation incident on a metallic surface forces electrons to move from the surface

photon the particle of light, a quantum of energy

photo-surface a metallic surface that ejects electrons when electromagnetic radiation is incident on it

photovoltaic cell a device that converts solar energy into electrical energy

plane polarised light whose electric field oscillates on one plane

plum pudding model the model, first described by J.J. Thompson, used to describe the structure of an atom before Rutherford had shown that an atoms consisted mostly of empty space. In the plum pudding model, the atom was shown as a sphere of positively charged material in which were embedded negatively charged electrons

point particle a particle that is assumed to be a mathematical point

polariser a device such that light passing through it emerges polarised

position generally a vector from some origin to the place where a particle is situated

positron the anti-particle of the electron

potential difference the work done per unit charge in moving a small point positive charge between two points

potential energy the energy a system has as a result of its state

power the rate at which work is being done or energy is being dissipated

precise measurements where the random error is small

pressure the normal force on an area per unit area

pressure law one of the three basic laws of gas behaviour. This law states that for a fixed amount of gas in a rigid container, the pressure of the gas is proportional to its absolute temperature

primary cell a source of emf that, once discharged, has to be discarded

primary energy energy that has not being processed in any way

principle of conservation of angular momentum the total angular momentum of a body remains constant unless it is acted upon by an external torque. This is analogous to the principle of conservation of linear momentum, where a body's total linear momentum remains constant unless subjected to an external force

principle of equivalence a principle used in general relativity, stating that the effects of a gravitational field are the same as the effects caused by a constant acceleration

proper length the length of an object measured by an observer in a frame of reference in which the object is a rest with respect to the observer

proper time the time interval between two events occurring in a frame of reference in which the two events occur in the same position

pulse an isolated disturbance in a medium carrying energy and momentum

pumped storage system plant in which water is pumped back up to higher elevations during off-peak hours so that it can again be released later during periods of high demand for electricity

quantised a quantity that can take on a discrete set of values

quantised energy energy that takes values from a set of values that are not continuous

quantum a unit of something, for example, energy

quark an elementary particle making up nucleons (and hadrons) appearing in six flavours

quark confinement the principle that free quarks cannot be observed

radial the direction towards or away from the centre of a spherical body

radiation energy in the form of electromagnetic waves

radioactivity the phenomenon in which nuclei emit particles and energy randomly and spontaneously

random uncertainty an error due to inexperience of the observer and the difficulty of reading instruments

rarefaction a point in a medium through which a wave is travelling that has minimum density

ray the direction of energy transfer of a wave

Rayleigh criterion the condition for resolving two objects; resolution is possible when the central maximum in the diffraction pattern of one source coincides with the first minimum of the diffraction pattern of the other

real gas a gas obeying the gas laws approximately for limited ranges of pressures, volumes and temperatures

red-shift an increase in the observed wavelength

reflection the scattering of radiation off a surface such that the angle of incidence is equal to the angle of reflection

refracting telescope an optical device using two or more (usually two) lenses to produce an image of a distant object

refraction the change in speed of a wave as it enters another medium and the subsequent change of direction (except at normal incidence)

refractive index the ratio of the speed of light in vacuum to the speed of light in a material

renewable sources of energy from a source that has, for all practical purposes, an infinite lifetime

resistivity the resistance of a conductor of unit length and unit cross-sectional area

resolution the ability to see as distinct two objects that are distinct

resolving power the ability of a diffraction grating to see as distinct two wavelengths that are close to each other

rest mass the mass of an object or particle that is stationary in its frame of reference

restoring force a force directed towards the equilibrium position of a system

right-hand grip rules the right-hand grip rule for a current-carrying wire gives the direction of the magnetic field due to the current in a wire; the right-hand grip rule for a solenoid gives the direction of the magnetic field due to the current in a solenoid; the right-hand rule gives the direction of the magnetic force on a moving charge

root mean square (rms) value of a current or a voltage that would give the same average power dissipation in a dc circuit component as in the ac circuit

Sankey diagram a pictorial way to represent energy losses and transfers

scalar a quantity that has magnitude but no direction

Schrödinger theory the theory that determines the wavefunction of a system

Schwarzschild radius the distance from the centre of a star where the escape speed is the speed of light

secondary cell a rechargeable source of emf

secondary energy energy that has been processed in some way so as to make it useful

second law of thermodynamics a concept based on the idea of the conservation of energy, which shows that real-life thermodynamic processes are irreversible. The second law is usually stated in two complementary ways: The Clausius version, which states that in a closed system it is not possible to transfer energy from a colder body to a hotter body without doing work on the system, and the Kelvin-Planck version which states that it is impossible to extract energy from a hot reservoir and transfer it completely into mechanical work

second postulate of relativity the speed of light in free space is the same in all inertial frames of reference

series connection resistances connected one after the other so they take the same current

simple harmonic motion (SHM) oscillatory motion in which the acceleration is opposite and proportional to displacement from equilibrium

simple pendulum a small mass attached to a fixed length of string that oscillates

slip rings conducting rings used to connect the rotating coil of a generator to the external circuit so that ac current is delivered to it

Snell's law the law relating the angles of incidence and refraction to the speeds of the wave in two media

solar constant the intensity of the Sun's radiation at the position of the Earth's orbit

solenoid a long, tightly wound coil

specific energy the energy that can be obtained from a unit mass of fuel

specific heat capacity the energy required to raise the temperature of a unit mass by one degree

specific latent heat of fusion   the energy needed to change a unit mass from the solid to the liquid phase at constant temperature

specific latent heat of vaporisation   the energy needed to change a unit mass from the liquid to the vapour phase at constant temperature

spherical aberration   the problem created by spherical lenses and spherical mirrors that causes light to focus at different places, thus producing a blurred image

standard deviation   a measure of the spread of a set of measurements around the mean

Standard Model   the presently accepted model of elementary particles and interactions for quarks and leptons

standing wave   a wave formed from the superposition of two identical travelling waves moving in opposite directions

state of a gas   a gas with a specific value of pressure, volume, temperature and number of moles

static friction   a force opposing the tendency to motion when a body is at rest

Stefan–Boltzmann law   the power radiated by a black body is proportional to the body's surface area and the fourth power of its kelvin temperature; $P = \sigma A T^4$

stopping voltage   the voltage in a photoelectric experiment that makes the photocurrent zero

strange   a flavour of quark with electric charge $-\frac{1}{3}$, but heavier than the down quark

strong nuclear interaction   an interaction mediated by the exchange of gluons

superposition   the displacement when two waves meet is the sum of the individual displacements

systematic error   an error due to incorrectly calibrated instruments – it is the same for all data points and cannot be reduced by repeated measurements

temperature   a measure of the 'coldness' or 'hotness'; the absolute temperature is a measure of the average random kinetic energy of the particles of a substance

tension   the force developed in a string or spring as a result of stretching and compressing

terminal speed   the eventual constant speed attained by a body experiencing a speed-dependent resistance force.

thermal conductor   a body that allows heat to be transferred by the process of conduction

thermal equilibrium   the state in which the temperature remains constant

thermistor   a resistor whose resistance varies strongly with temperature

thin film interference   a type of interference caused by reflected rays from the two boundaries of a thin film

Thomson model   an early model of the atom as a positive sphere of positive charge with electrons moving about in the sphere

threshold frequency   a term used to describe the frequency of light, f_0 , incident on a metal surface that is just sufficient to allow the ejection of photoelectrons $f_0 = \dfrac{\phi}{h}$, where ϕ

is the work function of the metal surface and h is Planck's constant

time constant   the time after which the charge on a discharging capacitor is reduced to about 37% of its original value

time dilation   a difference in elapsed time as measured by two observers moving relative to each other

top   a flavour of quark with electric charge $+\frac{2}{3}$, but heavier than the charm

total internal reflection   when the angle of incidence is greater than the critical angle, the incident ray only reflects with no refracted ray

total mechanical energy   the sum of the kinetic energy, gravitational potential energy and elastic potential energy of a body

transfer of thermal energy   the transfer of energy from one body to another as a result of a temperature difference

transformer   a device that takes a given ac voltage as input and delivers a higher or lower ac voltage

transition   the change from one energy level to another with the associated release or absorption of energy

transverse wave   a wave where the displacement is at right angles to the direction of energy transfer

trough   a point on a wave of minimum displacement

tunnelling   the ability of subatomic particles to move into regions forbidden by energy conservation

twin paradox   an example of time dilation (a thought experiment) where two identical twins measure their ages to be different because they have moved (at relativistic speeds) relative to each other. One twin flies off to a distant place and returns to find that the twin who remained on the Earth has aged more

ultrasound   sound waves at a frequency that is too high for a human to hear – usually taken to mean frequencies greater than about 20 kHz

uniform motion   motion with constant velocity

uniformly accelerated motion   motion with constant acceleration

unpolarised   light whose electric field oscillates on many planes

up   a flavour of quark with electric charge $+\frac{2}{3}$

upthrust   an upward force exerted on a body immersed in a fluid

vaporisation   the change from the liquid to the vapour state

vector   a quantity that has magnitude and direction

voltage   the potential difference between two points in a circuit

voltmeter   an instrument that measures the potential difference across its ends

wave   a periodic disturbance that carries energy and momentum with no large-scale motion of the medium

wavefront   surfaces of constant phase (usually only drawn through crests)

wavefunction a function of time and position whose magnitude squared is related to the probability of finding a particle somewhere

wavelength the length of a full wave; the distance between two consecutive crests or troughs

weakly interacting massive particles (WIMPs) a proposed example of dark matter; sub-atomic particles with mass that don't interact, or hardly interact, with normal matter. Examples suggested are neutrinos (that we know about) and axions and neutralinos (that are, so far, hypothetical)

weak nuclear interaction an interaction mediated by the exchange of W and Z bosons

weight the force of attraction between the mass of the Earth and a body

Wien's displacement law the wavelength at which most of the power of a black body is radiated is inversely proportional to the body's temperature; $\lambda = \dfrac{2.90 \times 10^{-3}}{T}$

work done the product of the force and the distance travelled in the direction of the force

work function the minimum amount of energy that must be supplied to an electron so it can escape a metal

work–kinetic energy relation the work done by the net force on a body equals the change in the body's kinetic energy

CD-ROM terms and conditions of use

CD-ROM Terms and conditions of use This is a legal agreement between 'You' (which for individual purchasers means the individual customer and, for network purchasers, means the Educational Institution and its authorised users) and Cambridge University Press ('the Licensor') for *Physics for the IB Diploma Workbook*. By placing this CD in the CD-ROM drive of your computer You agree to the terms of this licence.

1 **Limited licence**

   a You are purchasing only the right to use the CDROM and are acquiring no rights, express or implied to it or to the software ('Software' being the CD-ROM software, as installed on your computer terminals or server), other than those rights granted in this limited licence for not-for-profit educational use only.

   b Cambridge University Press grants the customer the licence to use one copy of this CD-ROM either (i) on a single computer for use by one or more people at different times, or (ii) by a single person on one or more computers (provided the CD-ROM is only used on one computer at any one time and is only used by the customer), but not both.

   c You shall not: (i) copy or authorise copying of the CD-ROM, (ii) translate the CD-ROM, (iii) reverse engineer, alter, adapt, disassemble or decompile the CD-ROM, (iv) transfer, sell, lease, lend, profit from, assign or otherwise convey all or any portion of the CD-ROM or (v) operate the CD-ROM from a mainframe system, except as provided in these terms and conditions.

2 **Copyright**

   a All original content is provided as part of the CD-ROM (including text, images and ancillary material) and is the copyright of, or licensed by a third party to, the Licensor, protected by copyright and all other applicable intellectual property laws and international treaties.

   b You may not copy the CD-ROM except for making one copy of the CD-ROM solely for backup or archival purposes. You may not alter, remove or destroy any copyright notice or other material placed on or with this CD-ROM.

   c The CD-ROM contains Adobe® Flash® Player. Adobe® Flash® Player Copyright © 1996−2010 Adobe Systems Incorporated. All Rights Reserved. Protected by U.S. Patent 6,879,327; Patents Pending in the United States and other countries. Adobe and Flash are either trademarks or registered trademarks in the United States and/or other countries.

3 **Liability and Indemnification**

   a The CD-ROM is supplied 'as-is' with no express guarantee as to its suitability. To the extent permitted by applicable law, the Licensor is not liable for costs of procurement of substitute products, damages or losses of any kind whatsoever resulting from the use of this product, or errors or faults in the CD-ROM, and in every case the Licensor's liability shall be limited to the suggested list price or the amount actually paid by You for the product, whichever is lower.

   b You accept that the Licensor is not responsible for the persistency, accuracy or availability of any urls of external or third party internet websites referred to on the CD-ROM and does not guarantee that any content on such websites is, or will remain, accurate, appropriate or available. The Licensor shall not be liable for any content made available from any websites and urls outside the Software.

   c Where, through use of the CD-ROM and content you infringe the copyright of the Licensor you undertake to indemnify and keep indemnified the Licensor from and against any loss, cost, damage or expense (including without limitation damages paid to a third party and any reasonable legal costs) incurred by the Licensor as a result of such infringement.

4 **Termination**

Without prejudice to any other rights, the Licensor may terminate this licence if You fail to comply with the terms and conditions of the licence. In such event, You must destroy all copies of the CD-ROM.

5 **Governing law**

This agreement is governed by the laws of England, without regard to its conflict of laws provision, and each party irrevocably submits to the exclusive jurisdiction of the English courts.